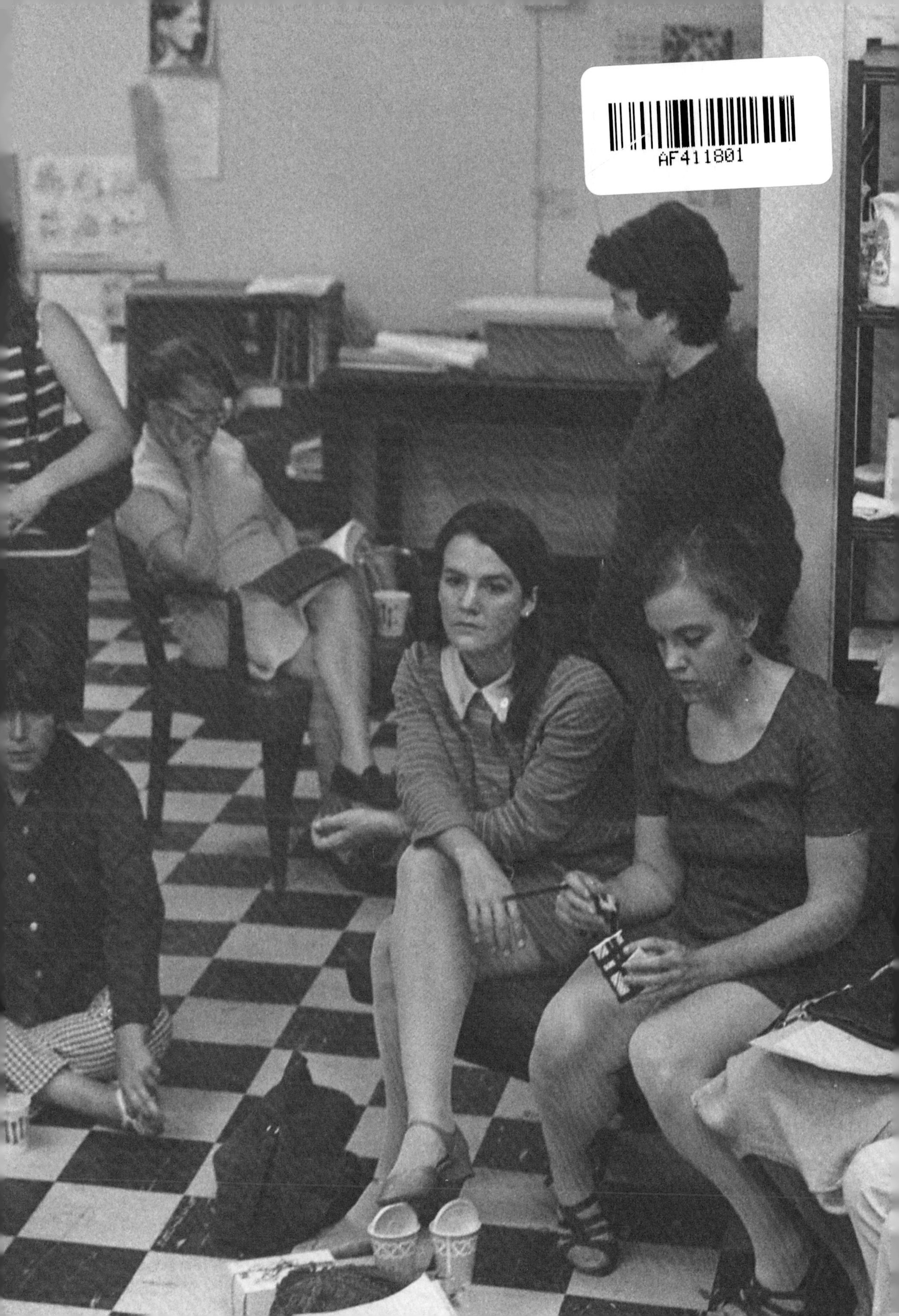
AF411801

Bev Grant
Photography 1968-1972

Edited by
Cay Sophie Rabinowitz

Essays by
William Cordova and Johanna Fernández

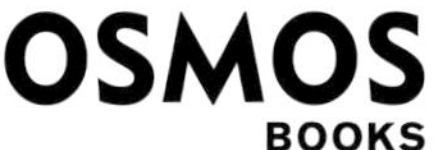

OSMOS
BOOKS

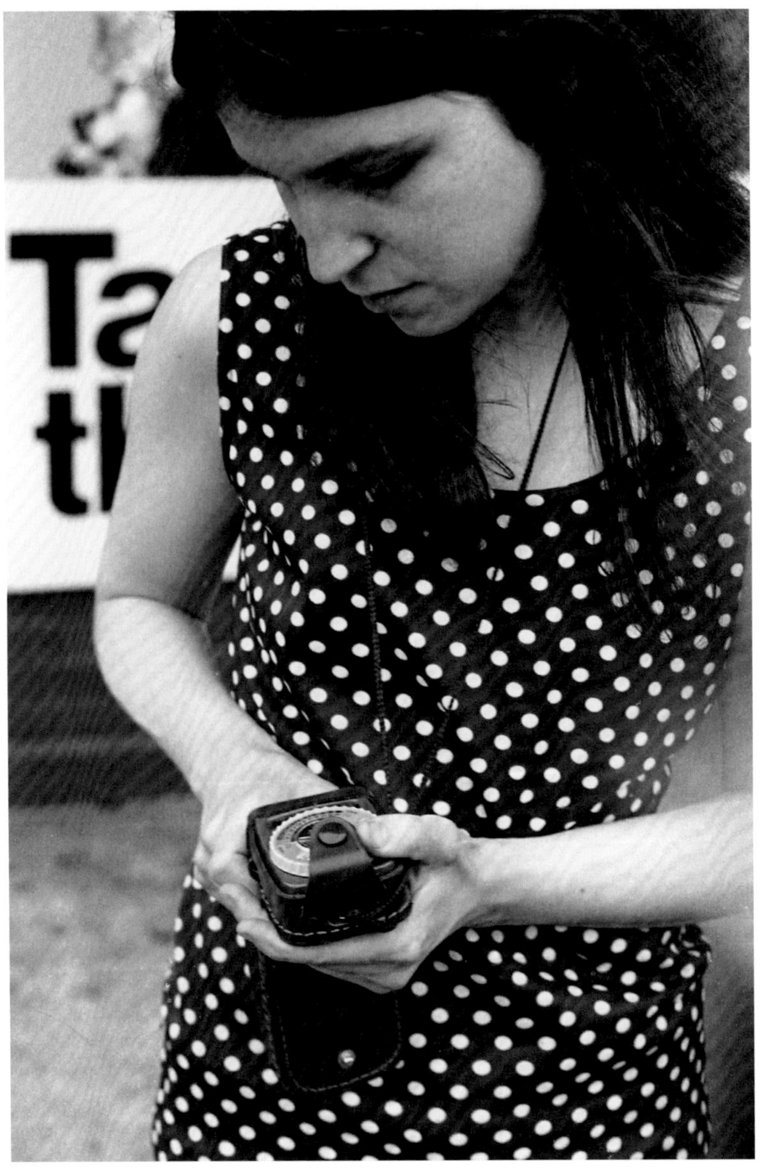

Bev Grant, Coney Island, New York, July 4, 1968
Photo by Juan Julien Caicedo

Contents

Introduction

by Wiilliam Cordova

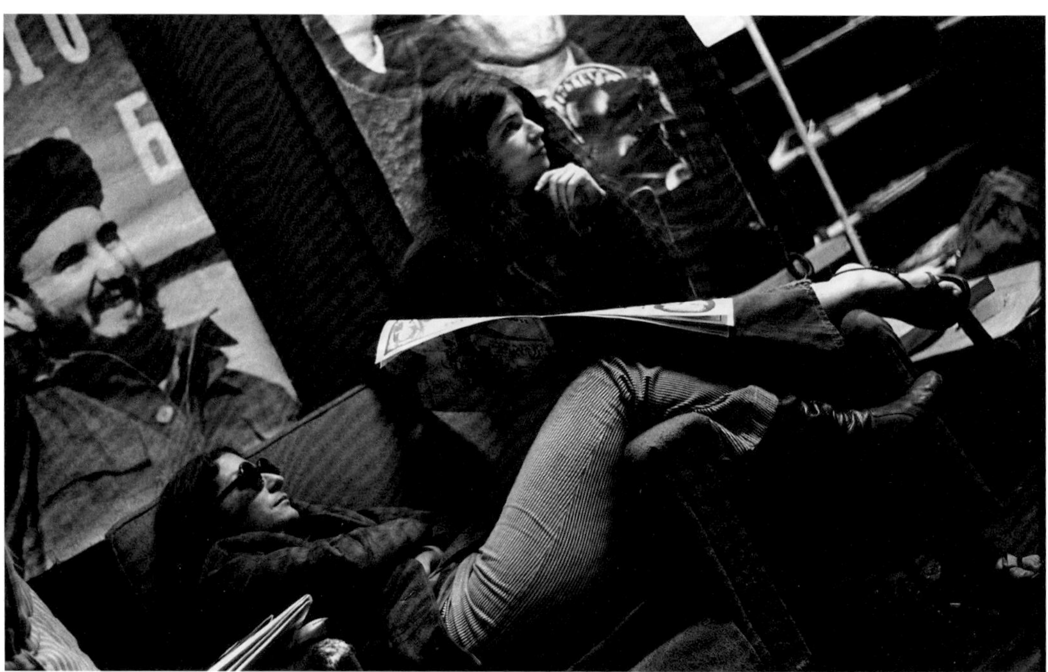

Roz Payne and Bev Grant, Young Lords Office, East Harlem, New York, Summer 1969
Photographer unknown

Jorge Aponte, Fred "Solitaire" Fernandez, Sylvia Perez, Richard Rodriguez, Christina Choy, Juan "John" Martinez, Pedro "Chango" Monges, Ricardo de Leon, Mike Gillespie, David Castro, Victor Perez, Carlos Rodriguez, Gabriel "Tea" Torres, Francisco Torres, Marion Hilliard, Julio Lopez, Guy Kurose, Angel Cruz, José Rene Gonzalvez, Ronny Hajopian, Eugene Reyes, Lee Lew Lee, Carlos Perez.... These are only a few of the names in a longer list of Latino, Asian, and Indigenous rank and file members of the Black Panther Party I came across during research visits to the Schomburg Center for Research in Black Culture in New York City.

It was fall of 2004 and I had just started the Artist-in-Residence or AIR program at The Studio Museum in Harlem. I was working on what would eventually turn out to be a long-term project focused on the multiethnic and multiracial makeup of the memberships of the Black Panther Party or BPP and Young Lords Party or YLP, two community activist organizations that were primarily composed of young folks, students, activists, and the lumpenproletariat. YLP was primarily a Puerto Rican-led organization, but it also included Filipinos, Dominicans, Cubans, Mexicans, and Black Americans. I was drawn to both organizations because of their abilities to work side by side and often share group members. I began searching for visual representations of such solidarity. As my project progressed over several years, I eventually arrived at photographer Bev Grant, whose personal and photographic works are evidence of radical approaches to racial coalition that are still unfolding.

During this time, I initially came across Roz Payne, a photographer whose photo *Yellow Peril Supports Black Power* (1968) depicts Asian men on the steps of the Alameda County Courthouse in California holding protest signs in support of BPP Minister of Defense Huey P. Newton. Another photo by Payne, *Cops and Panthers on Courthouse Steps for the Panther 21 Trial* (1969), shows a long row of BPP members confronting armed police officers on the stairs of the New York City Criminal Court.[1] The photo is a symbol of civil disobedience. The police, armed with billy clubs and riot helmets, menace the young Panthers, who resist these staunch representations of authority by standing defiantly with arms crossed and dignity intact. This photo showed me the first example of a Latino BPP member: Fred "Solitaire" Fernandez, who was Puerto Rican and captain of the Corona, Queens, branch of the BPP, standing next to Nile Rodgers, then age nineteen, who would later form the 1970s R&B group, Chic.

As political activist and journalist Mumia Abu-Jamal notes: "New York's branches were also unique in the racial composition of party members, for it was the only site where Puerto Ricans served as Panthers. While they seemed to make up a higher percentage in Brooklyn, there were also some in our Bronx and Harlem branches. Some were former members of the Young Lords Party, who, because of their African heritage or their radicalism, felt more at home en el Partido Pantera Negra. They gave the Party a deeper penetration in the communities of color in New York and served with both pride and distinction."[2]

Roz Payne and I corresponded between travels, but at that time, I had not yet encountered Bev Grant, so I wasn't able to find more visual evidence of Latino Panthers or of a supposed historic Rainbow Coalition meeting between the Young Lords, Black Panthers, and the Patriot Party (originally the Young Patriots Organization) on the East Coast. This gathering was intended to bring Black, Latino, and White activists and their respective communities together. The Patriot Party, an activist organization of young, working-class White people that originally formed in Chicago, was part of the first Rainbow Coalition formed by Fred Hampton, chairman of the Illinois chapter of the BPP. On December 4, 1969, Chicago police assassinated Hampton while he was sleeping in his bed.

Payne and I finally met in person on January 25, 2009, in Richmond, Vermont, and she opened her archive of Newsreel films, photography, and ephemera to me. I came across stacks of wrinkled and stained contact sheets, which included images of the Bedford-Stuyvesant, Brooklyn branch of the BPP and a very youthful Panther standing in front with other men and a group of children. Payne informed me that another photo, *Try Police Not Huey*, was taken at the same time in 1968 as *Yellow Peril Supports Black Power*. This picture, though, includes Richard Rodriguez, a Latino Black Panther wearing dark shades with his long, jet-black hair in a pompadour. I had read about him in *Agents of Repression: The FBI's Secret Wars Against the Black Panther Party and the American Indian Movement* by Ward Churchill and Jim Vander Wall. Later, I asked Churchill about Rodriguez, but his reply was limited: "I've no additional information on Rodriguez. Should anything further come my way, I'll be happy to share it with you."

> *Race is a social discourse that has a visual history. The collection and display of bodies, images, and artifacts in museums and elsewhere is a primary means by which a nation tells the story of its past and locates the cultures of its citizens in the present. —Jennifer A. González, Subject to Display: Reframing Race in Contemporary Installation Art (2008)*

Time passed and my research project evolved, taking me to Cuba, Germany, the United Kingdom, Spain, and France. Then, in summer 2017 while going through a social media website, I came across the same photos I had scanned at Roz Payne's house eight years earlier. These images were sharper, clearer, wrinkle-free versions, but they were all credited to Bev Grant. Who was Bev Grant? Why had I not seen any of these pictures before? I learned she was an accomplished folk singer/songwriter—and there were dozens of uploaded photos on her profile page. Some were familiar, but most were completely new to me. Most notably, they all seemed to be candid, revelatory moments.

Both Bev Grant and Roz Payne had been members of Third World Newsreel. As described by producer Danny Schechter, while working as "decentralized film collectives in several cities" the Newsreel organization "produced many, many films, mostly shot on 16 mm. Most were in black and white, as gritty and realistic as the subjects they depicted. These were films of civil rights and civil wrongs, of uprisings in communities and on campuses, about the Vietnam War and the war at home against it."[3]

I contacted Bev Grant, asking how Roz came across the photos. Simple, she explained—they had been friends since their days at Third World Newsreel in 1967. Payne had stored copies of both of their photographs and probably didn't recall which photos belonged to whom. The story made sense, especially since Grant remembered the names and places of all her photos.

I mentioned a group of pictures she took in 1969 of the Black Panther Party's Free Breakfast for School Children Program that I thought captured something extremely rare. The program was well-documented by mainstream and independent print and television journalists, including photographers Pirkle Jones and Ruth-Marion Baruch. Their examples gave insights into the BPP's Survival Programs and did much to humanize the Party and its community-driven goals. But all of those examples were often staged for the press. Grant's photos documented an unrehearsed, intimate perspective of the breakfast program that included Black, Brown, and White children eating together. This illustration of racial diversity had not been part of the broader conversation about most activist organizations. If more examples like this had been document-ed, they certainly hadn't been made public until now. In hindsight, it makes sense that both the Young Lords and the Black Panther Party would have shared not only in Survival Programs, but also that the rank and file would become members of both organizations, especially on the East Coast.

One of Grant's exemplary photos was of Joudon Ford, a former member of the Student Nonviolent Coordinating Com-mittee or SNCC, who became a captain and minister of defense for the Brook-lyn branch of the BPP at the age of eighteen.[4] His likeness had appeared in many now-historic photos by well-known photographers. All of these photos, though, were of public places or events, such as the United Nations headquar-ters, the U.S. Federal Courthouse in New York, and countless demonstrations. But none of these images were like Grant's photograph, which captured Ford in such a candid moment looking comfortable and unassuming with a relaxed smile. Of course, it is obvious why an activist

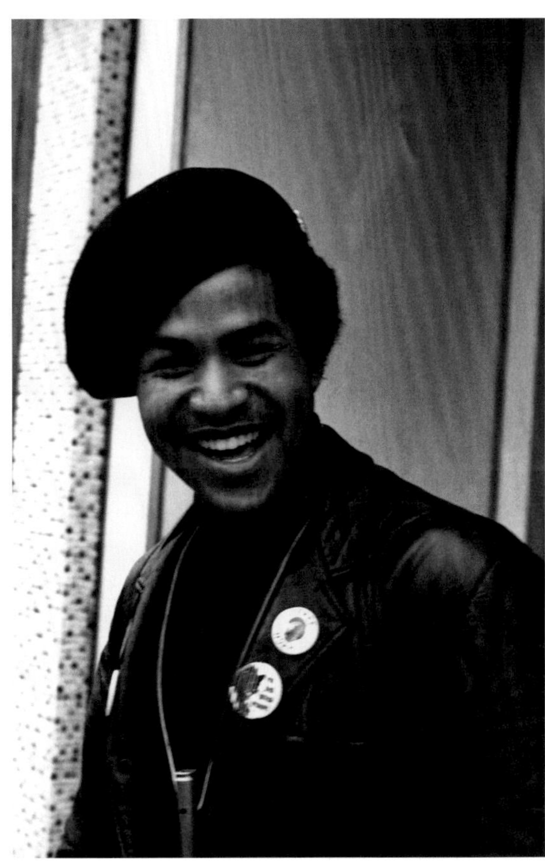

Joudon Ford, Brooklyn Black Panther Party Captain and Minister of Defense
Brooklyn, New York, Summer 1968

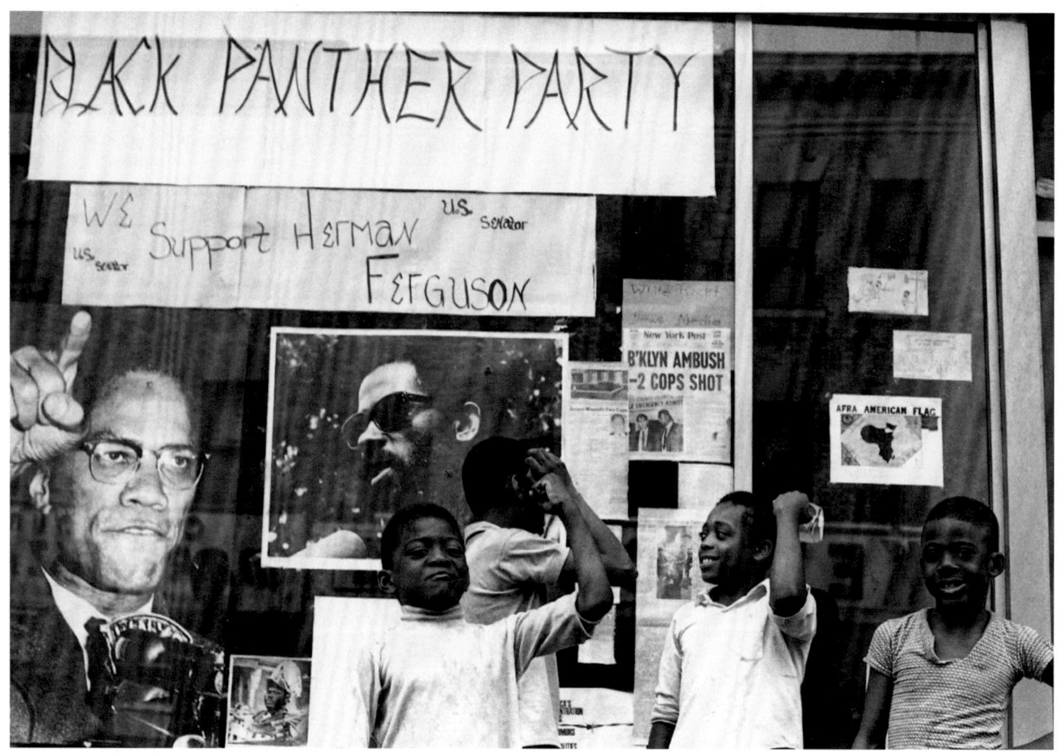

Brooklyn Black Panther Party office, Nostrand Avenue, Brooklyn, New York, Summer 1968

would not want to appear vulnerable during a public program, especially given the intensity of the civil rights movement in the 1960s and early 1970s.

This wasn't the only photo by Bev Grant that had resonated with me for almost a decade. One set shows four children striking spontaneous poses for the camera in front of the BPP Bedford-Stuyvesant branch office. They were at ease but self-conscious and, in some cases, mimicked the defiant poster images of Malcolm X, H. Rap Brown (now Jamil Al-Amin), Marcus Garvey, Huey P. Newton, and Eldridge Cleaver taped onto the interior of the branch's storefront window facade. The power of these photos is not in the documentation of Black iconographic nostalgia or popular culture appropriation turning the image into "Black currency." Instead, their strength is found in the intentional collapse of the photos' foregrounds and backgrounds in ways that contextualize both simultaneously. The scattered handbill headlines illuminate and build content like algorithms with the posters, window frames, and our assumption of the children's innocence and their brazen awareness.

This mode of visual construction is also at work in another photo, which depicts two of the boys with their fists in the air outside the Black Panther offices, surrounded by headlines and quotes such as, "We support Herman Ferguson U.S. Senator," Sniper Wounds Two Cops," "White Racist News Media New York Post B'KLYN AMBUSH—2 COPS SHOT," "AFRA AMERICAN FLAG," "American concentration camp," "BLACK LIBERATION," "SET HUEY FREE," "What we want, What we need," and "780." As the image shows, Grant's photos are cinematic in that she is sculpting in time fragile, obvious, hidden narratives, much like Manuel Álvarez Bravo's Parábola óptica (Optical Parable) (1931), Gordon Parks's Harlem Newsboy (1943), Ilka Hartmann's Boys Hold Signs at Rally (1970), Carrie Mae Weems' From Here I Saw What Happened and I Cried (1995-1996), and Deborah Willis's Shotgun House series (2002).

Another rare photographic moment Grant captured was the first Rainbow Coalition meeting on the East Coast between the Young Lords, the Black Panther Party, and the Patriot Party in New York. This historic meeting took place in mid 1969 at the Young Lords' office in El Barrio (Spanish Harlem) at 1678 Madison Avenue. The attendees included Lords central committee members Felipe Luciano, David Perez, Juan "Fi" Ortiz, and Pablo "Yoruba" Guzmán, along with BPP Field Marshal Don "D.C." Cox and Circulation Manager Sam Napier. William "Preacherman" Fesperman, the Patriot Party's national chairman, and Arthur Turco, its chief of staff, were also present. The photos are revelatory in showing the steps the three activist organizations were taking to build a coalition similar to what Fred Hampton started in Chicago. The meeting was a serious move toward uniting racial, class, ethnic, and social struggles.

Unfortunately, the Patriot Party's entire central committee and seven of its cadre were arrested on February 21, 1970. The group never recovered from the arrests and resulting legal costs and constant police surveillance. Within a few months, Cox of the BPP fled to Algiers and later France, where he remained in exile until he passed away in 2011. Of the Lords, Luciano and Guzmán became print and television journalists and are still very active today.

> *We need to document the existence of living traditions, both past and present, that can heal our wounds and offer us a space of opportunity where our lives can be transformed. —bell hooks, Art on My Mind (1995)*

Grant later explained to me that as a member of Newsreel, she was often at the right place at the right time. Indeed, she happened to be the only unaffiliated photographer at the Young Lords' first

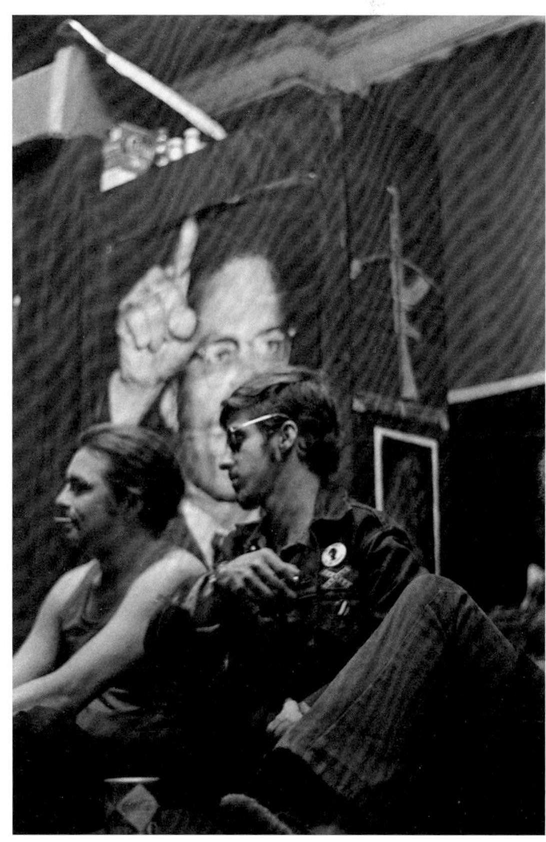

William "Preacherman" Fesperman with Young Patriots, Young Lords, and Black Panthers, Rainbow Coalition meeting, East Harlem, New York, Summer 1969

public action, the Garbage Offensive. Garbage was a serious issue in El Barrio due to a lack of waste disposal trucks picking up neighborhood trash, which would pile up like mountains for months. The city's neglect made for a deplorable state of living, as the stench, rats, and unsanitary conditions affected the young, the old, families—everyone.

In the summer of 1969, the Young Lords blocked both north and southbound traffic at East Third Avenue and 110th Street with trash and "someone" set it all on fire. It was an effective strategy that led to an immediate response from the press and the city. In communities of color across the city, neglect was common, and the Lords challenged the status quo by drawing attention to the government's lack of responsibility. Bev Grant's photographs tell this story candidly and affectionately. Hiram Maristany, a photographer who was a member of the Lords, was the only other individual who documented the Garbage Offensive. Most of his photos were published in the journal Caribe.[5]

Grant's photos tend to focus not only on the Lords but also on the people—women, children, elders—who took it upon themselves to play a role in purging the trash from their buildings and into the heart of Uptown traffic. That image brings to mind the fiery multi-car pileup in Jean-Luc Godard's film Weekend (1967). The heap of debris along a tattered motorway echoes any rebellion waiting to be lit. Grant's photography has a similar cinematic poise. Her work riffs on characteristics found in French New Wave and Italian neorealism, including their visual styles, narratives, and themes of the working class, poverty, oppression, injustice, and social progress.

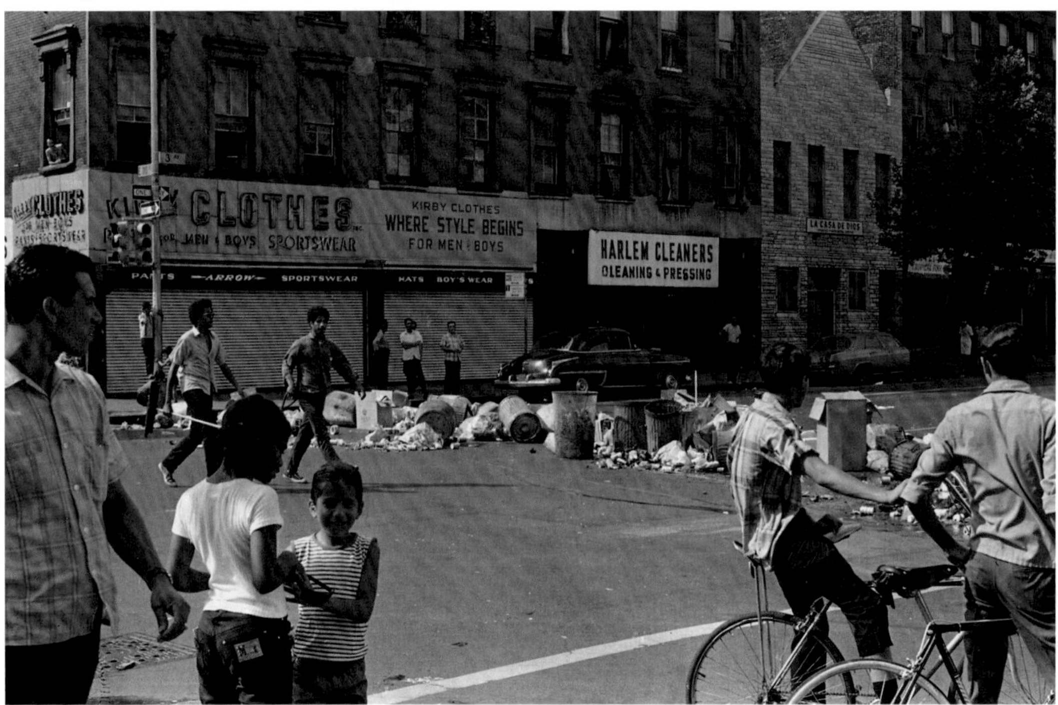

Young Lords Garbage Offensive, 110th Street and Third Avenue, New York, August 17, 1969

In documenting the activism of the Young Lords, Grant's photographic work naturally intersected with the struggles of other groups. For example, take her portrait of sorts of the Lords Minister of Finance Denise Oliver as she participated in a New York demonstration protesting the assassination of Black Panther Party leaders Fred Hampton and Mark Clark by Chicago police in December 1969. Grant's image reveals the climate of mortality on the faces of the young demonstrators, including Oliver's. Their awareness and the emotional toll are apparent. Nothing seemed right. It is interesting to note that Oliver is Afro American, yet she became one of the highest-ranking women in both the Young Lords and the Black Panther Party.[6]

Fin, pero no es el fin. —Nicolás Guillén Landrián, En un barrio viejo (1963)

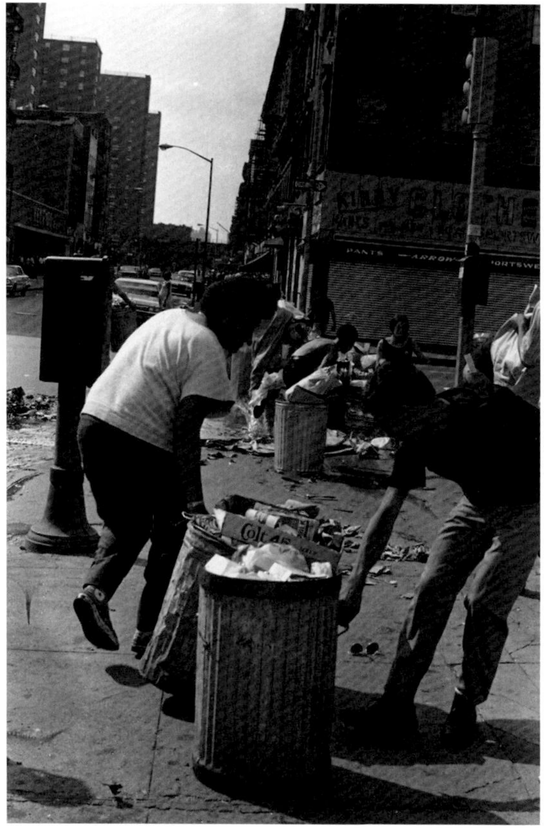

Young Lords Garbage Offensive
110th Street and Third Avenue, New York, August 17, 1969

The directness of radical racial coalitions in action is evident in Grant's photography. Historical photography tends to be plural through content building—an essay here, a lecture there—to construct and convince us of the significance of a static moment. In contrast, Grant's photography is Cinema Novo (New Cinema), as she uses an approach like Third Cinema that, according to Fernando Solanas, "aspires to prove that another world is possible."[7] When I think of her work, films like Mikhail Kalatozov's *Soy Cuba* (I Am Cuba) (1964), Sara Gómez's *Iré a Santiago* (I'll Go to Santiago) (1964), Vittorio De Sica's *Ladri di biciclette* (Bicycle Thieves) (1948), and Octavio Getino and Fernando Solanas's *La hora de los hornos* (The Hour of the Furnaces) (1968) all come to mind. Much like those films, Grant compels us to narrate our own experience in what we see. Everything is transparent in order to be transformative in Third Cinema. In that context, Grant's work echoes Argentinian filmmaker Raymundo Gleyzer's assertion: "We think of film as a bullet that ignites consciousness. We must serve as the stone that breaks silence, or the bullet that starts the battle. Poetry is not a goal in itself. Among us poetry is a tool to transform the world."[8]

Many know about the widely documented "Free Bobby Seale May Day" demonstration on the New Haven Green on May 1, 1970, but Grant photographed a different unique event that

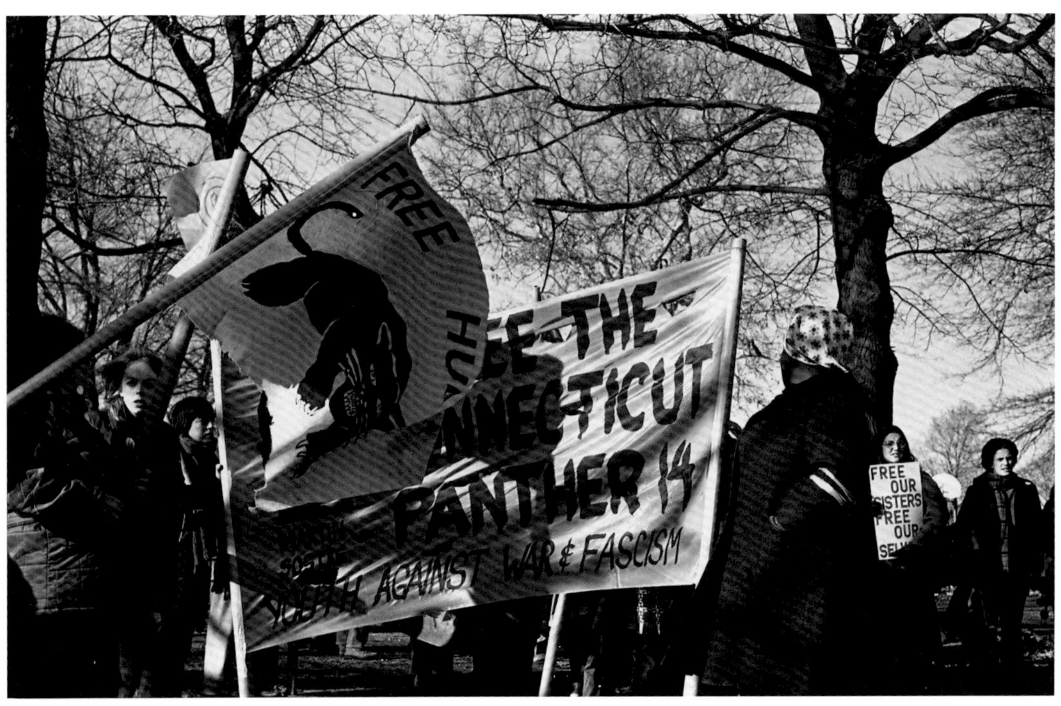

Women's demonstration
Free Ericka Huggins and Bobbie Seale Protest, New Haven, Connecticut, November 22, 1969

took place in New Haven the previous year. On November 22, 1969, members of the Women's Liberation Movement, the Young Lords, and the Black Panther Party assembled at the "Free Bobby! Free Ericka!" demonstration in New Haven. Mothers with babies, children, teenagers, younger and older women of different races, sizes, and colors collectively worked toward one goal. They battled the cold Northern winds, the police, and time before it ran out. Everything was about timing; it was like a game of Monopoly in which most players went directly to jail and there were no real estate properties—only an Empire State. Although men were present at this event, this diverse and organized march was about the women harnessing political power. It was visible in the photos Grant captured of the event all those years ago. And it is still active in more recent events such as the Women's March on Washington in 2017, the March for Sandra Bland in Dallas in 2017, and the Sister March for Breonna Taylor on Staten Island in 2020.

My search for evidence of activists passing through and beyond self-imposed racial lines as a way of building different dimensions of awareness has been a long process, particularly in finding how they evoke other spaces of consciousness and bring them to the forefront. But discovering Bev Grant's work and then meeting her makes the struggle worth it for that evidence. Her photography, music, and generosity as a friend who shared a deeper understanding of diversity and sacrifices has been "guided by a great feeling of love."

Notes

1.	Artist/Author Coco Fusco and curator Brian Wallis included *Yellow Peril Supports Black Power* (1968) in their 2003 publication *Only Skin Deep: Changing Visions of the American Self*. The *Cops and Panthers on Courthouse Steps for the Panther 21 Trial* (1969) photo was used for the cover of historian Jeffrey O.G. Ogbar's 2005 book, *Black Power: Radical Politics and African American Identity*.

2.	Mumia Abu-Jamal, *We Want Freedom: A Life in the Black Panther Party* (Cambridge, MA: South End Press, 2004), 199.

3.	Danny Schechter, "They called themselves NEWSREEL," Newsreel, accessed February 22, 2021, http://www.newsreel.us.

4.	I later learned that Joudon Ford and Minister of Education George Murray were the first Black Panther Party members to be officially invited by the Cuban government. They traveled to Cuba on August 18, 1968. Ford eventually left the BPP due to "bad-jacketing" courtesy of the FBI's COINTELPRO (Counter Intelligence Program). He finished his studies as a writer at City College of New York and Yale University.

5.	See *Caribe* VII, no. 4 (1983).

6.	Denise Oliver (now Oliver-Velez) is a professor of anthropology and women's studies at SUNY New Paltz and a contributing editor for the progressive political blog Daily Kos.

7.	Fernando Solanas, who conceptualized Third Cinema with Octavio Getino in 1970, used this phrase to describe his 2004 film *Memoria del saqueo* (A Social Genocide). See "Press Release: Jan 20, 2004: Berlinale 2004: An Honorary Golden Bear for Fernando Solanas," Berlin International Film Festival, accessed February 22, 2021, https://www.berlinale.de/en/archive/jahresarchive/2004/08_pressemitteilungen_2004/08_pressemitteilungen_2004-detail_655.html.

8.	The quote is sometimes attributed to Ernesto Ardito, who co-directed the documentary *Raymundo* (2002) with Virna Molina.

9.	Ernesto "Che" Guevara, "El socialismo y el hombre en Cuba," March 12, 1965.

Following spread
Women's demonstration
Free Ericka Huggins and Bobbie Seale Protest, New Haven, Connecticut, November 22, 1969

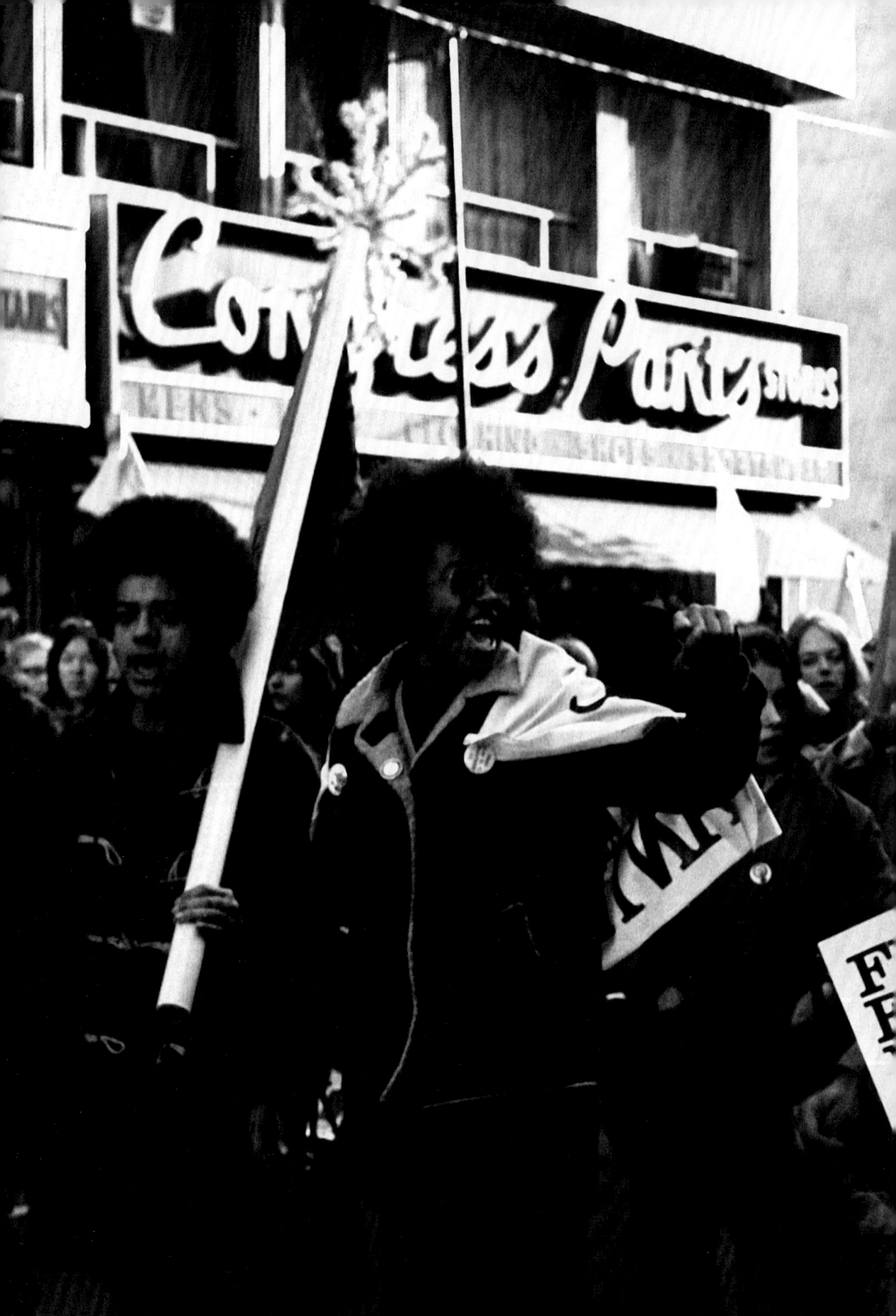

Countess Party STORES
MERS

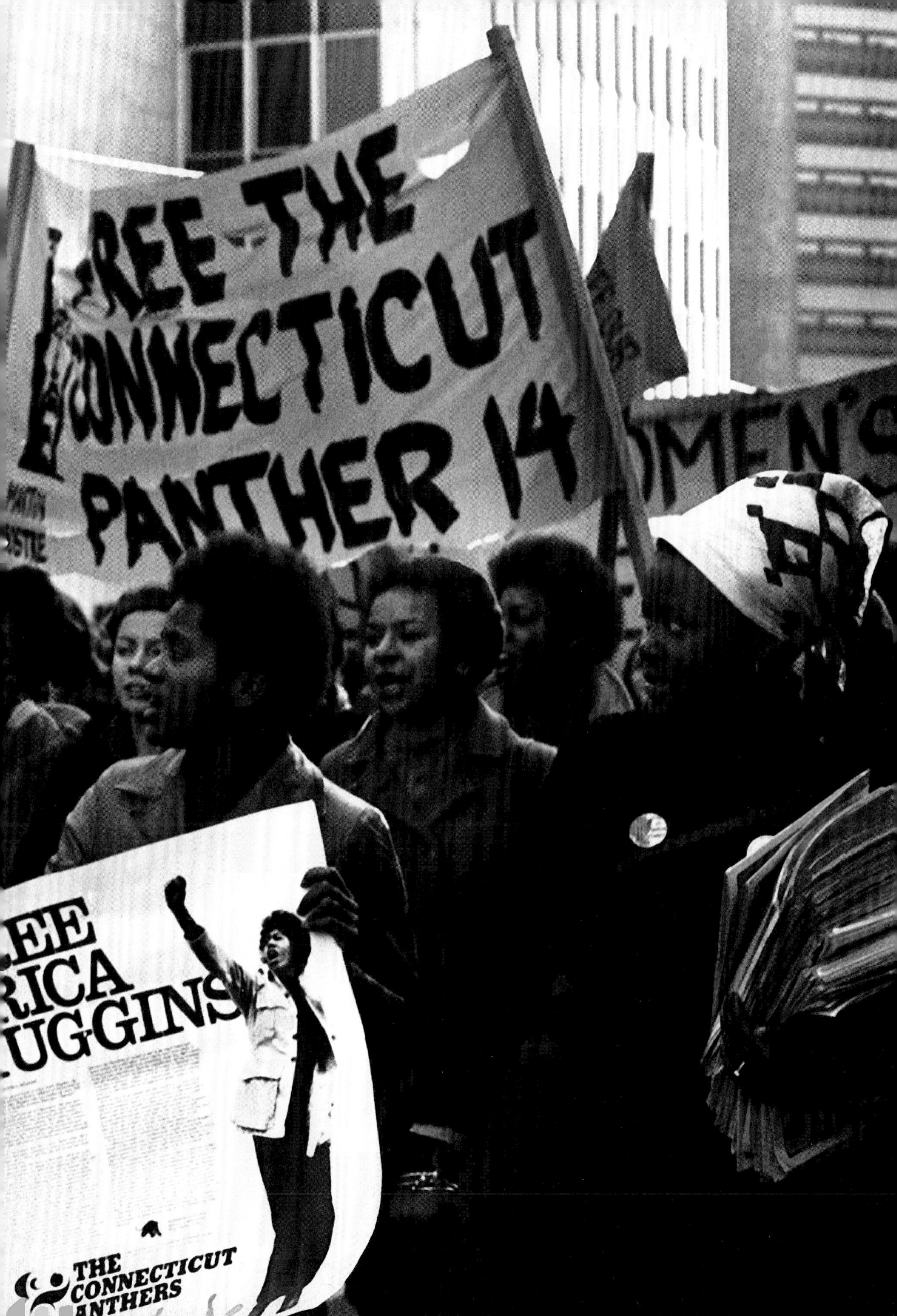
FREE THE
CONNECTICUT
PANTHER 14
WOMEN'S
FREE
ERICA
HUGGINS
THE
CONNECTICUT
PANTHERS

Jeannette Rankin Brigade
Washington, DC

In 1967, I began attending a women's consciousness raising group that met weekly on the Lower East Side, organized by Pam Chude (Allen), with Peggy Powell Dobbins, Kathy Barrett, Carol Hanisch, and Shulamith Firestone, among others. It soon coalesced into a group we called New York Radical Women or NYRW. There was already a women's movement, the National Organization for Women, or NOW, whose co-founder, Betty Friedan, was the author of The Feminine Mystique, published in 1964. She addressed issues related to the experience of white middle class women. The movement she helped found advocated working within the system. In NYRW we believed that the only way to gain real freedom was to overthrow the system.

Our first organized action was on January 15, 1968, when we attended the Jeannette Rankin Brigade in Washington, DC. A group of women's pro-peace organizations, led by Women's Strike for Peace, joined together to confront Congress on its opening day with a display of female opposition to the Vietnam War. At age 87, Jeannette Rankin, a pioneering suffragist, pacifist, and former congresswoman from Montana, led the march of approximately 5,000 women. She was elected to Congress in 1916, the first woman and only Member of Congress to vote against U.S. participation in both World War I and World War II.

It was a rather sedate event, with mostly well-dressed middle-class women politely marching, while we, the radical women, wore pots and pans on our heads. We banged on our pots and chanted, calling for the burial of traditional womanhood. We proclaimed that women must unify into a force to be reckoned with so as not to be patronized and ridiculed into total political ineffectiveness. This was my first foray into participant-based photo-journalism.

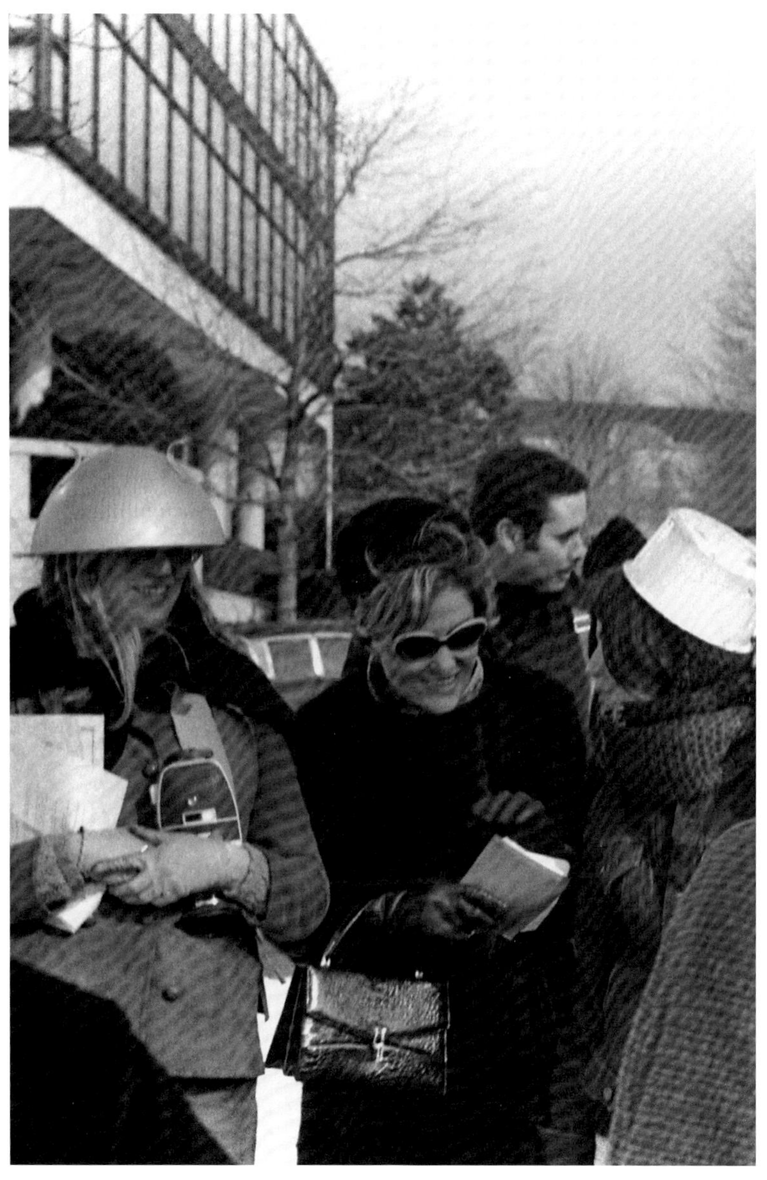

Peggy Powell Dobbins and Bev Grant
Jeannette Rankin Brigade, Washington, DC, January 15, 1968

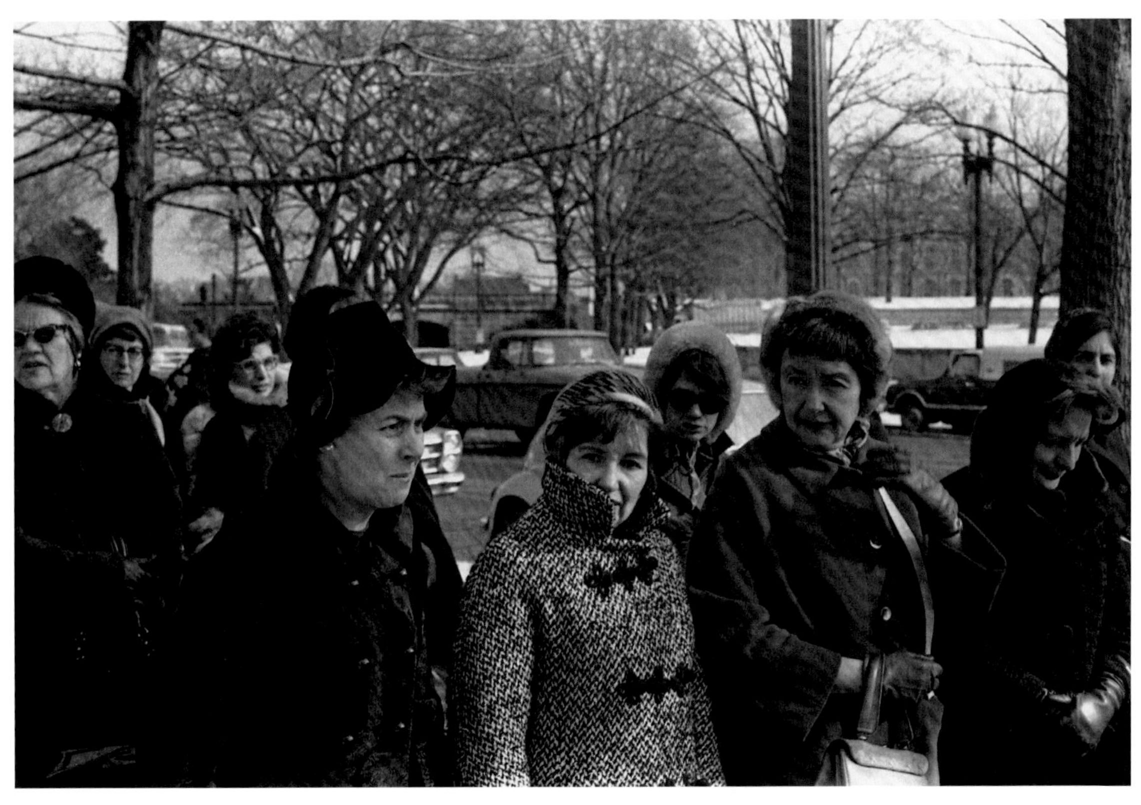

Jeannette Rankin Brigade, Washington, DC, January 15, 1968

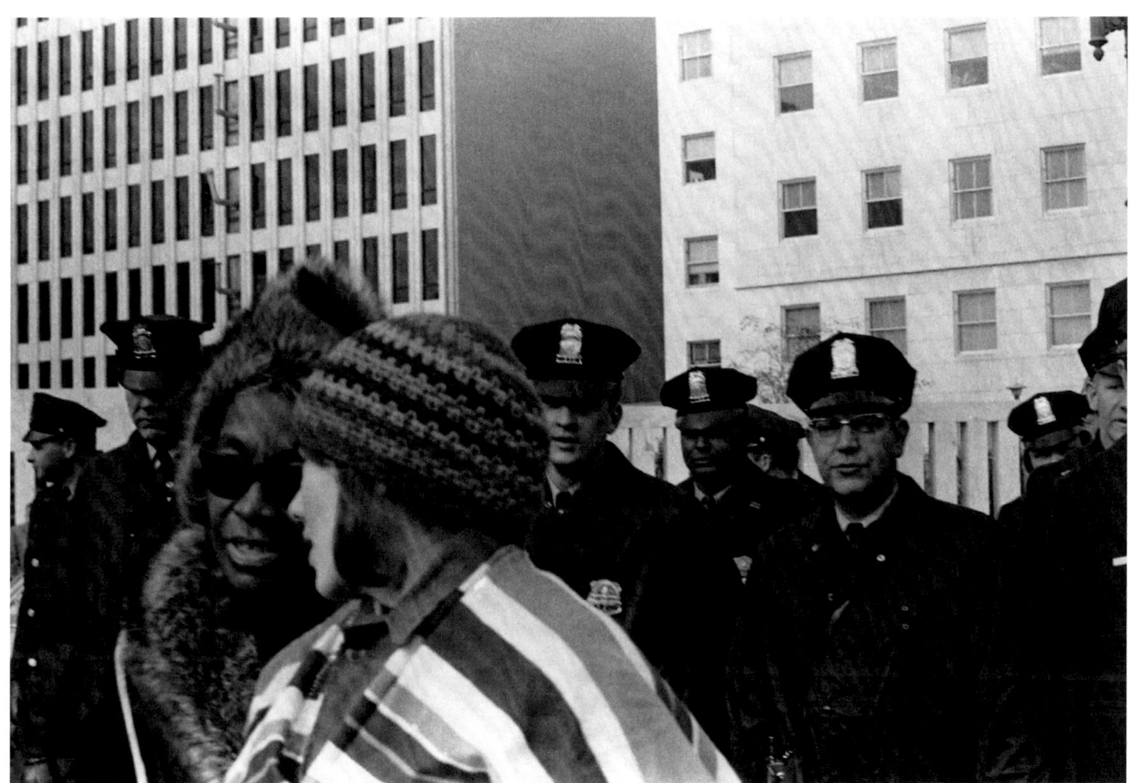

Feminist and Civil Rights attorney, Flo Kennedy and Kathy Barrett of New York Radical Women,
Jeannette Rankin Brigade, Washington, DC, January 15, 1968

Following spread
Jeannette Rankin Brigade, Washington, DC, January 15, 1968

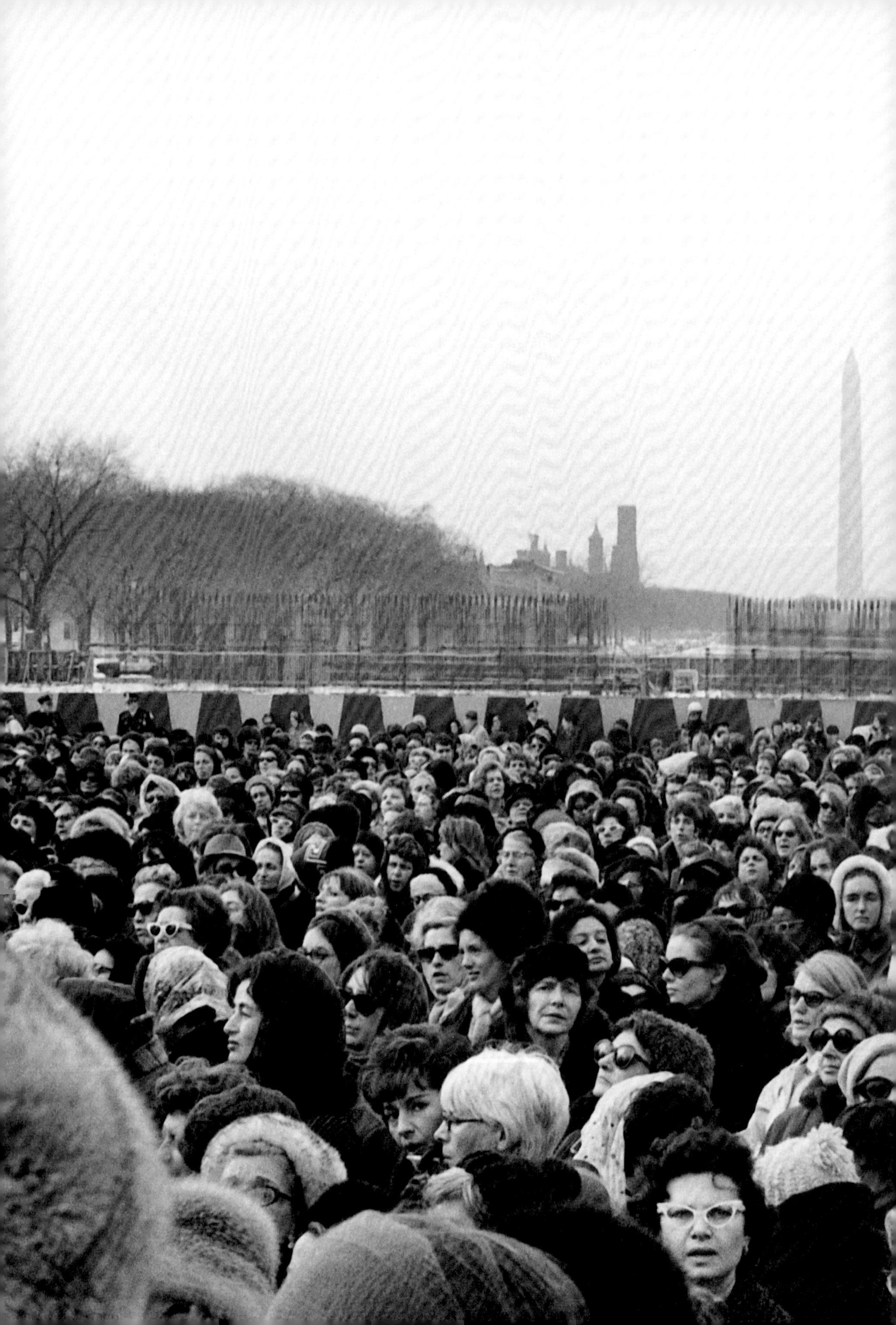

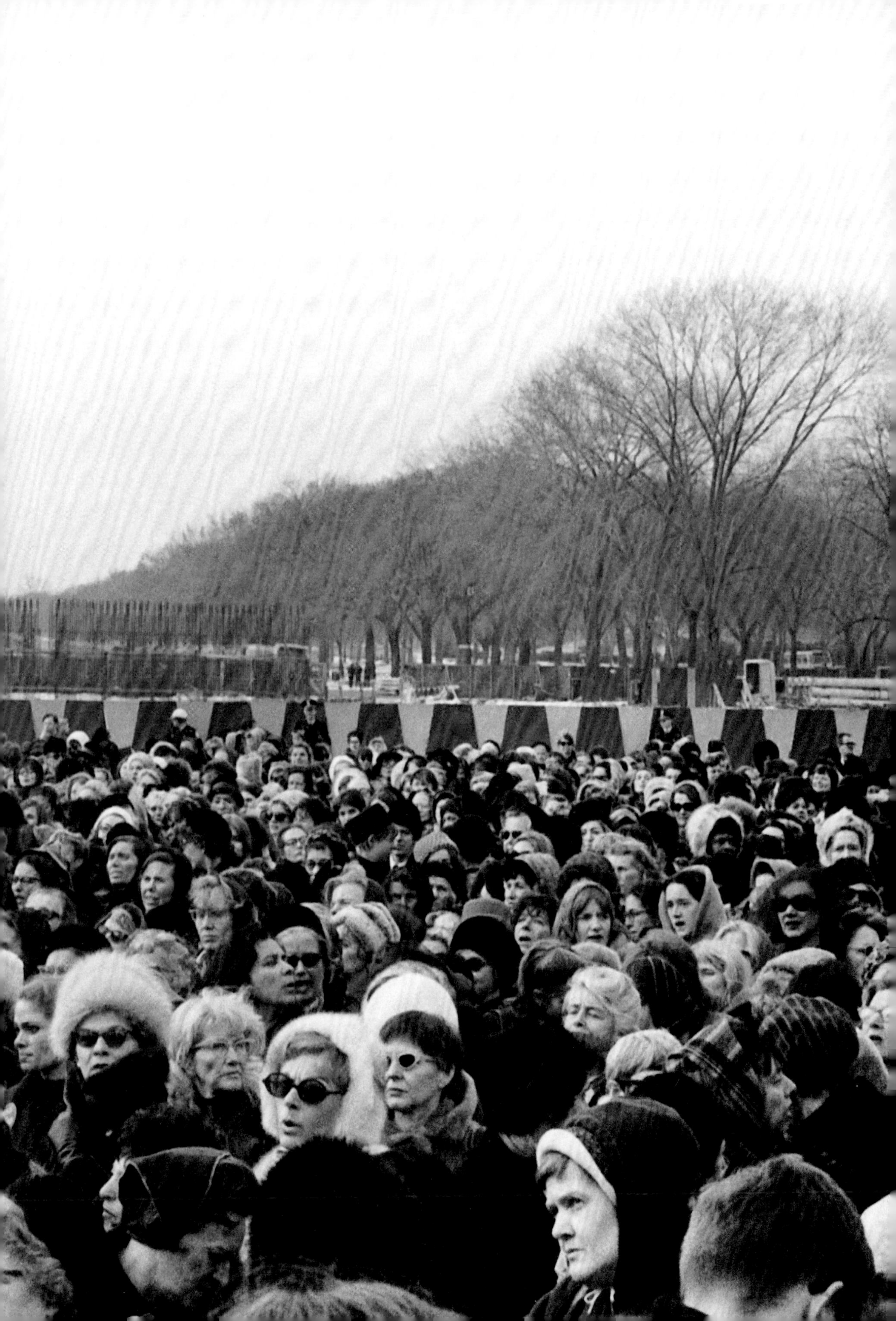

March 24, 1968

Legalize Abortion Rally
Rockefeller Center, New York

On March 24, 1968, New York Radical Women or NYRW participated in a Legalize Abortion rally organized by the Parent's Aid Society of Hempstead, New York. Bill Baird, their director, had been a long-time advocate for reproductive rights. He helped win two US Supreme Court cases that resulted in positive decisions on reproductive rights and a landmark bill in Congress legalizing contraception for all Americans. We marched up Fifth Avenue to Rockefeller Center and set up a large "Legalize Abortion" banner directly facing St. Patrick's Cathedral.

Shulamith Firestone, one of the founders of NYRW, gave a speech in which she expressed our rage and frustration with the patriarchy:

> We want a society that exists for our good as well as yours! We are not just grease between men, links between generations, not just the mothers of sons and their future wives! We are tired of being pawns in a male power game. Tired of being bought and sold and traded and used to sell your deodorants and hair sprays. [...] So: we must say to those bishops and pompous lawmakers and self-righteous men, we will no longer be shoved around. We will no longer submit to your definitions of what we should or should not be or do to become truly feminine in your eyes. For unless we have a part in creating the laws which govern our fate, then we will refuse to follow those dictates and laws.

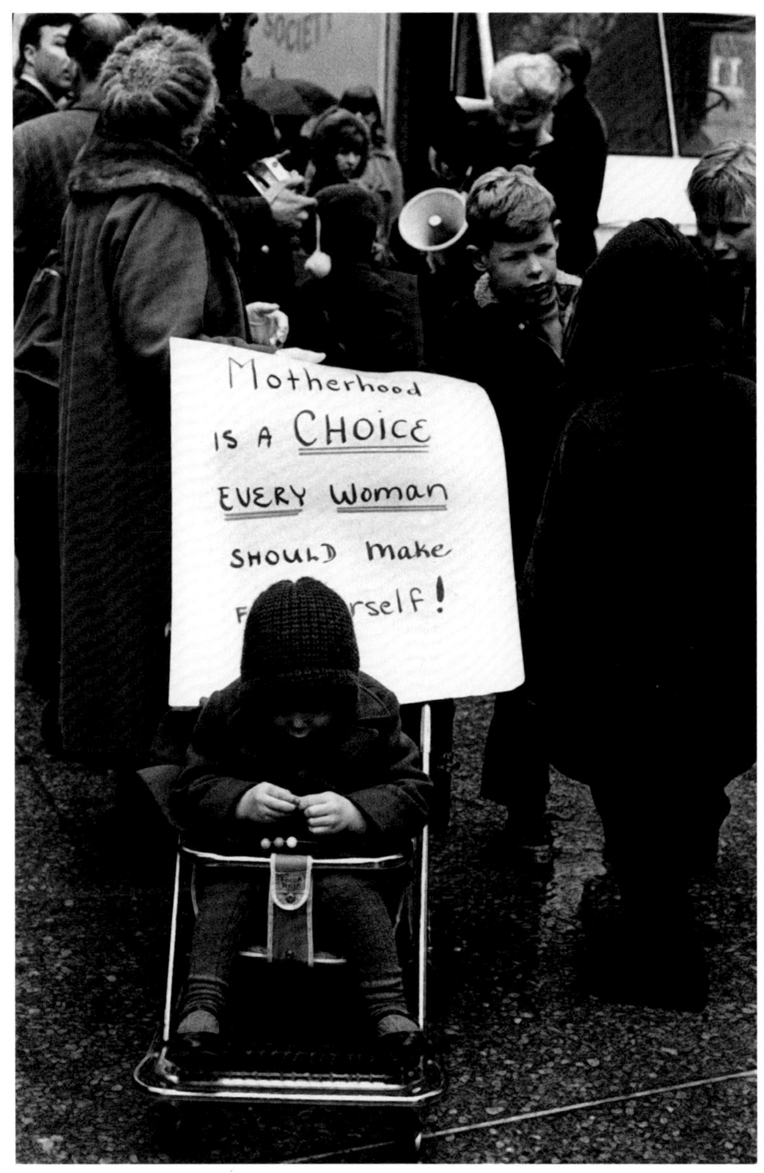

Legalize Abortion Rally, Rockefeller Center, New York, March 24, 1968

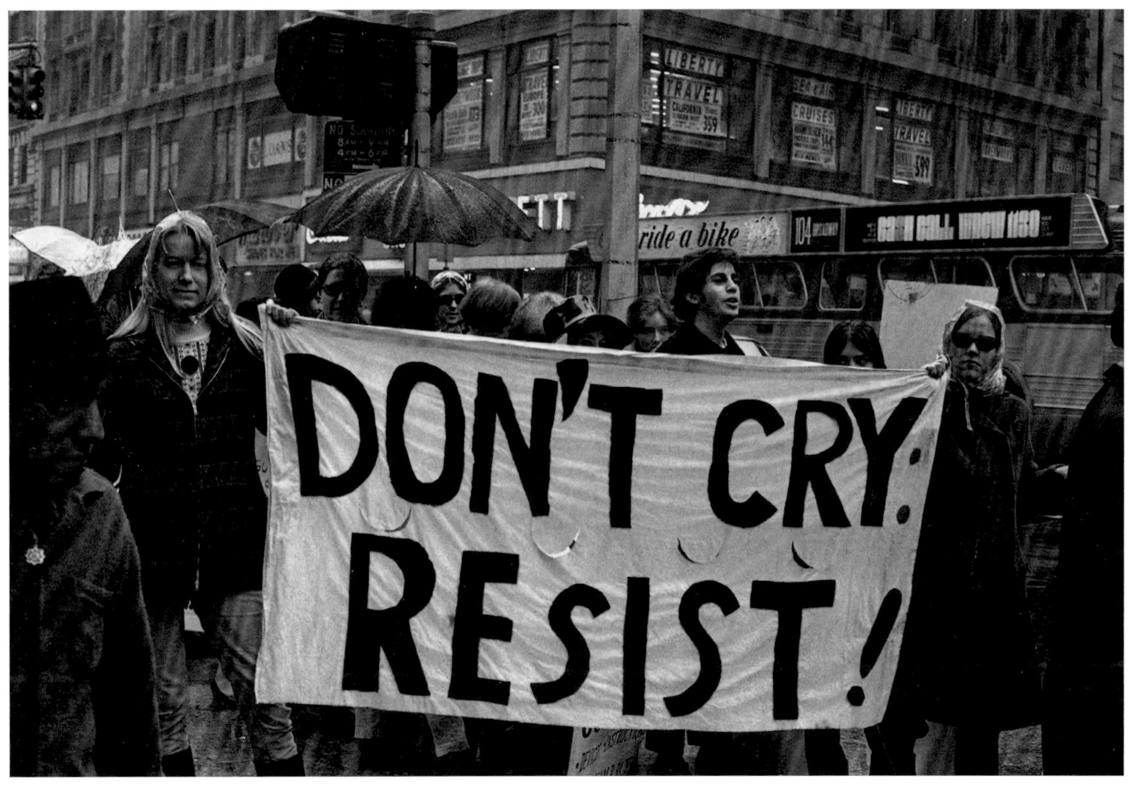

Legalize Abortion Rally, Rockefeller Center, New York, March 24, 1968

Following spread
Legalize Abortion Rally, Rockefeller Center, New York, March 24, 1968

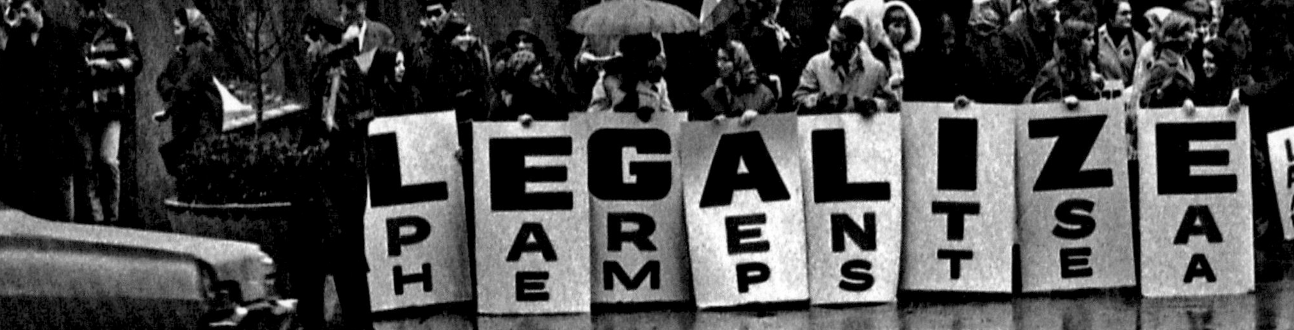

LEGALIZE
PARENTS
PHEASE ATTEMPT SAA

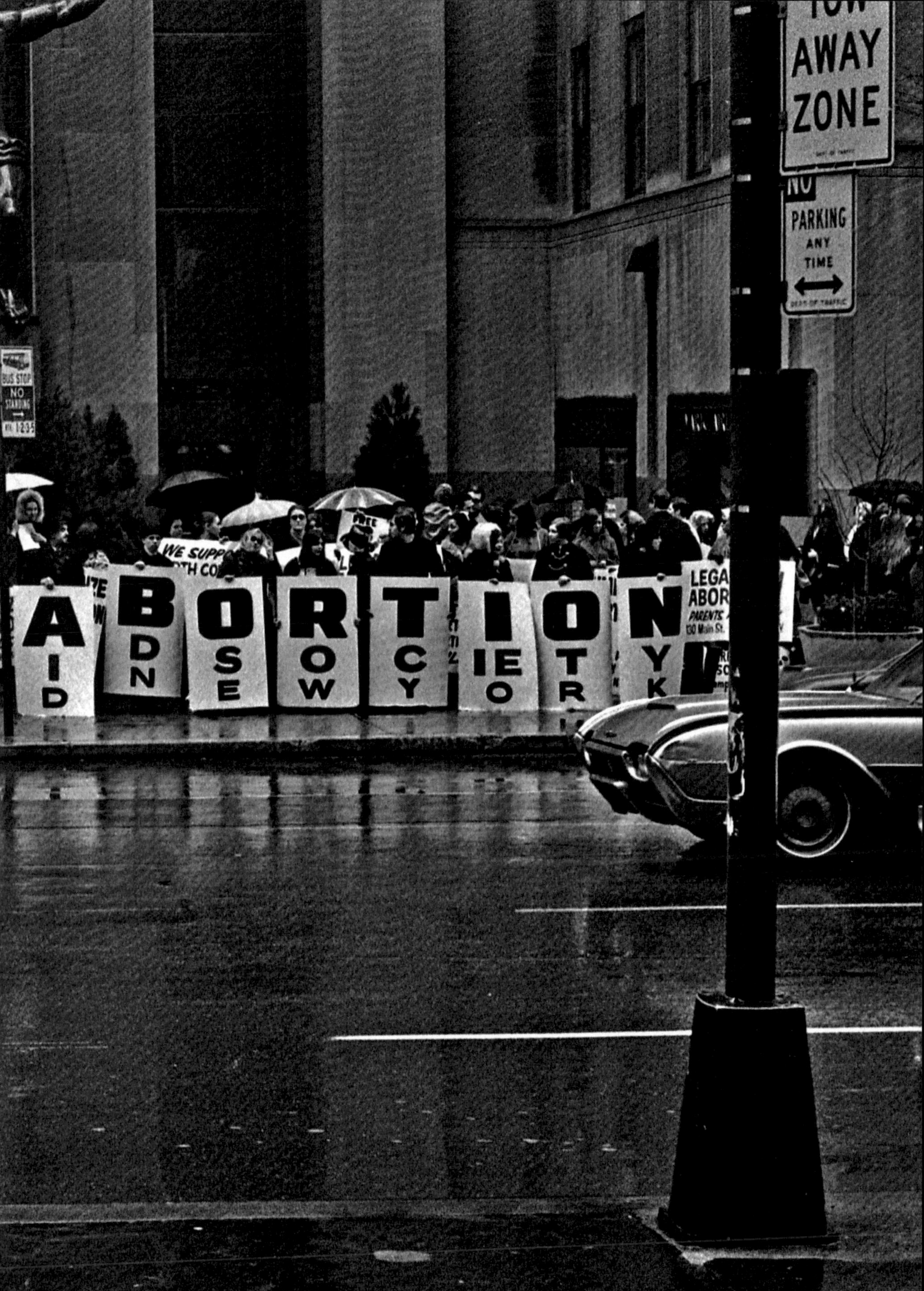

AID
ABORTION
DN
SE
OW
CY
IE
TR
OR
YK
WE SUPP
TH CO
LEGA
ABOR
PARENTS A
130 Main St.
AWAY
ZONE
NO
PARKING
ANY
TIME
BUS STOP
NO
STANDING

GIs Against the War in Vietnam
Central Park, New York

On April 27, 1968, I attended one of many demonstrations in New York City that was led by GIs and veterans against the war in Vietnam. It was said that nearly 90,000 people attended the rally at Sheep Meadow and the bandshell in Central Park. Similar demonstrations on the same day drew thousands in Chicago and San Francisco. It was a rainy day, but one guy managed to burn his draft card. Abbie Hoffman and Jerry Rubin, founding members of the Yippies, both spoke at the bandshell, with Ossie Davis as the emcee. Only three weeks after Dr. Martin Luther King Jr.'s murder, his widow Coretta Scott King gave a speech in Sheep Meadow, in which she read her late husband's *Ten Commandments on Vietnam*:

> Thou shalt not believe in a military victory.
> Thou shalt not believe in a politicalvictory.
> Thou shalt not believe that they, the Vietnamese, love us.
> Thou shalt not believe that the Saigon government has the support of the people.
> Thou shalt not believe that the majority of the South Vietnamese look upon the
> Vietcong as terrorists.
> Thou shalt not believe the figures of killed enemies or killed Americans.
> Thou shalt not believe that the generals know best.
> Thou shalt not believe that the enemy's victory means communism.
> Thou shalt not believe that the world supports the United States.
> Thou shalt not kill.

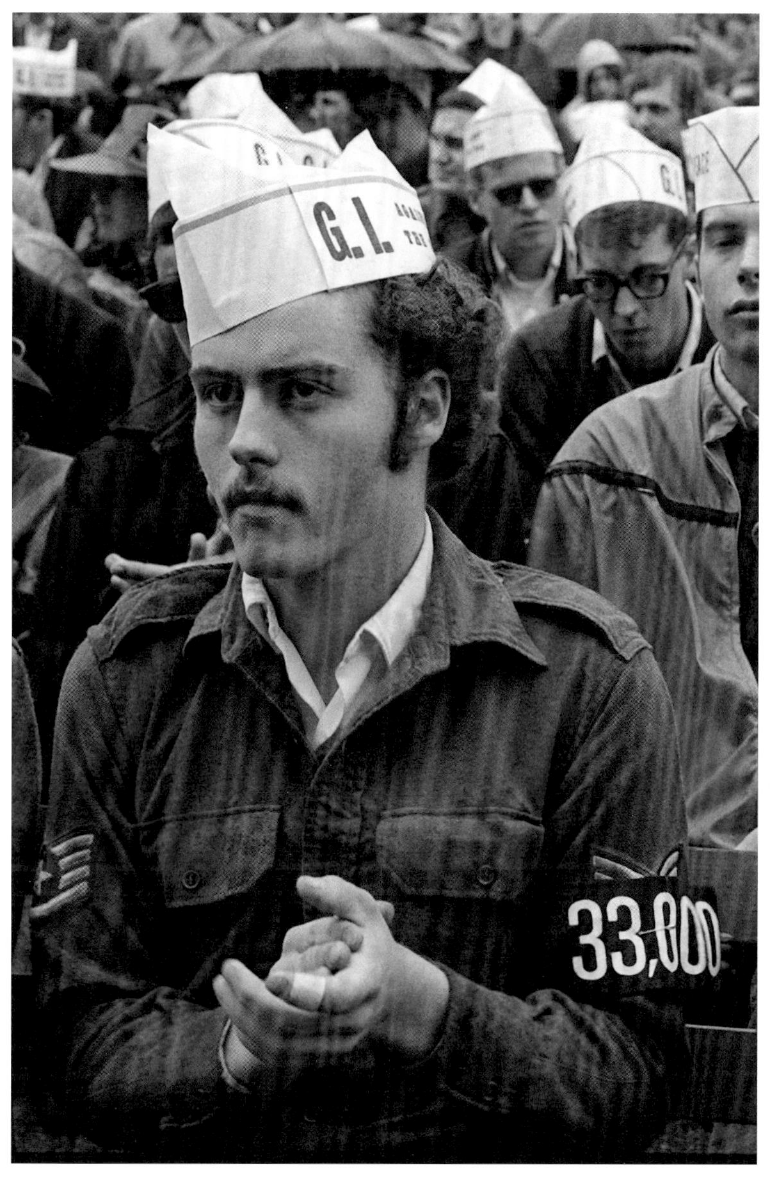

GI wearing armband with death toll
GIs Against the War in Vietnam, Central Park, New York, April 27, 1968

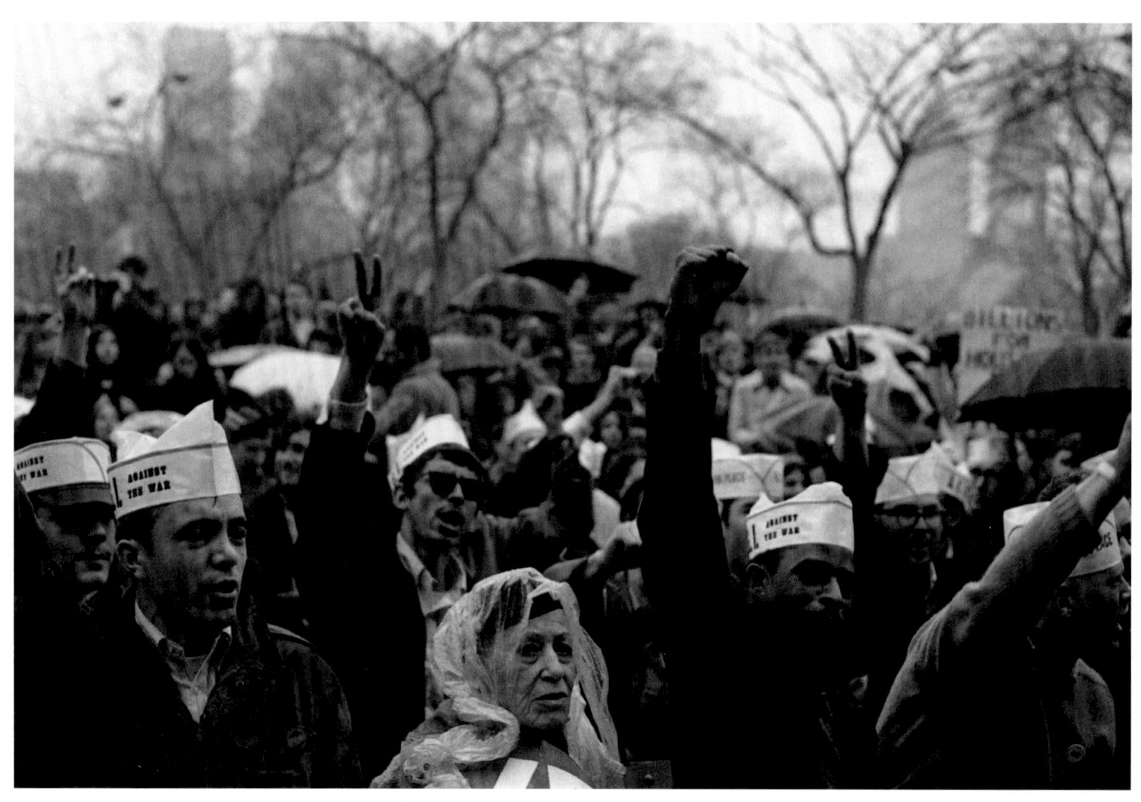

GIs Against the War in Vietnam, Central Park, New York, April 27, 1968

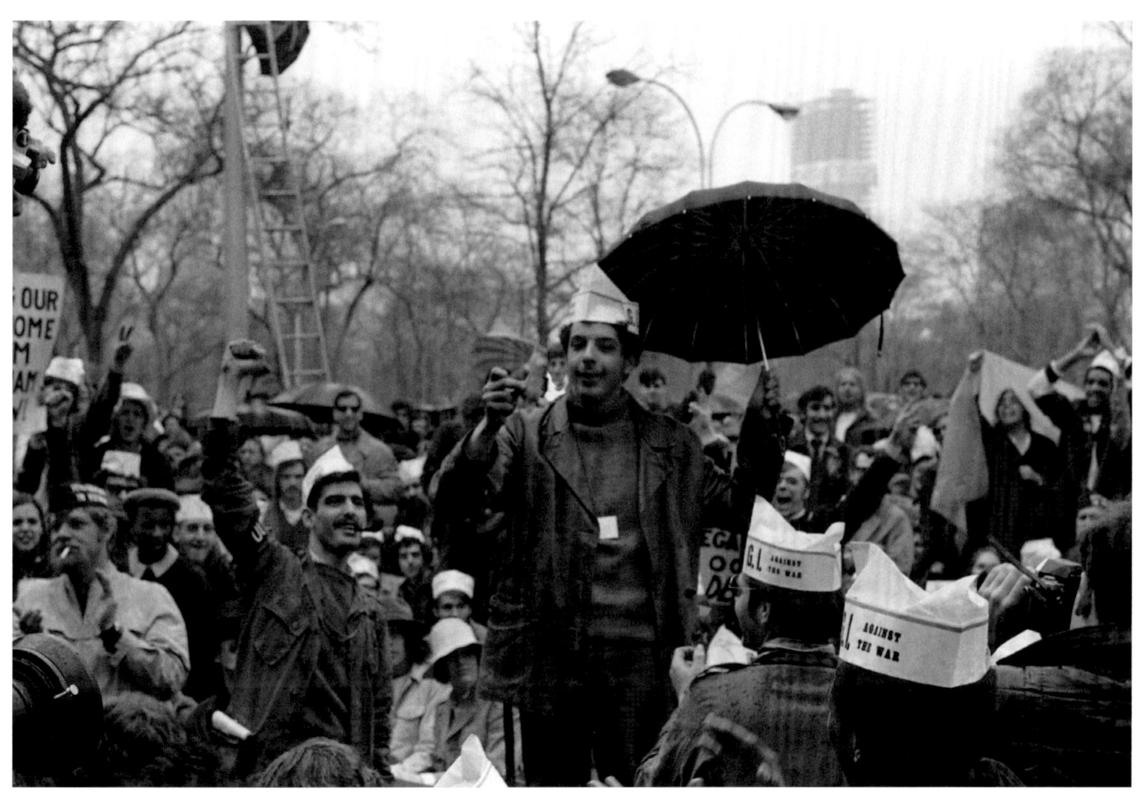

GI burning his draft card
GIs Against the War in Vietnam, Central Park, New York, April 27, 1968

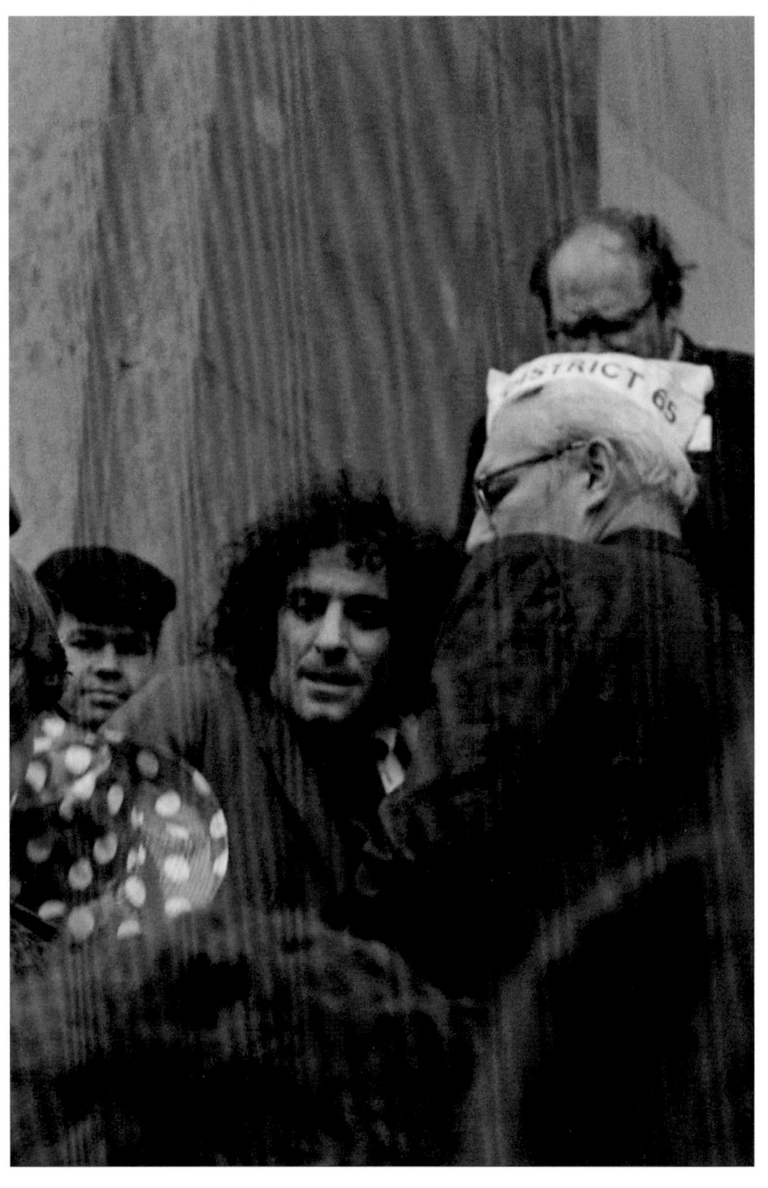

Abbie Hoffman, cofounder of the Yippies
GIs Against the War in Vietnam, Central Park, New York, April 27, 1968

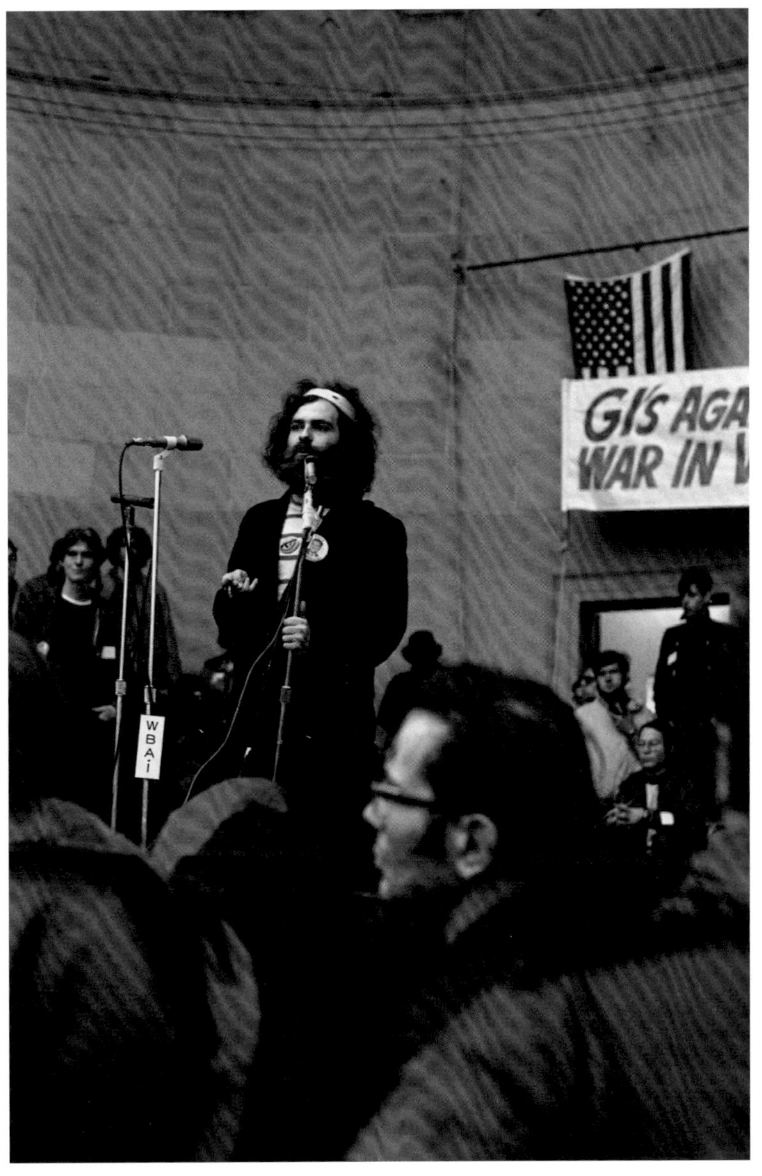

Jerry Rubin, cofounder of the Yippies
GIs Against the War in Vietnam, Central Park, New York, April 27, 1968

Following spread
GIs Against the War in Vietnam, Central Park, New York, April 27, 1968

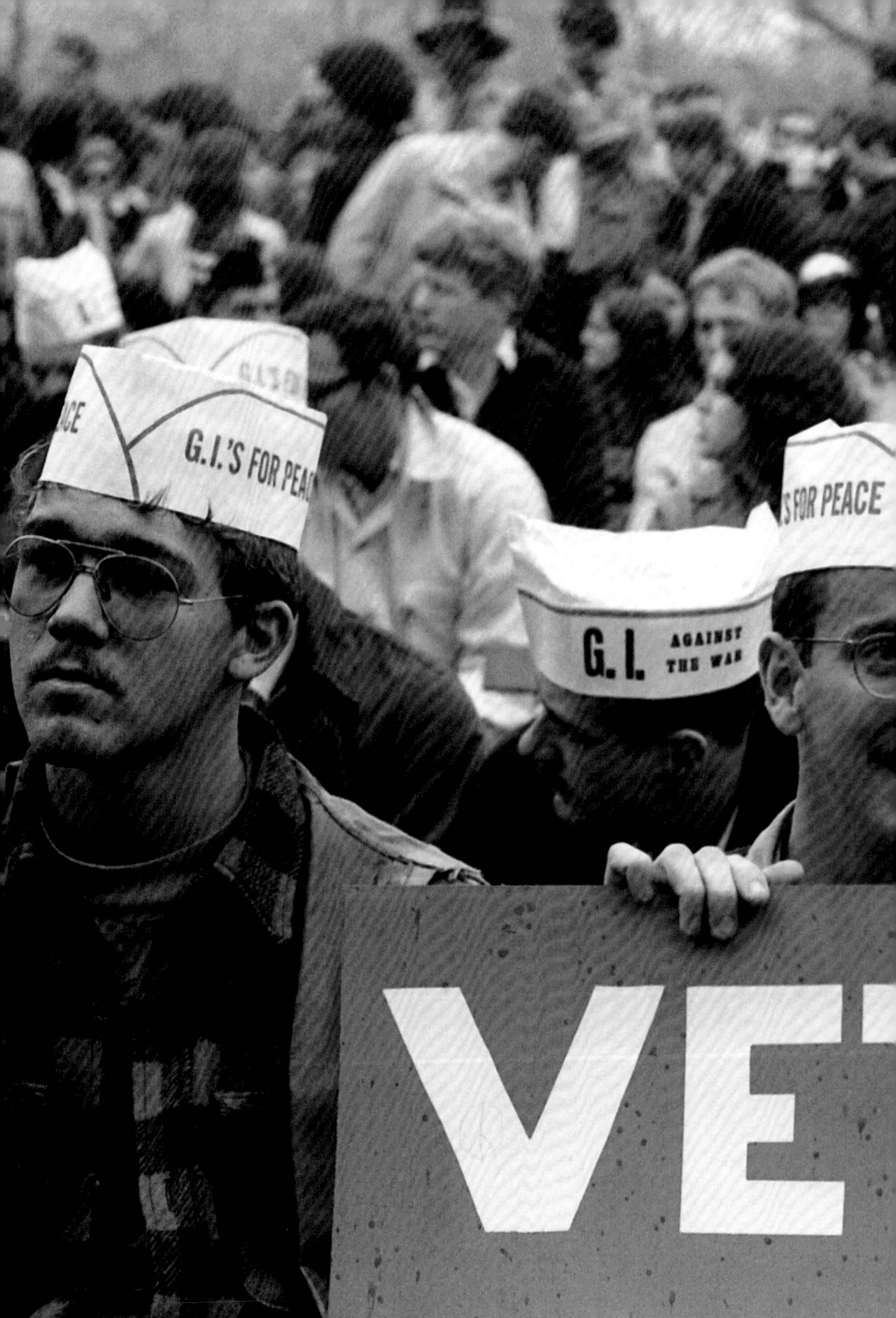
G.I.'S FOR PEACE
ACE
G.I. AGAINST THE WAR
S FOR PEACE
VE

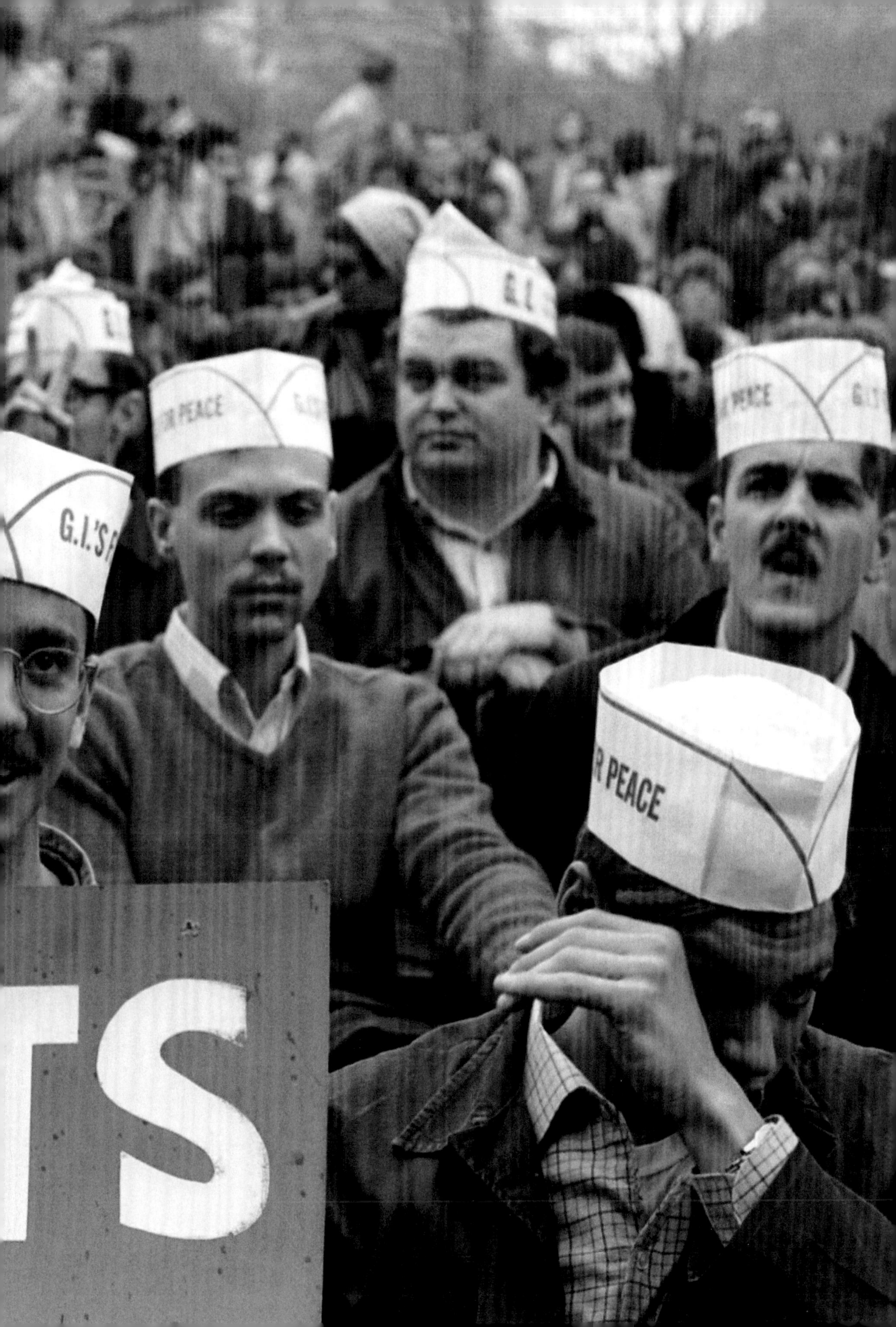
G.I.'S FOR PEACE
G.I.'S FOR PEACE
G.I.'S
FOR PEACE
G.I.'S
FOR PEACE
TS

Poor People's Campaign
New York City

On April 29, 1968, two days after Coretta Scott King's promise that we will "kick off this poor people's campaign" and will be "marching towards Washington," the Poor People's Campaign established Resurrection City in Washington, DC, an encampment of people of all races gathered to confront the power structure. Dr. Martin Luther King Jr. had called for America to "bridge the gulf between the have and the have-nots" and to end the war in Vietnam. He was assassinated in Memphis, Tennessee, on April 4, only twenty-five days before the campaign was to begin. The Poor People's Campaign went forward under the leadership of Dr. Ralph Abernathy and the Southern Christian Leadership Conference or SCLC, which was founded in 1957 to help coordinate Civil Rights protest activity across the south.

Organizers spread out to head up regional caravans that would bring people to occupy Resurrection City and to demonstrate for economic rights. On May 9, the Eastern Caravan started in Boston, and two days later rallied in New York City on their way to Washington. We gathered at the 369th Infantry Armory in Harlem, home to the Harlem Hellfighters, an all-Black regiment in World War I, before marching to Central Park.

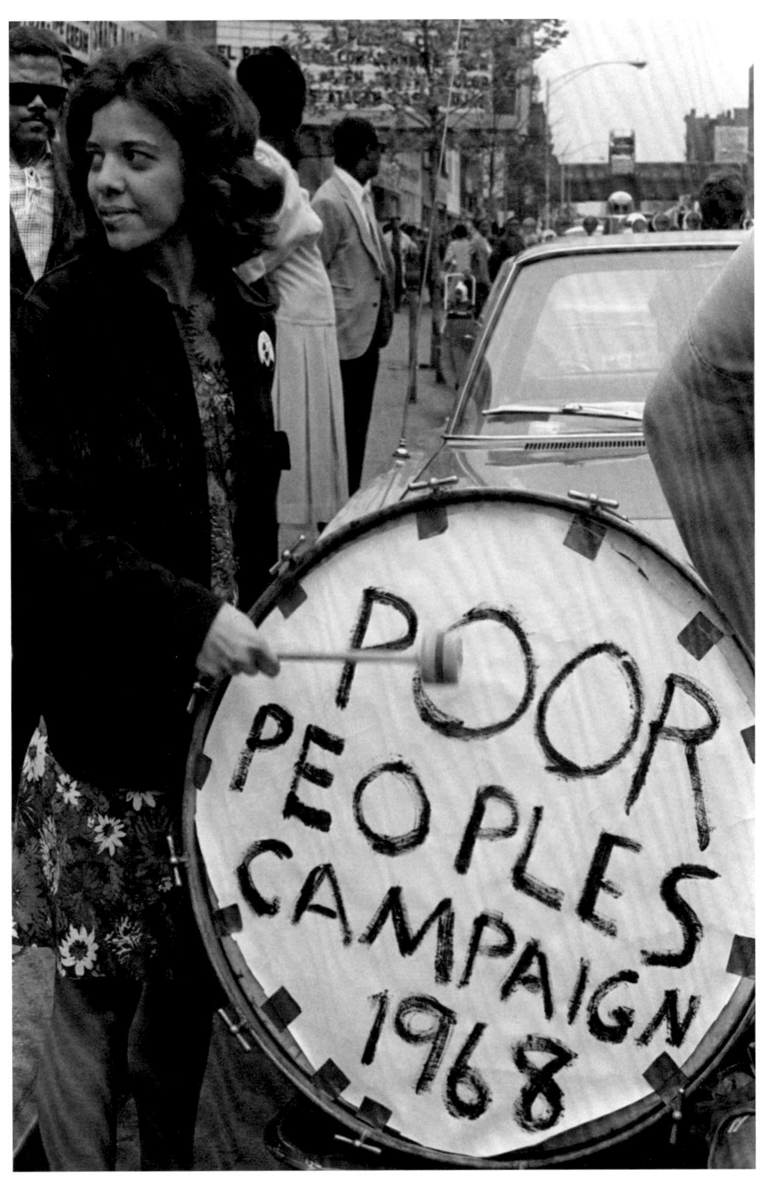

The Eastern Caravan is greeted with music
Poor People's Campaign, New York City, May 11, 1968

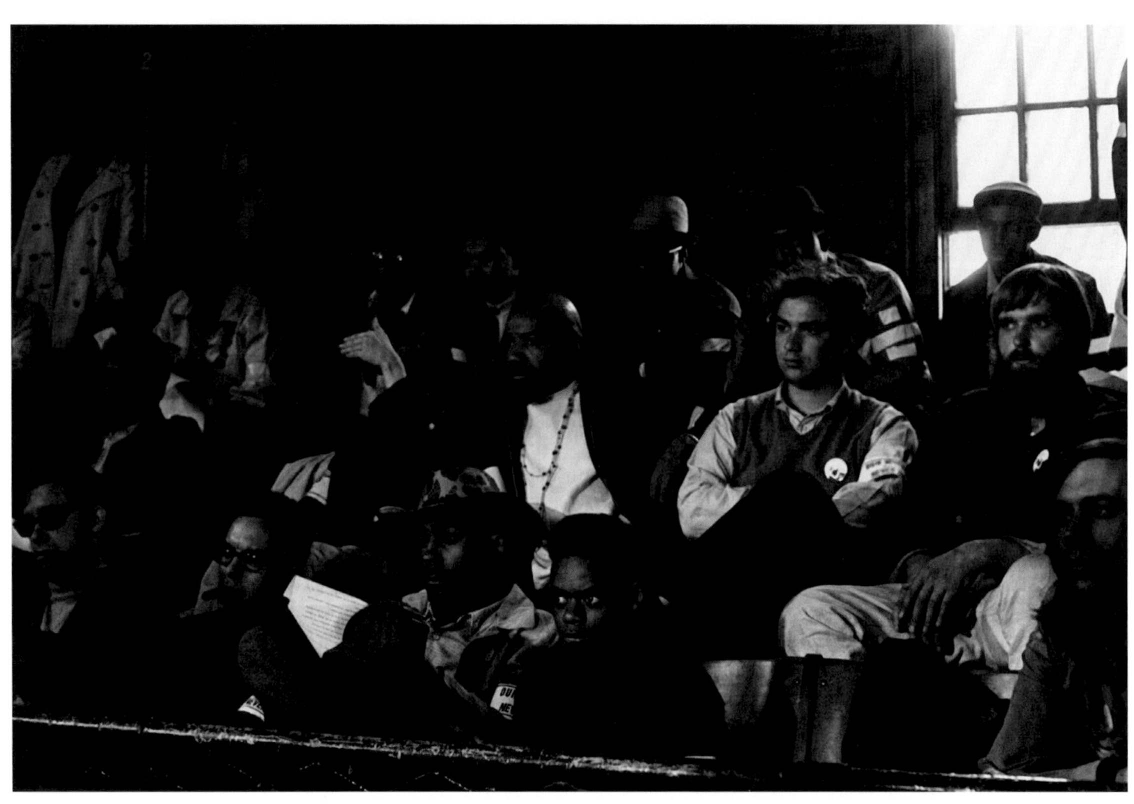

Gathering at the 369th Infantry Armory
Poor People's Campaign, New York City, May 11, 1968

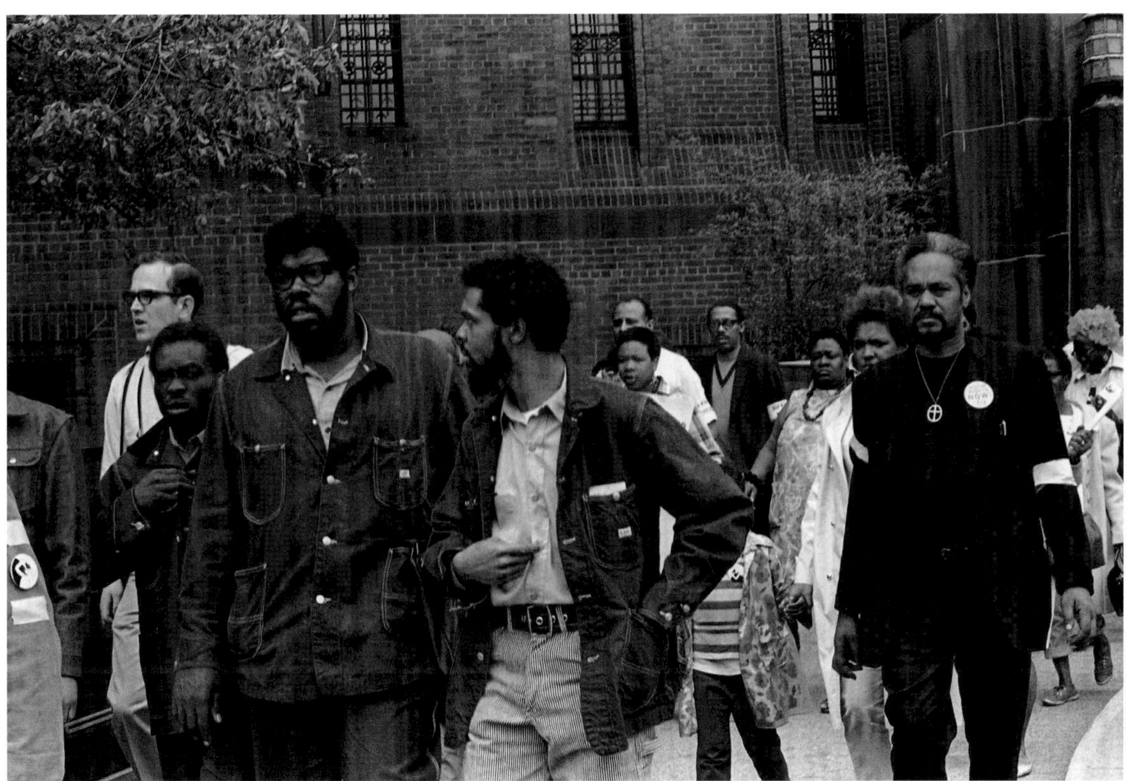

James Orange and Jimmy Collier, 369th Infantry Armory
Poor People's Campaign, New York City, May 11, 1968

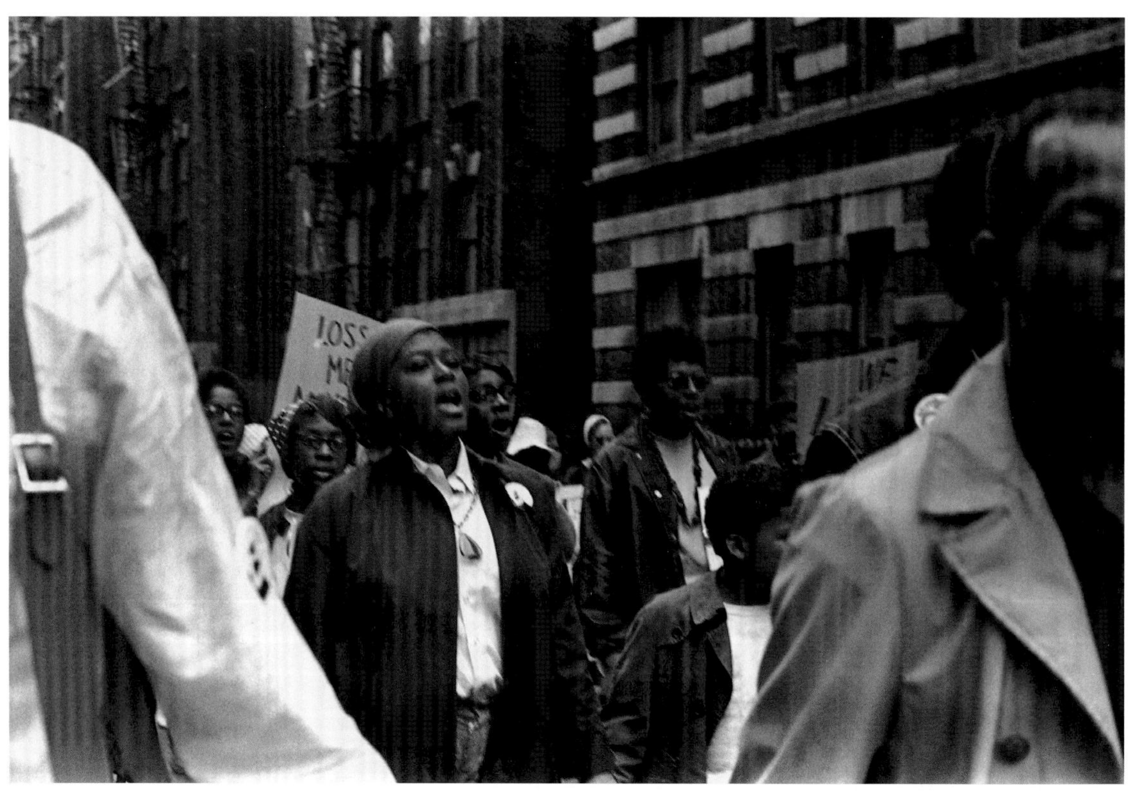

Eastern Caravan
Poor People's Campaign, New York City, May 11, 1968

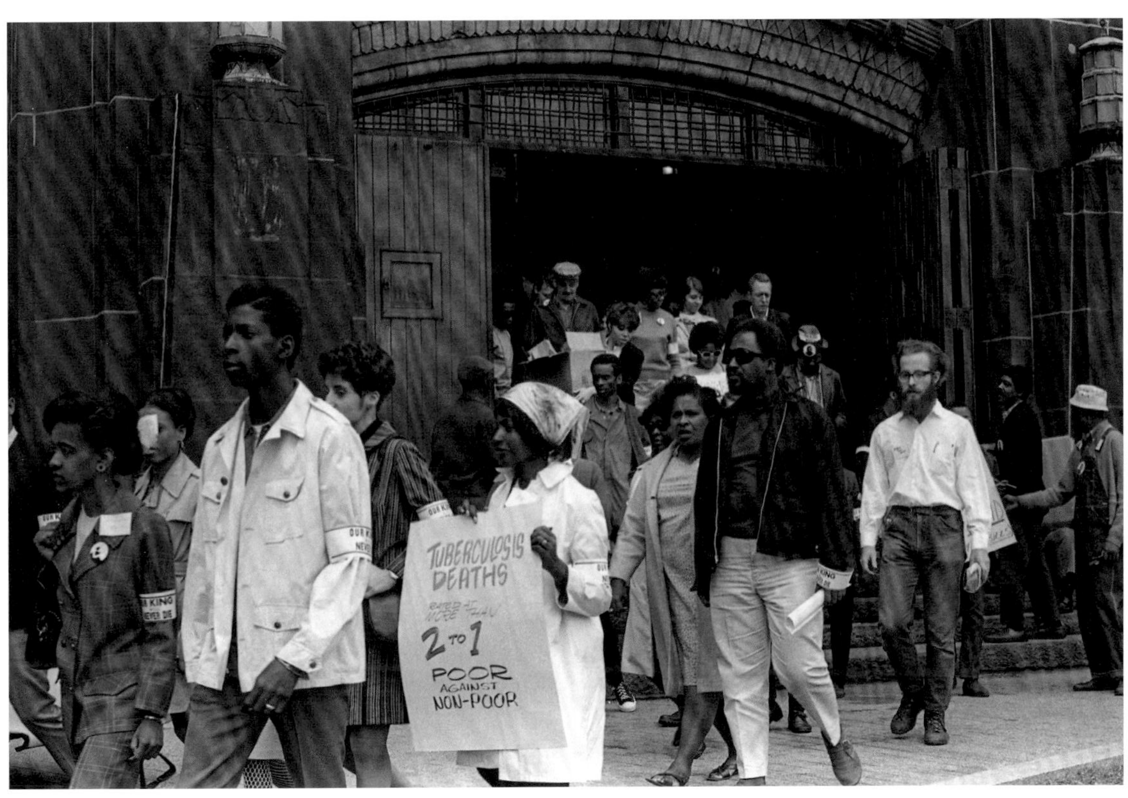

Eastern Caravan, 369th Infantry Armory
Poor People's Campaign, New York City, May 11, 1968

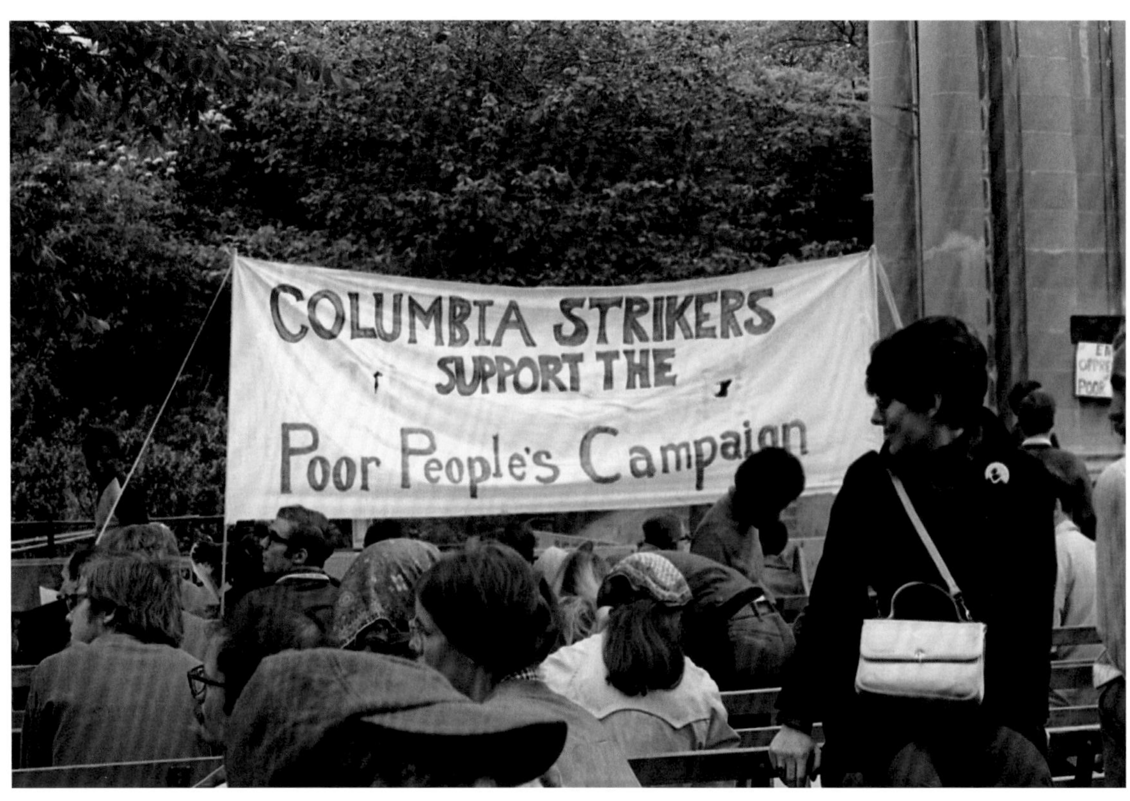

Columbia University Strikers support banner
Poor People's Campaign, New York City, May 11, 1968

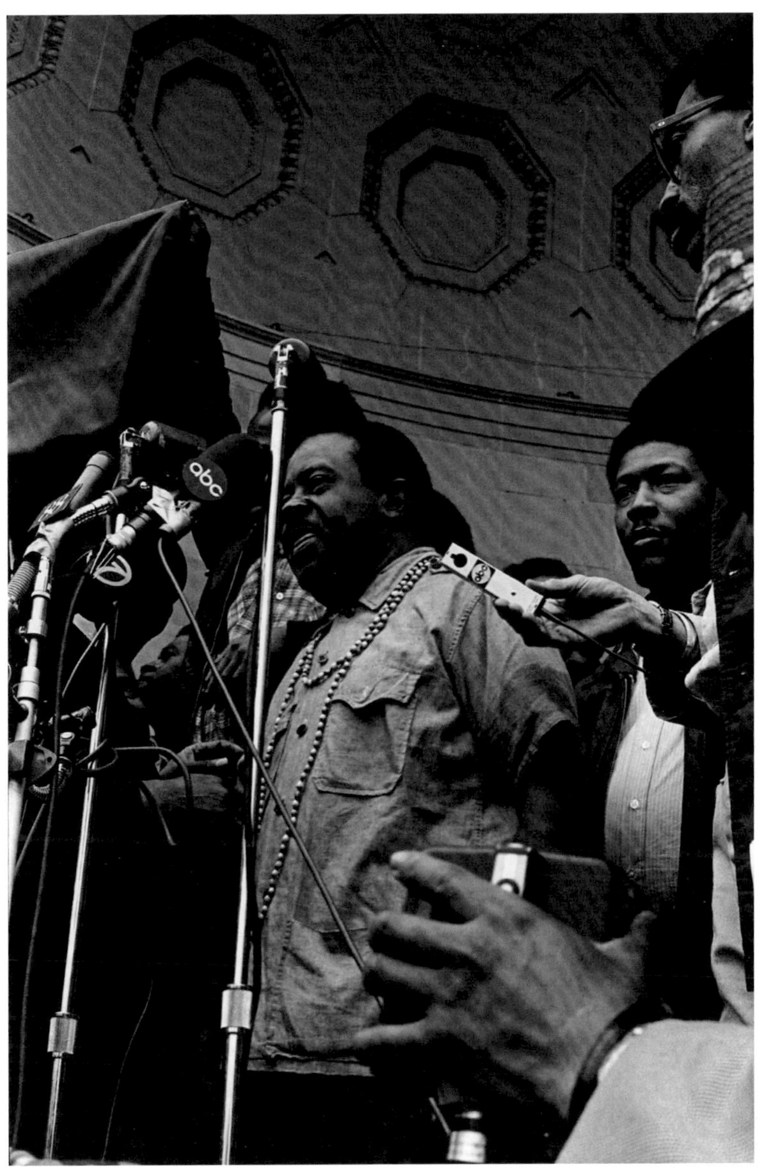

Dr. Ralph Abernathy, Central Park Bandshell
Poor People's Campaign, New York City, May 11, 1968

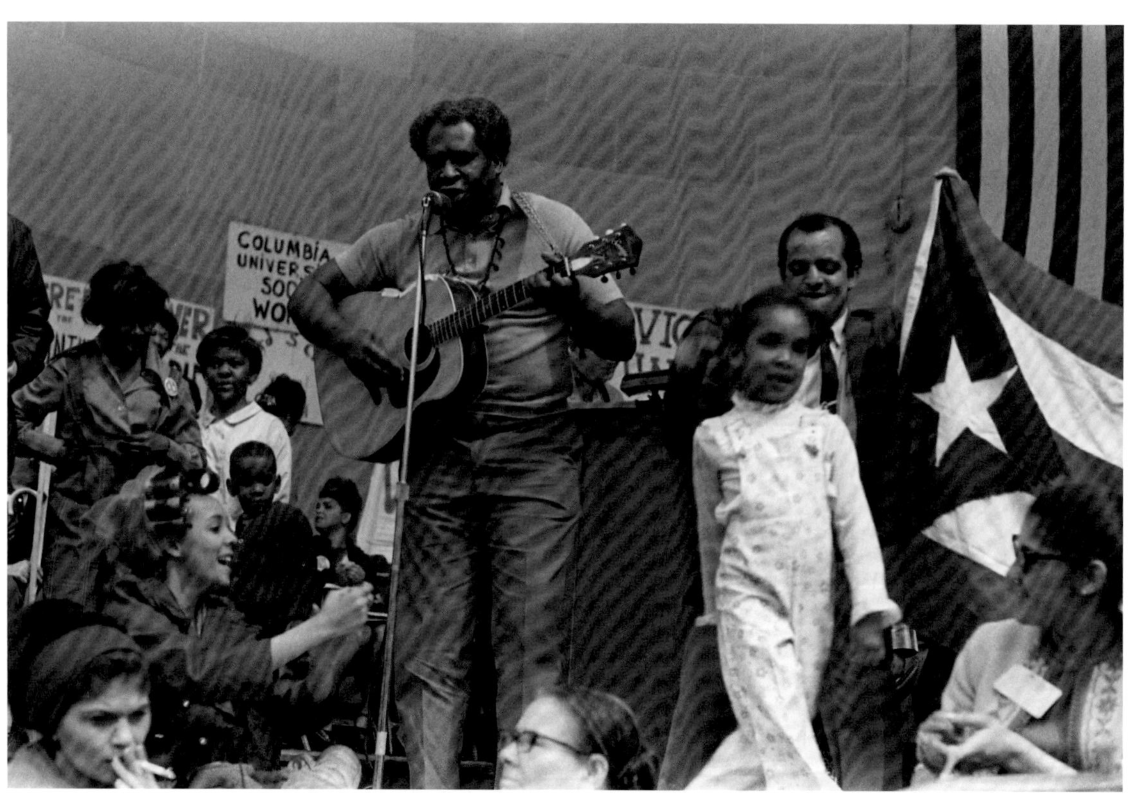

Reverend Frederick Douglass Kirkpatrick
Poor People's Campaign, New York City, May 11, 1968

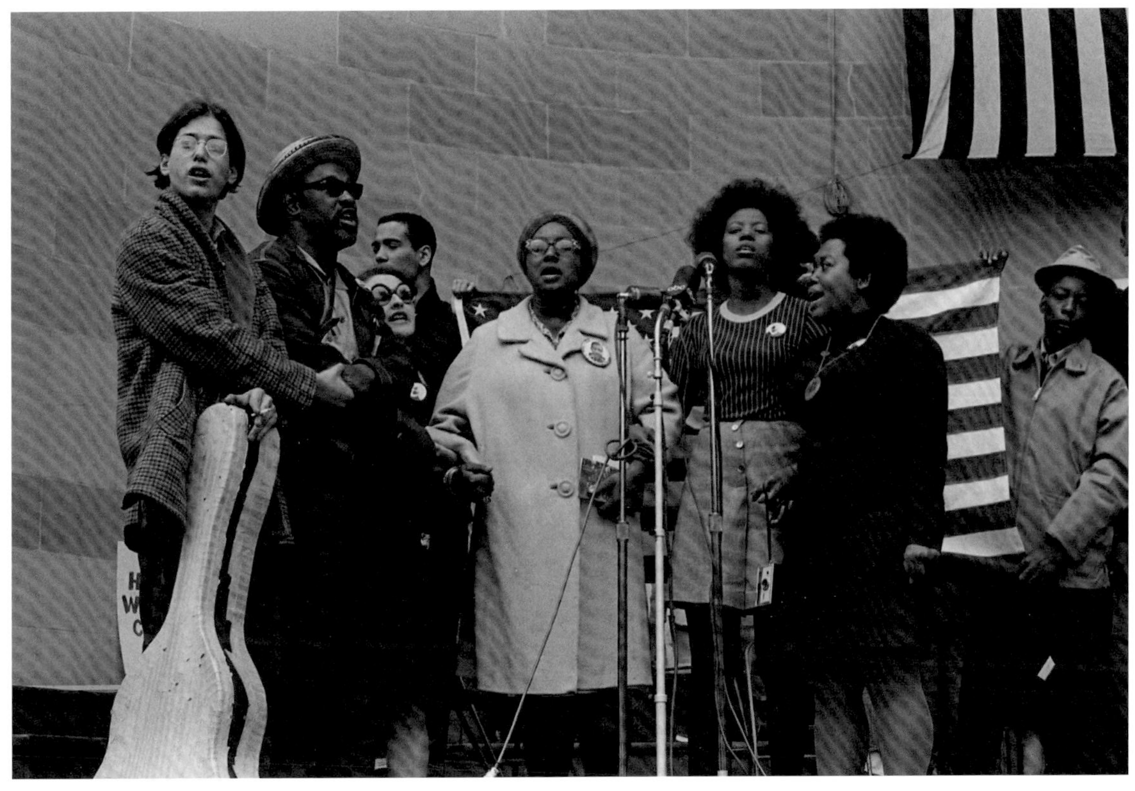

Freedom singers
Poor People's Campaign, New York City, May 11, 1968

Following spread
Welcoming the Eastern Caravan
Poor People's Campaign, New York City, May 11, 1968

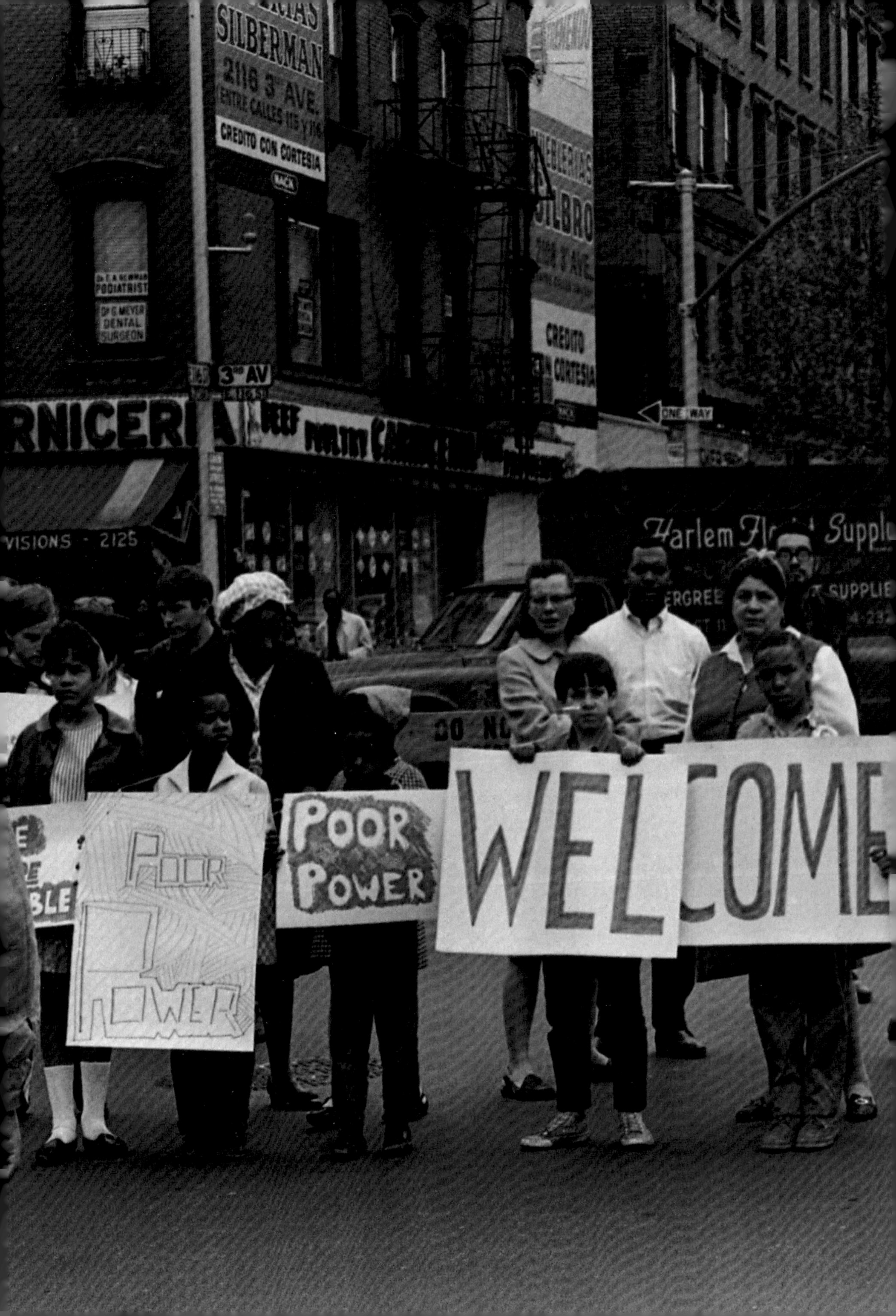

SILBERMAN
2116 3 AVE.
(ENTRE CALLES 115 Y 116)
CREDITO CON CORTESIA
Dr. E. A. NEWMAN
PODIATRIST
Dr. G. MEYER
DENTAL SURGEON
3RD AV
MUEBLERIAS
SILBRO
CREDITO CON CORTESIA
ONE WAY
RNICERIA
BEEF
VISIONS · 2125
Harlem Florist Supply
SUPPLIE
DO NO
POOR POWER
POOR POWER
WELCOME

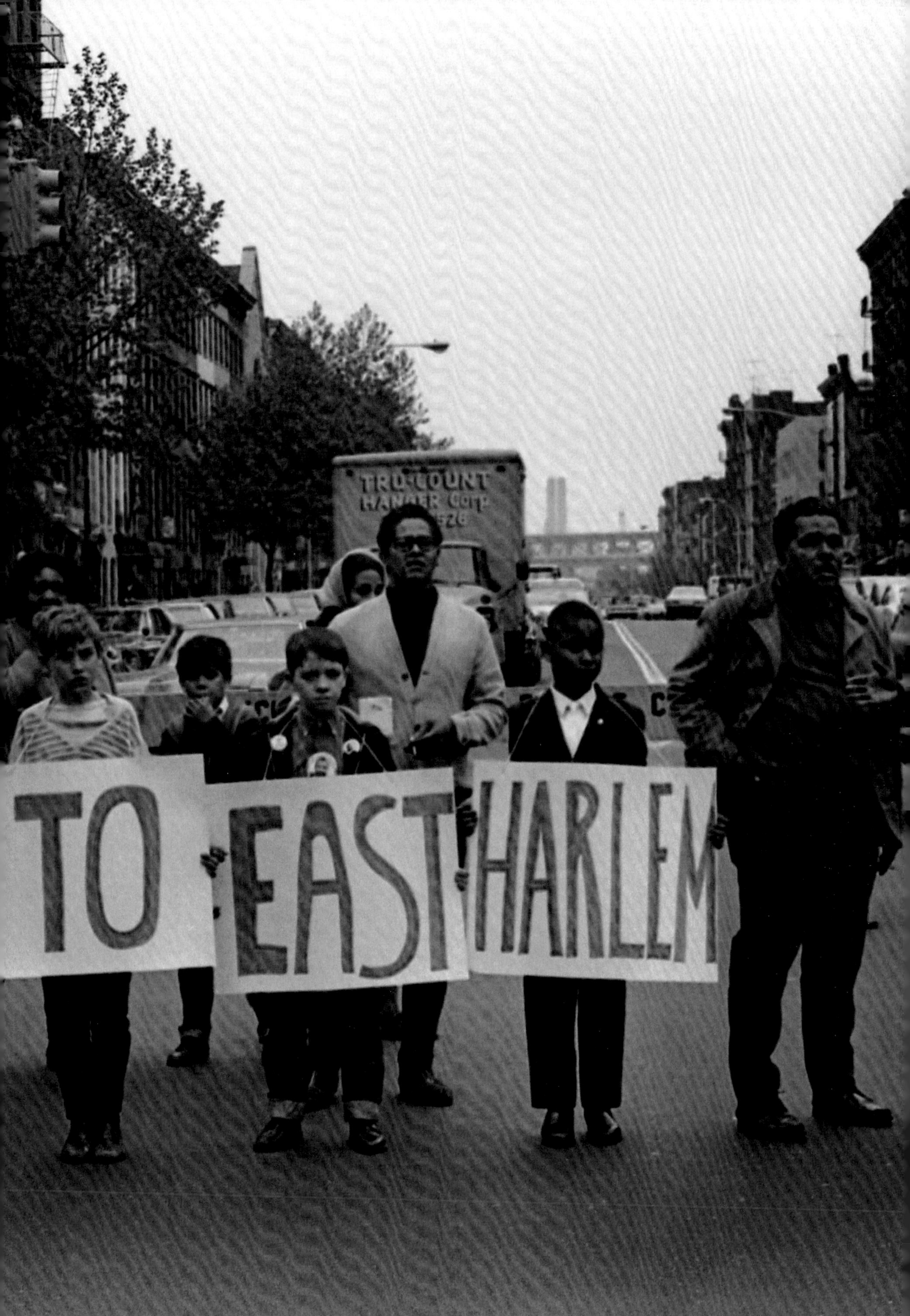

TO
EAST
HARLEM
TRU-COUNT
HANGER CORP

May 18, 1968

Anti-Imperialist Demonstration
New York City

On May 18, 1968, I covered a large Anti-Imperialist demonstration that began in Washington Square Park and ended in Union Square. It was a large umbrella event, with groups representing Puerto Rican independence, Dominican independence, anti-draft and anti-Vietnam war, economic justice, anti-secret police as well as socialist and anarchist sentiment. People milled around in the park, children waded in the fountain pool, others blew bubbles while a group of musicians jammed. Somehow, someone managed to get on top of the arch and wave a Viet Cong flag. There were many placards and banners proclaiming the views of the various constituencies. We marched out of the park and across West Fourth Street through the Lower East Side and up to Union Square.

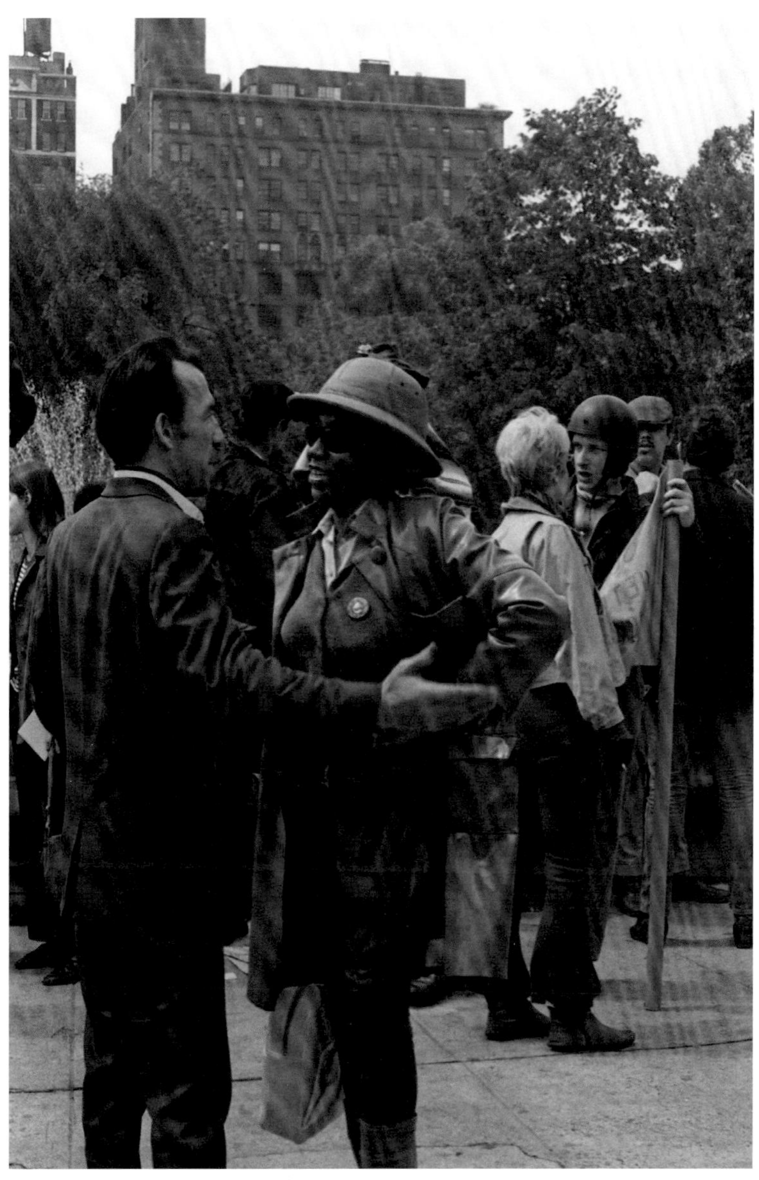

Feminist and Civil Rights attorney, Flo Kennedy, Washington Square Park
Anti-Imperialist Demonstration, New York City, May 18, 1968

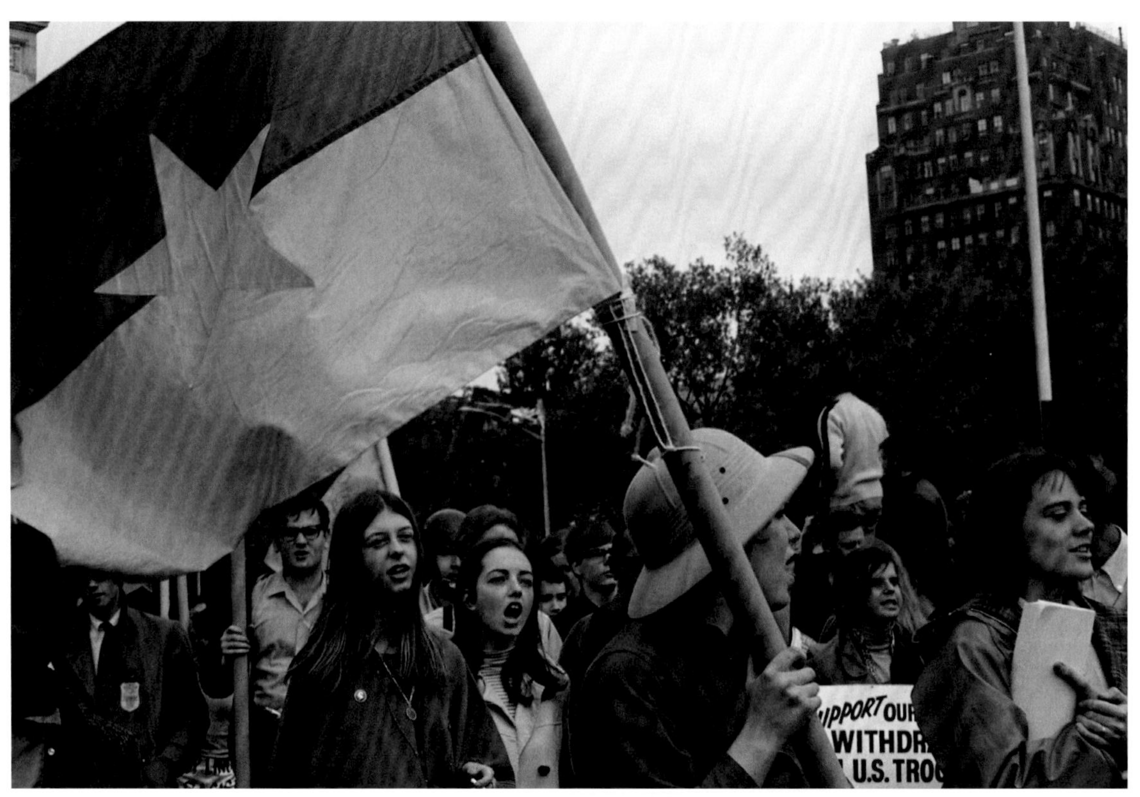

Marchers with Viet Cong flag, Washington Square Park
Anti-Imperialist Demonstration, New York City, May 18, 1968

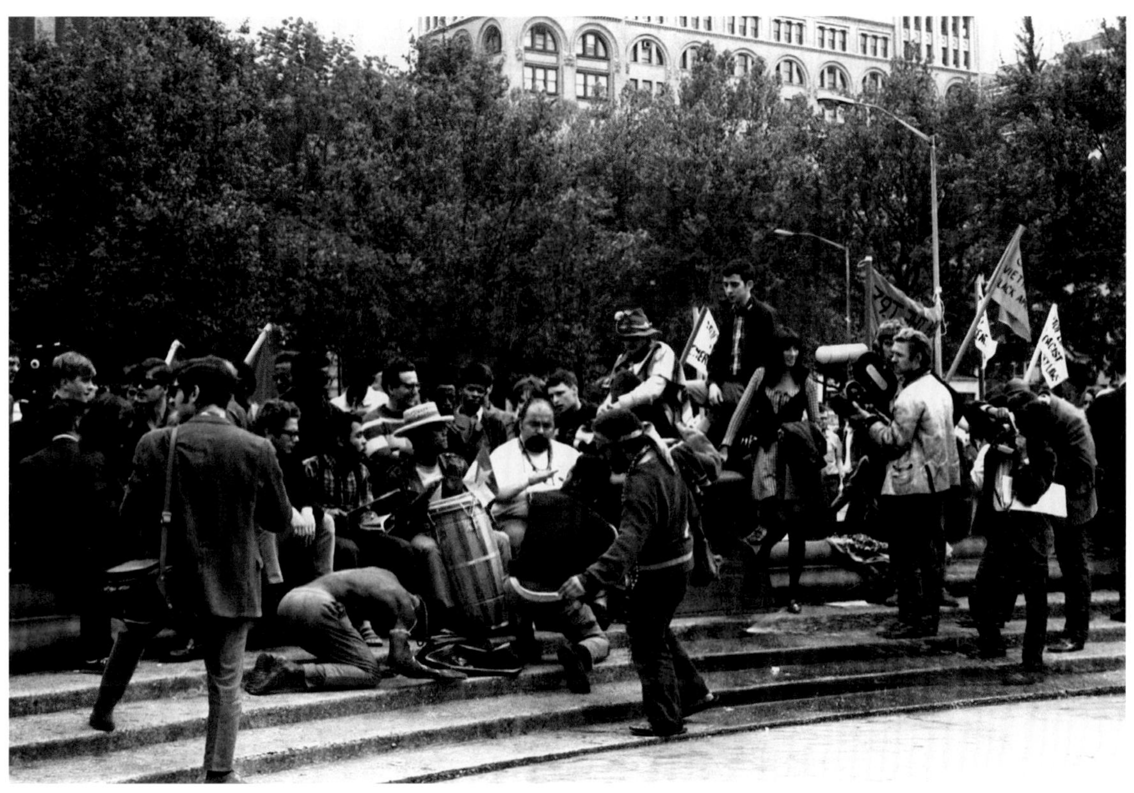

Musicians and demonstrators, Washington Square Park
Anti-Imperialist Demonstration, New York City, May 18, 1968

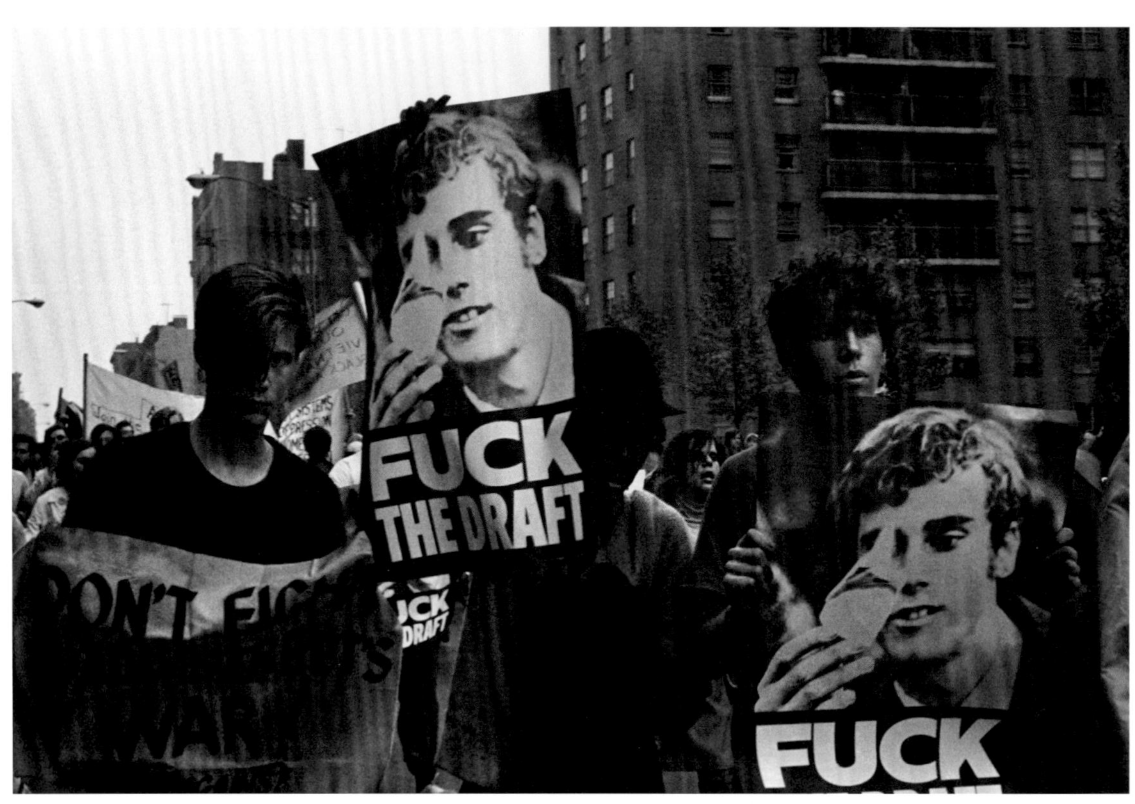

Demonstrators at Fourth Street and First Avenue
Anti-Imperialist Demonstration, New York City, May 18, 1968

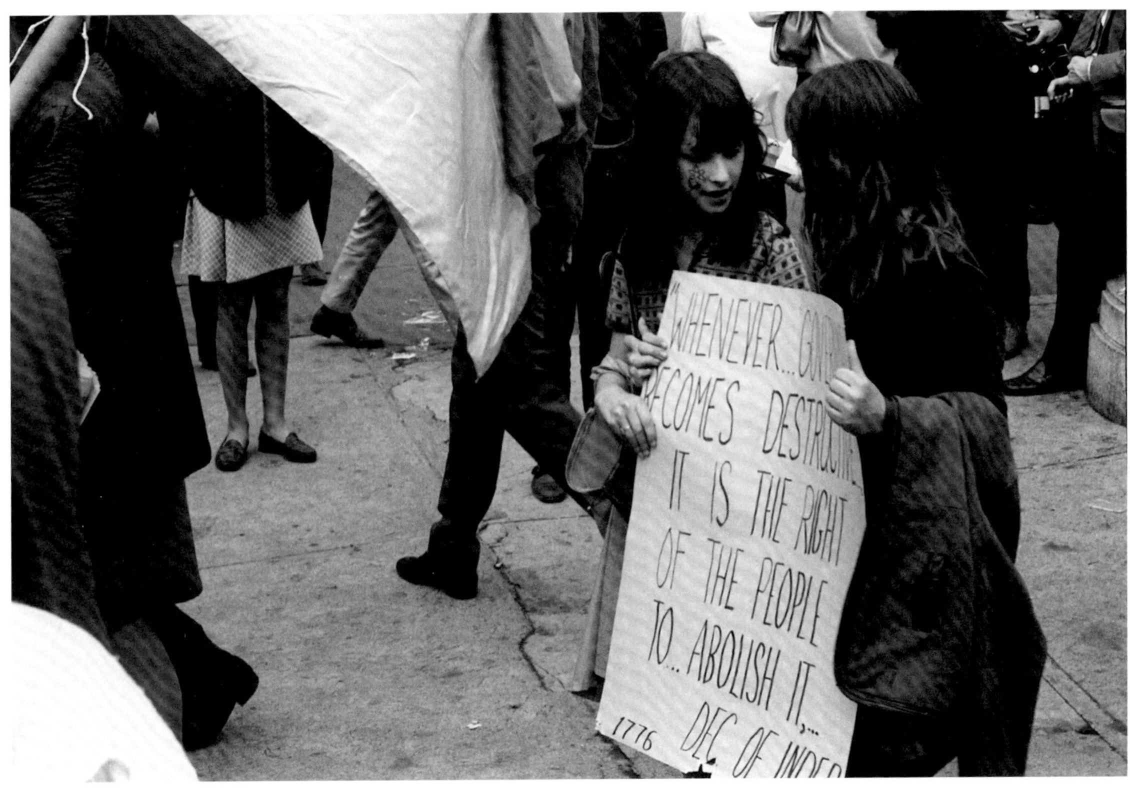

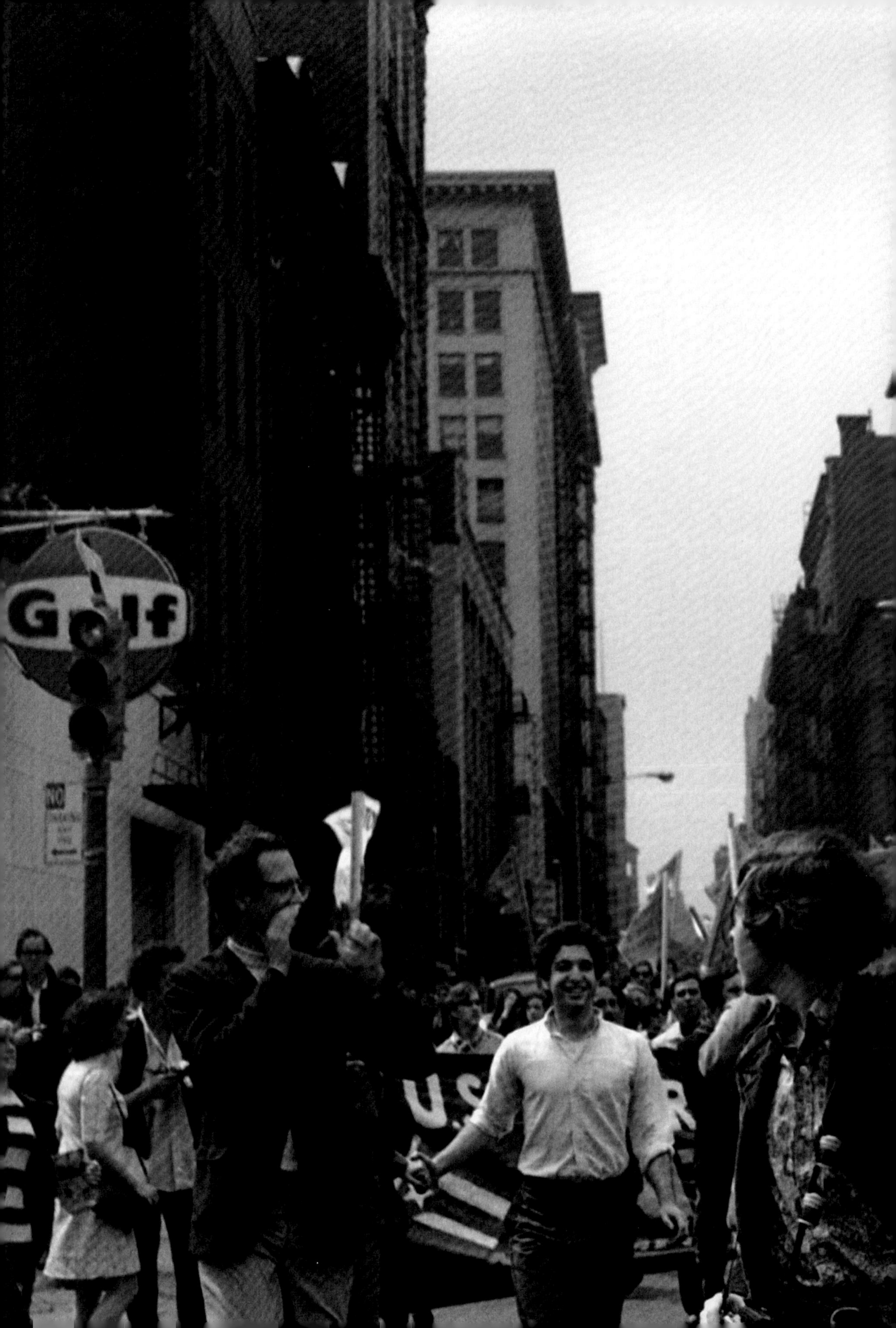

Gulf

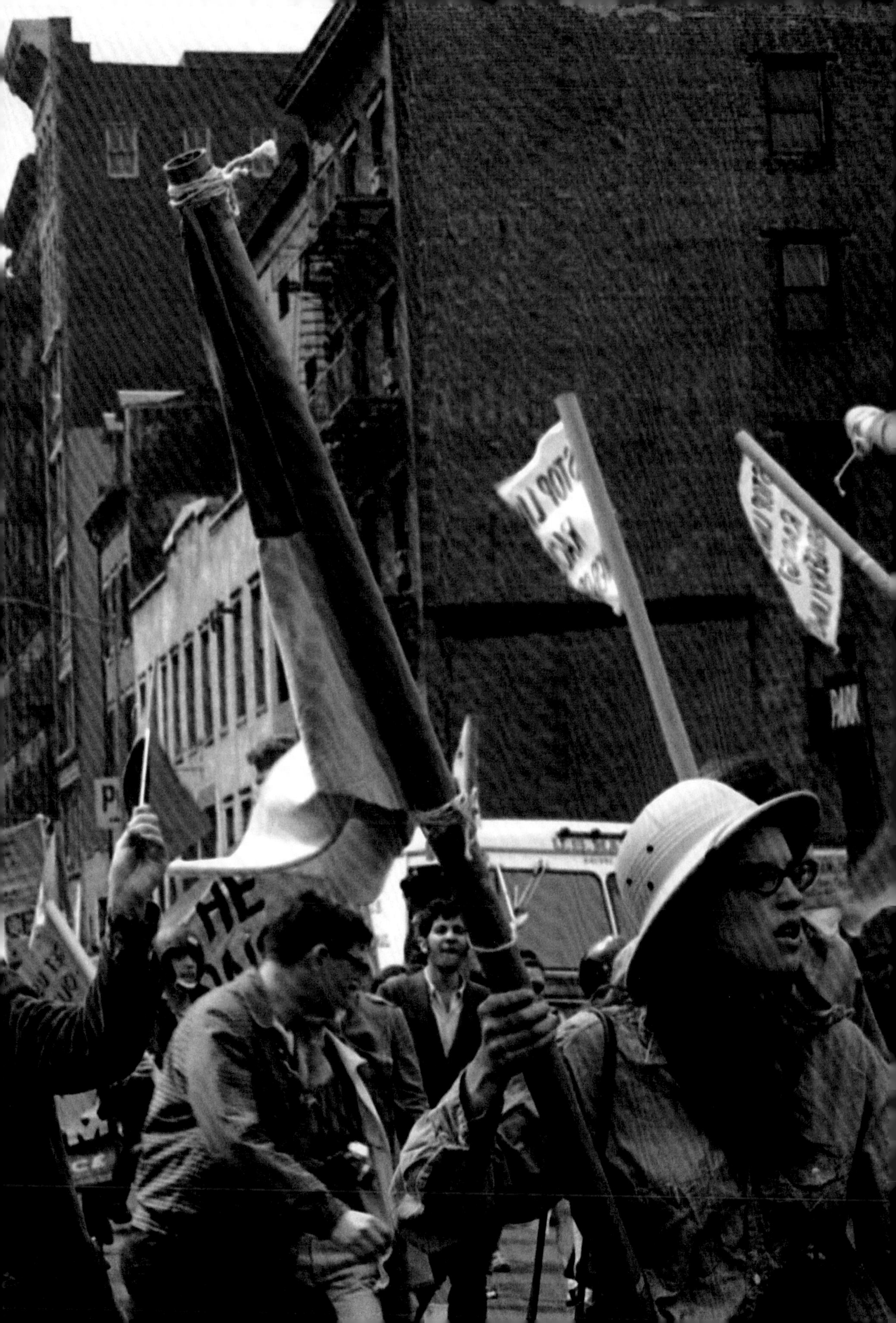
STOP
PARK

May 24, 1968

Support Rally for the Poor People's Campaign
Lower East Side, New York

Support for the Poor People's Campaign continued in New York City after the rally in Central Park and during the occupation of Resurrection City in Washington, DC.

On May 24, 1968, from 1 to 3pm, a group of New Yorkers marched from the Smith Houses on Madison and Catherine Street on the Lower East Side to the Jackson Park Amphitheater at Grand Street and the East River to rally for food, money, sleeping bags, and other provisions for the residents of Resurrection City. At the time, I lived nearby. I carried a banner part of the way and took photos for the rest. The marchers reflected the diversity of the neighborhood and the demonstration itself was spirited and friendly.

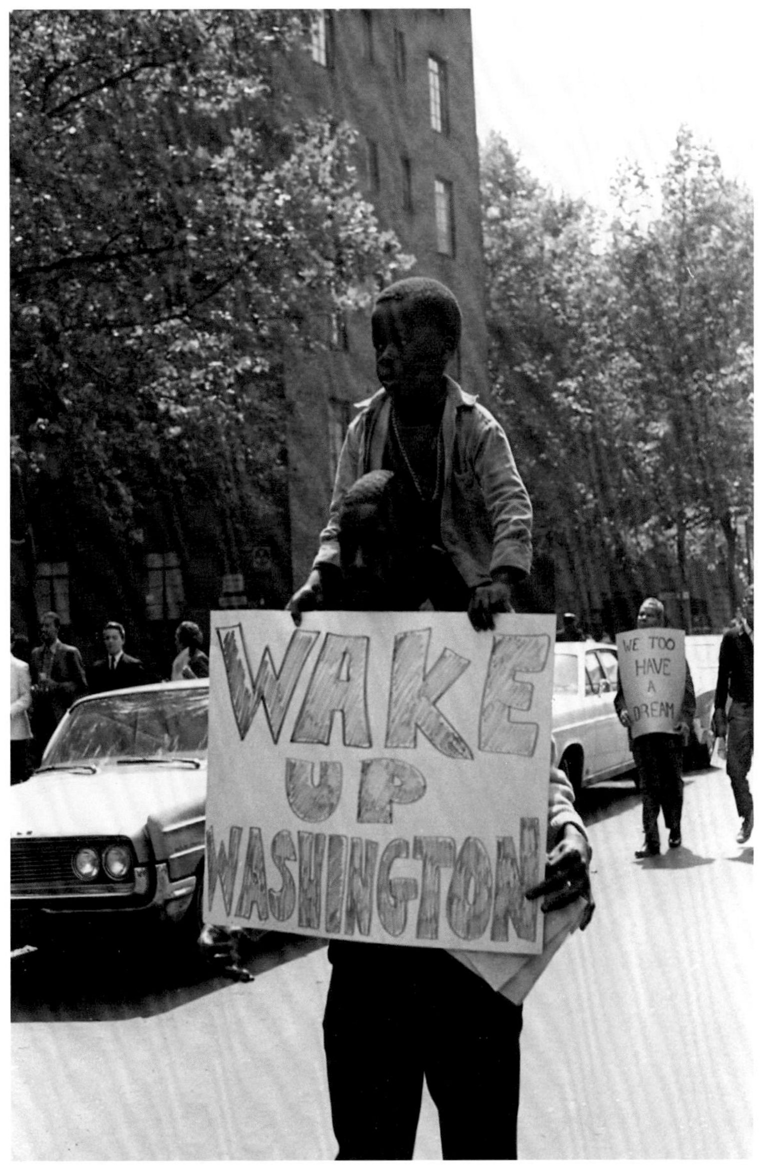

Support Rally for the Poor People's Campaign, Lower East Side
New York, May 24, 1968

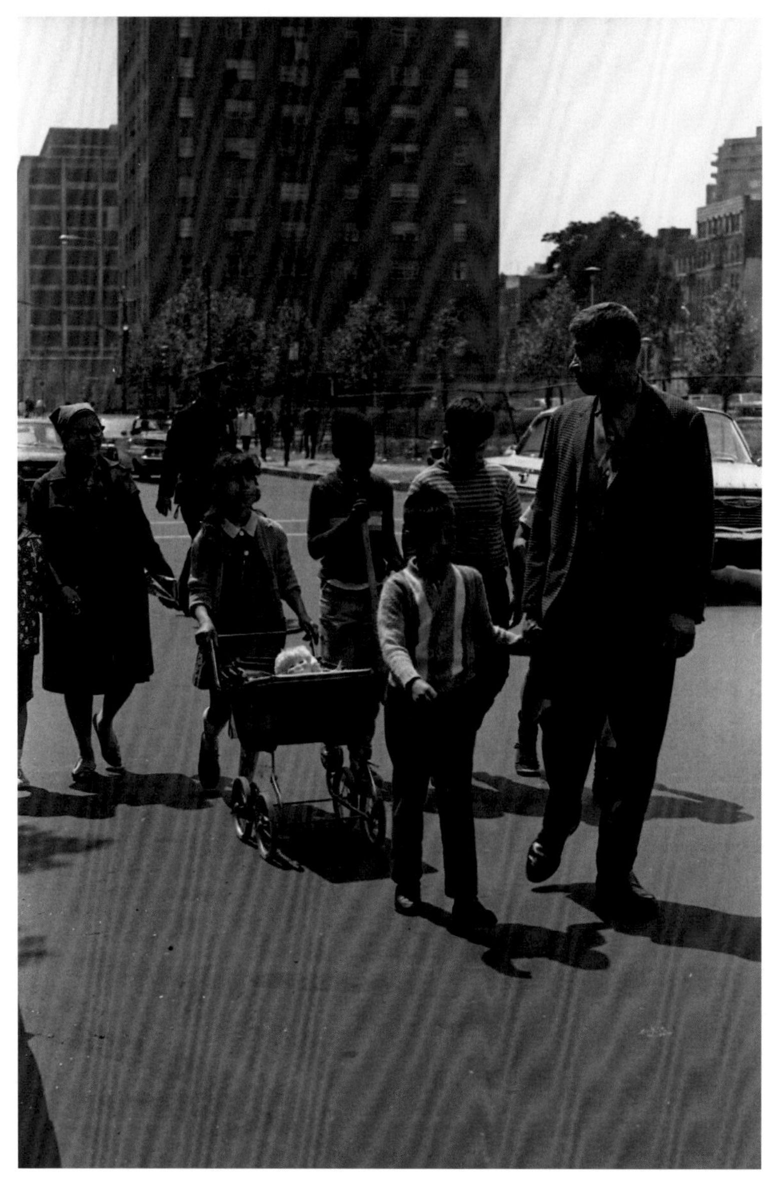

Support Rally for the Poor People's Campaign, Lower East Side
New York, May 24, 1968

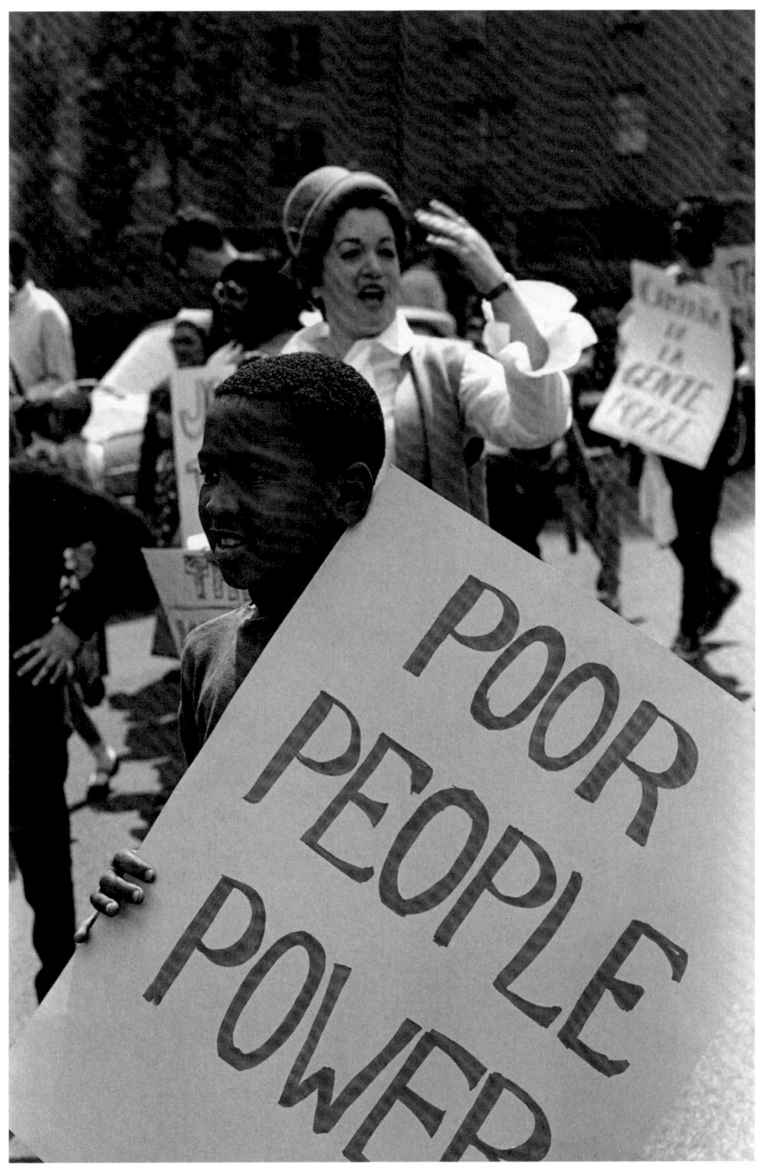

Support Rally for the Poor People's Campaign, Lower East Side
New York, May 24, 1968

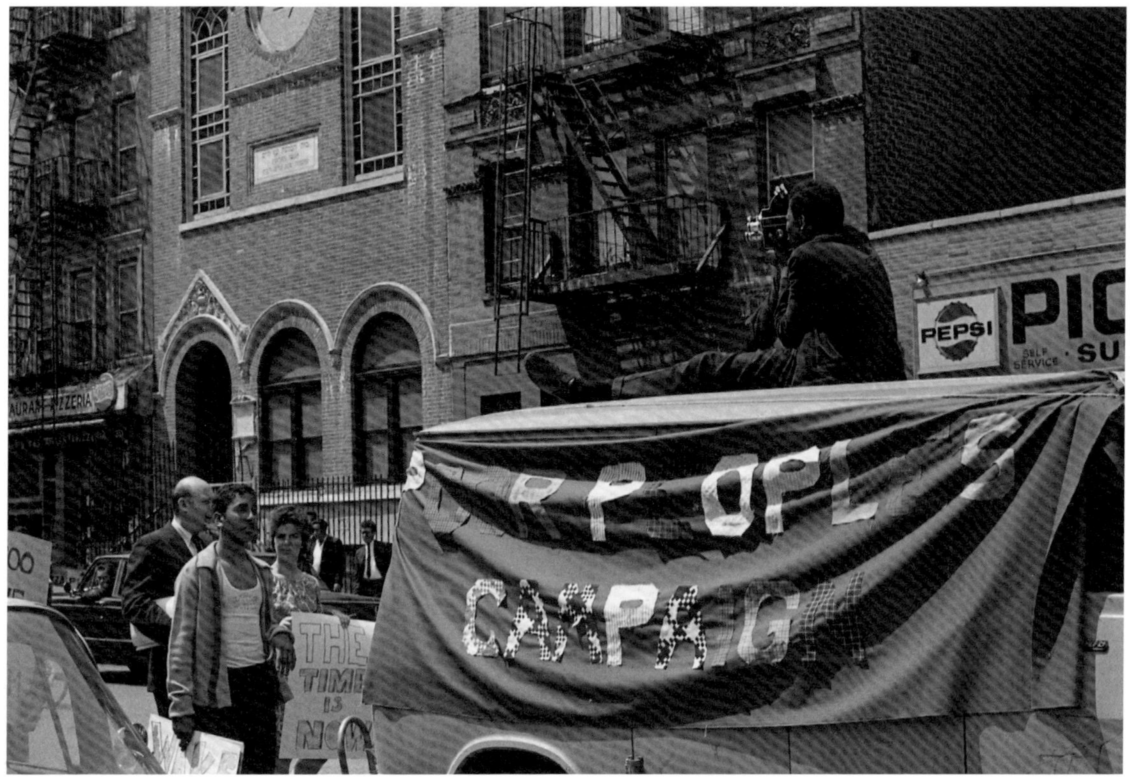

Support Rally for the Poor People's Campaign, Lower East Side, New York, May 24, 1968

Following spread
Support Rally for the Poor People's Campaign, Lower East Side, New York, May 24, 1968

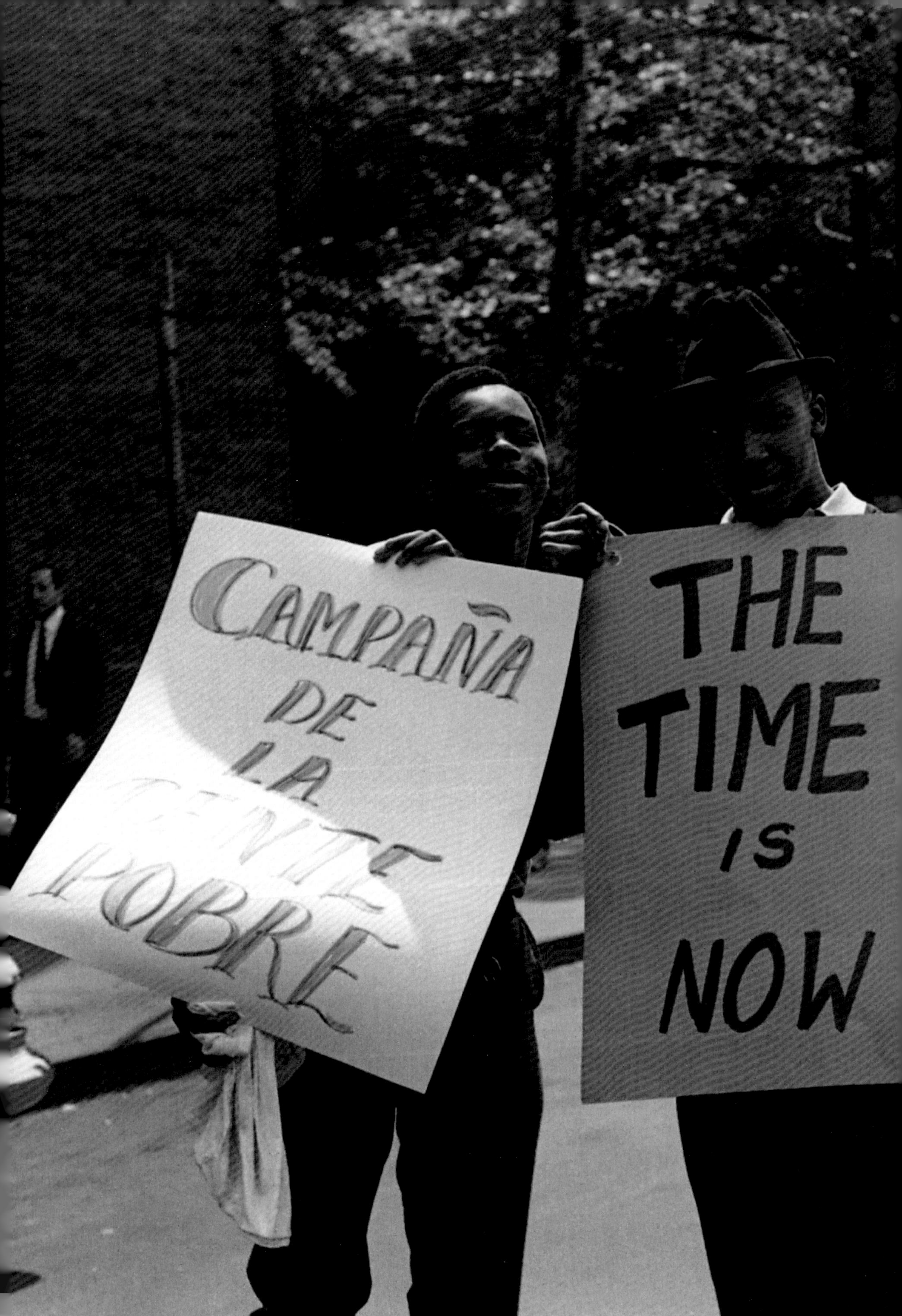

CAMPAÑA DE LA GENTE POBRE
THE TIME IS NOW

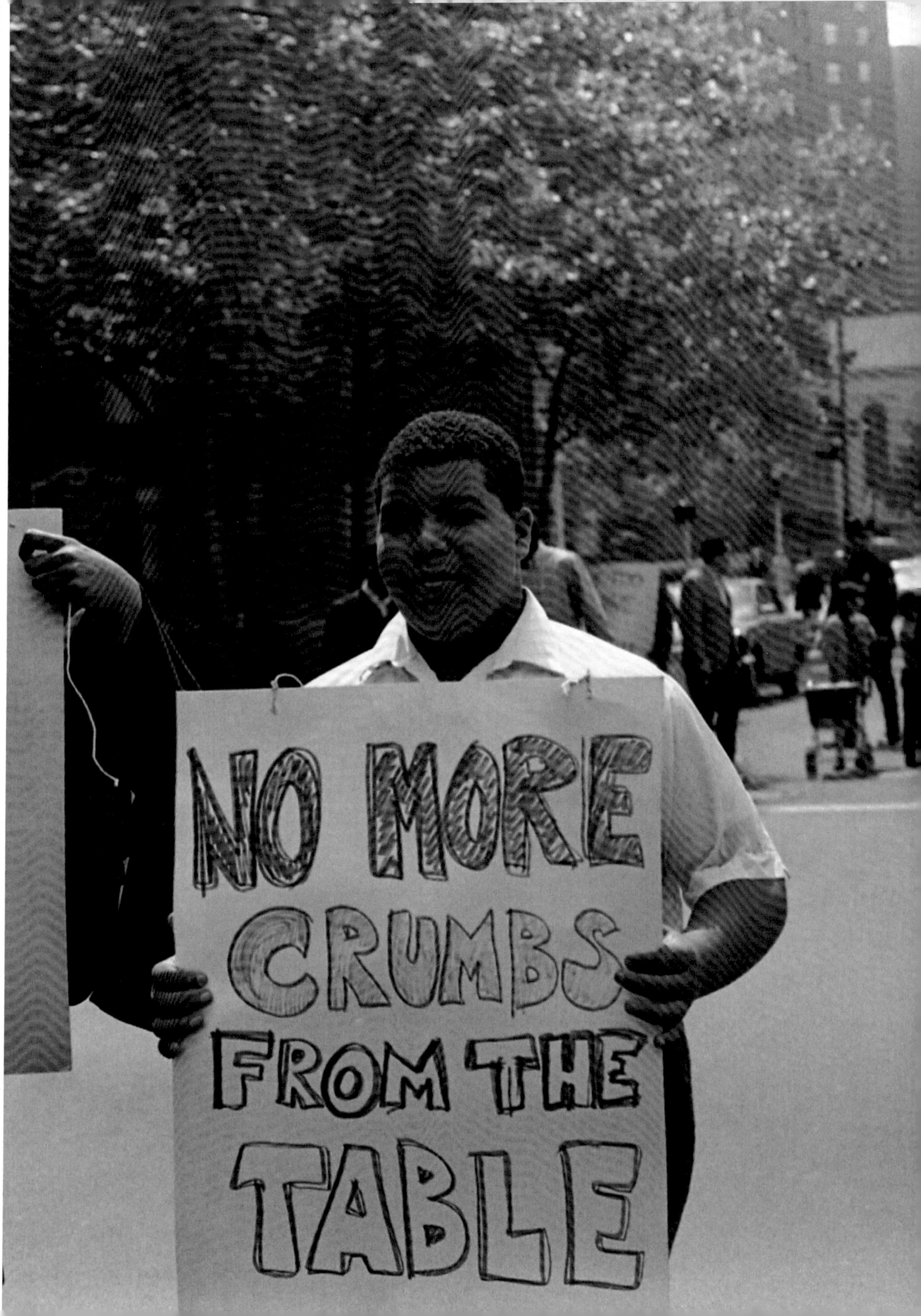

NO MORE
CRUMBS
FROM THE
TABLE

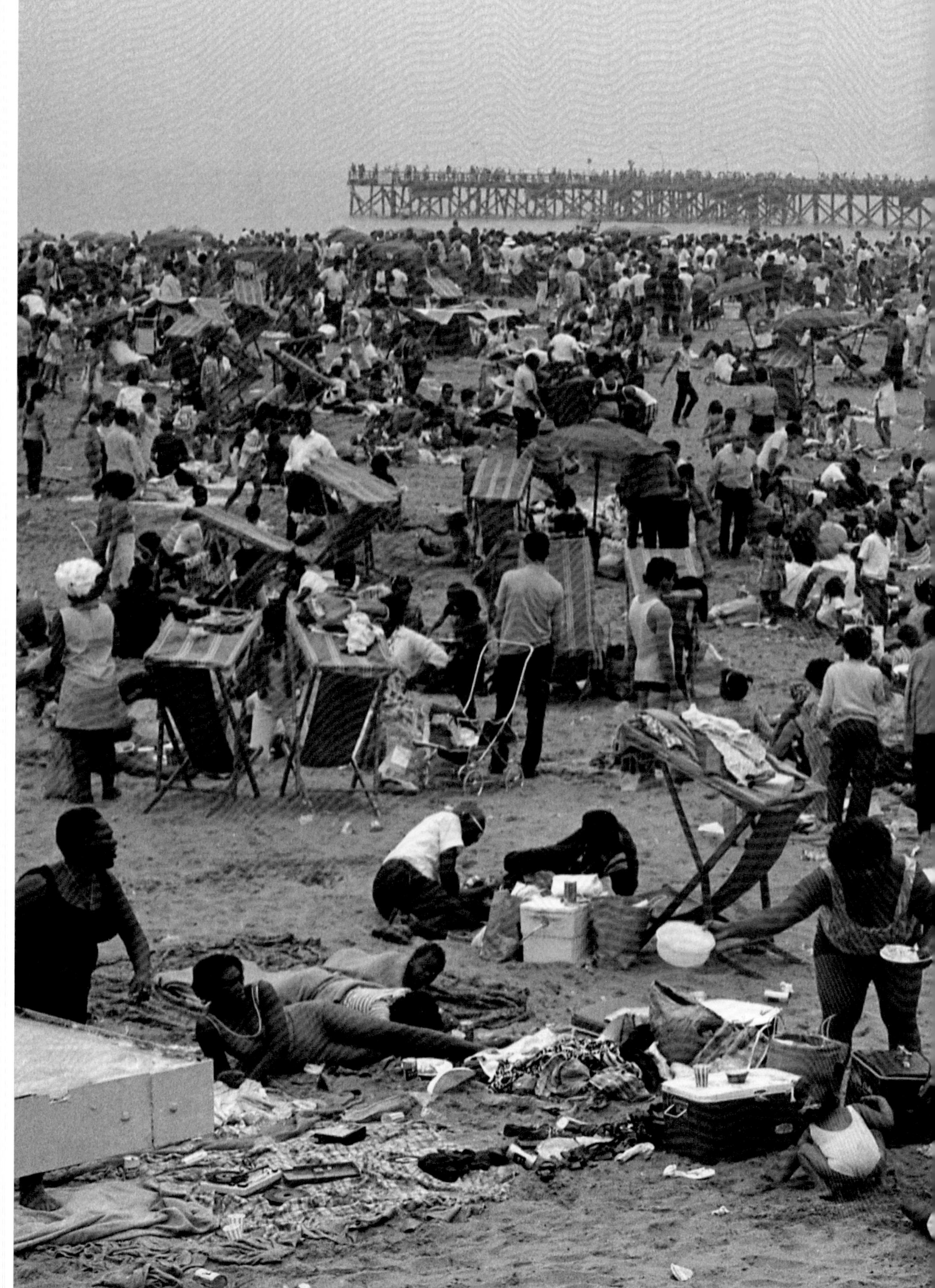

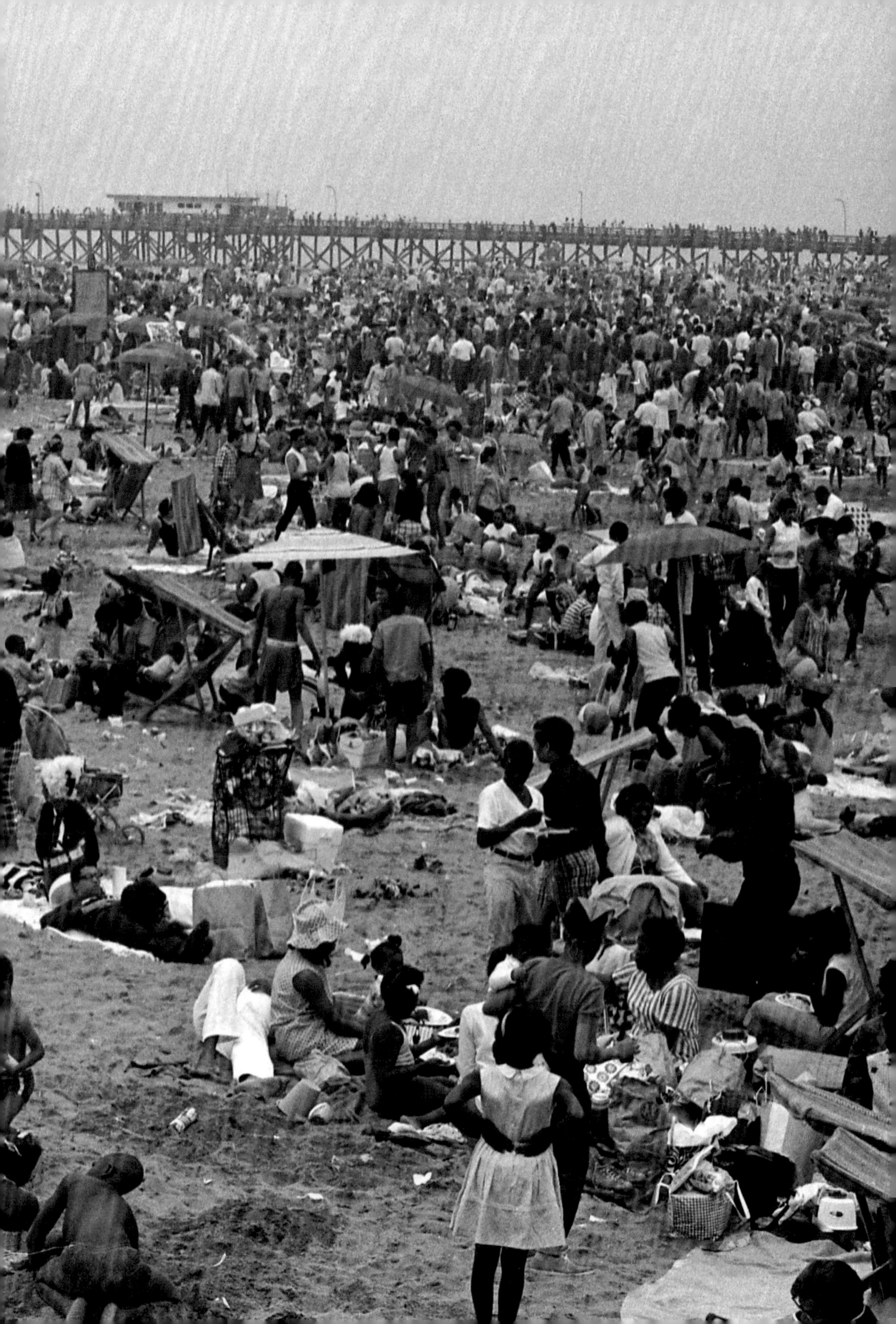

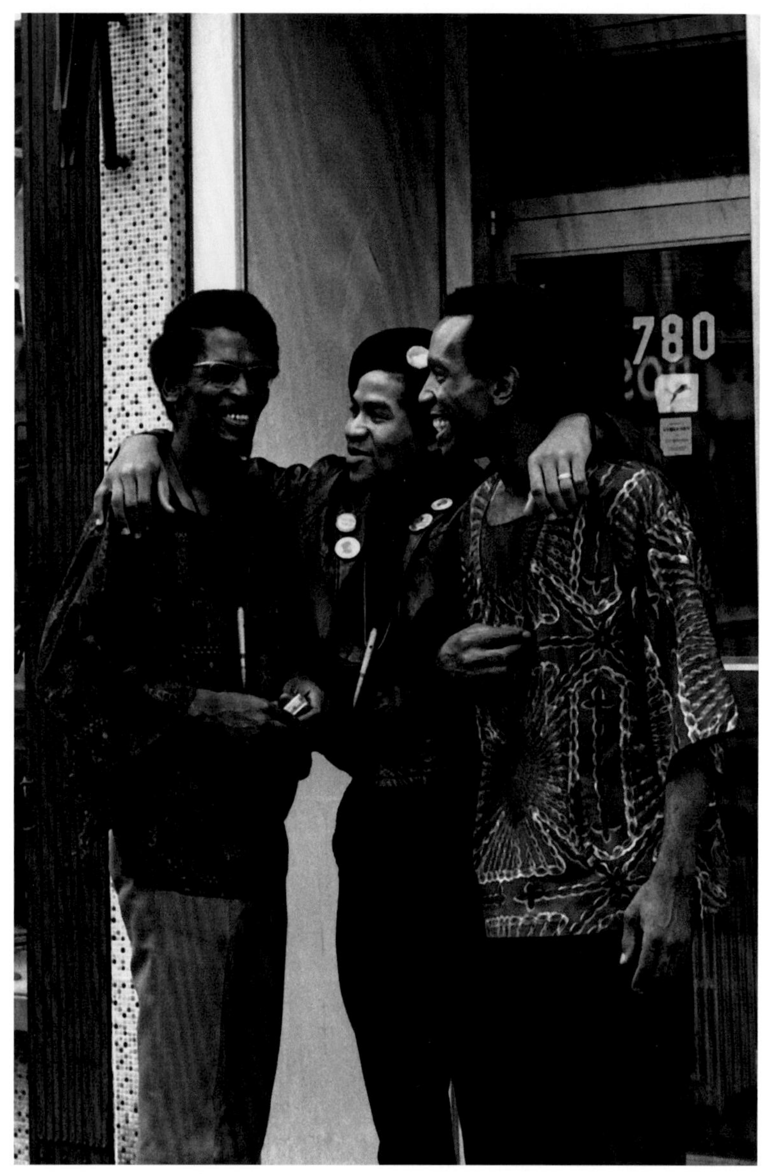

Joudon Ford, Brooklyn Black Panther Party Captain and Minister of Defense
Black Panther Party Office, Brooklyn, New York, Summer 1968

Black Panther Party Office
Brooklyn, New York

The Black Panther Party was founded in 1966 in Oakland, California, by Huey P. Newton and Bobby Seale, who were college buddies. Their original purpose was to patrol Black neighborhoods to protect residents from acts of police brutality. They developed a ten-point program, more or less summarized in their tenth point: "We want land, bread, housing, education, clothing, justice, peace and people's community control of modern technology."

My brother-in-law, Sundiata Acoli, recalls that David Brothers established the Brooklyn chapter of the Black Panther Party in the summer of 1968 at 780 Nostrand Avenue. A few months later, Lumumba Shakur set up a branch in Harlem (although the Panthers had been active in Harlem since 1966) and Sekou Odinga set up offices in the Bronx. Some of the Brooklyn members were Thomas "Blood" McCreary, Jorge Aponte, Janet Cyril and a young man named Joudon Ford, a former SNCC field marshall, who would become the Minister of Defense for the new Brooklyn office and Captain for the New York City Harlem Branch of the Black Panther Party.

Following spread
Black Panther Party Office, Brooklyn, New York, Summer 1968

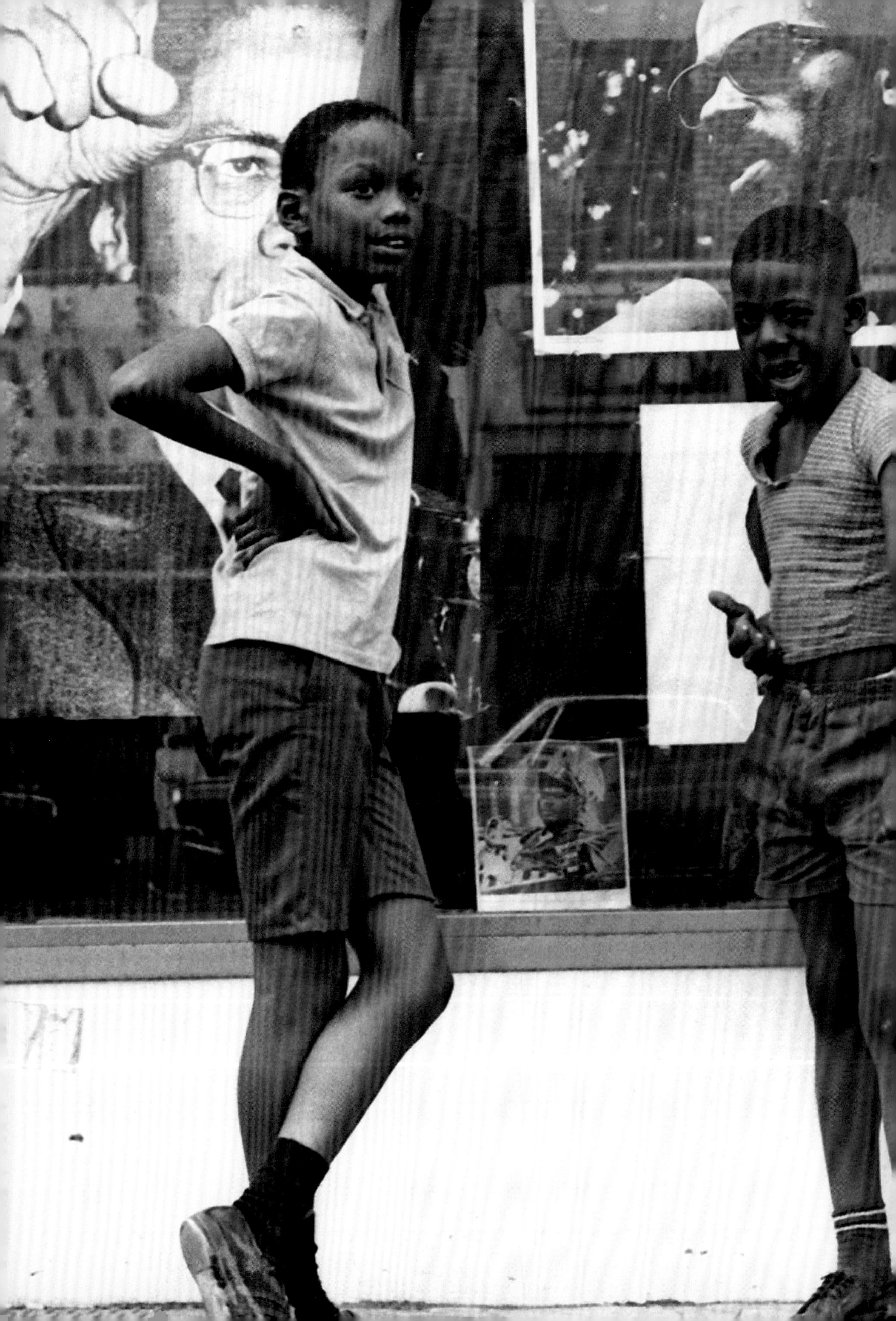

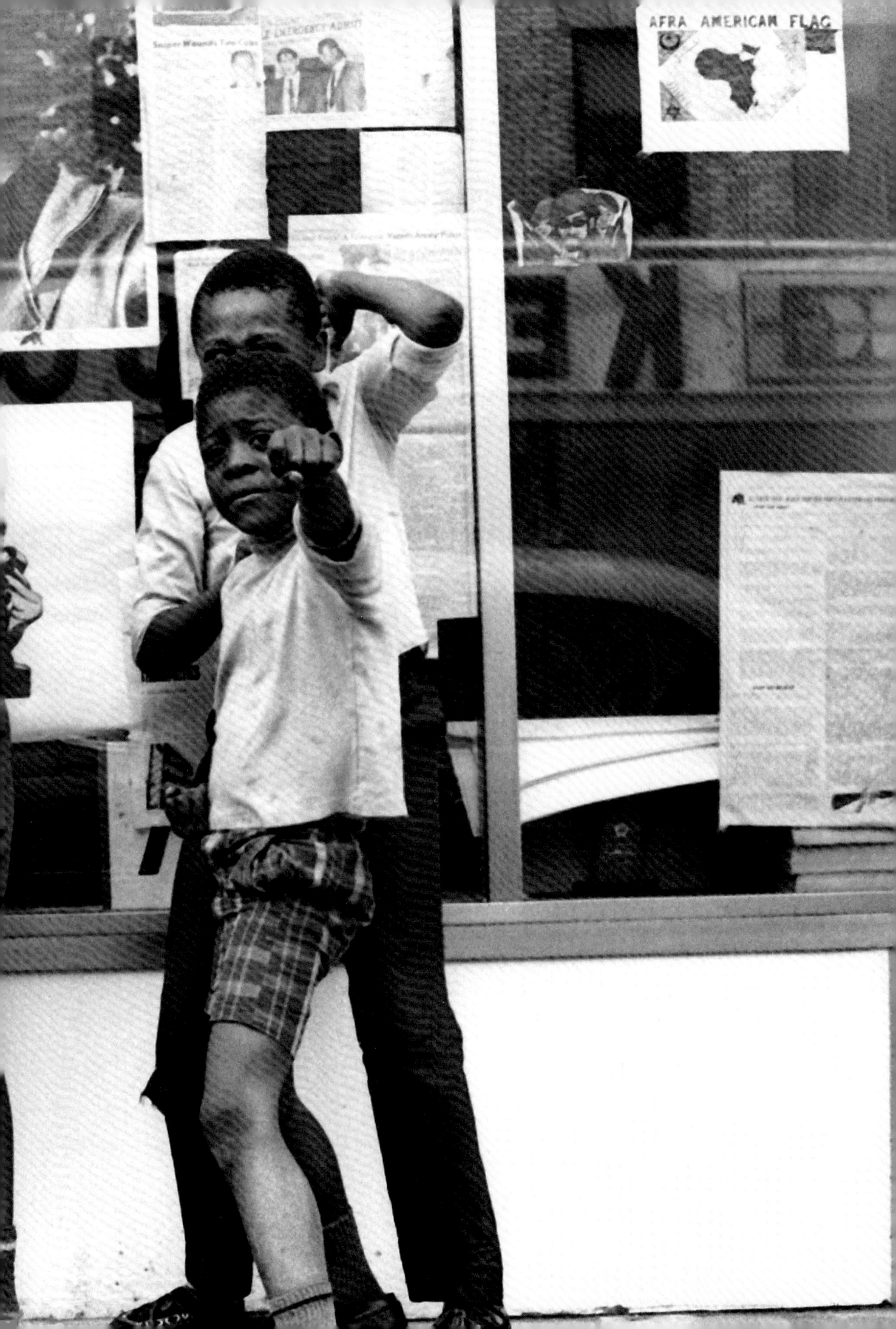

Sniper Wounds Two Cops
EMERGENCY ADMIT
AFRA AMERICAN FLAG

Miss America Pageant Protest
Atlantic City, New Jersey

In the Spring of 1968, New York Radical Women or NYRW, began meeting at the Southern Conference Educational Fund or SCEF office in Manhattan to plan the Miss America Pageant Protest. Carol Hanisch, who worked as the office manager for SCEF, proposed the protest. SCEF was a civil rights organization that educated about discrimination and provided support to organizers, notably to the early Student Nonviolent Coordinating Committee movement, commonly known as SNCC, who were working on voter registration and running freedom schools in the South. Many of the women who returned from the South brought back organizational skills and also consciousness of gender inequality that they experienced within SNCC and other left organizations they worked in. Our meetings were a combination of consciousness raising and logistical discussion about the planned protest. We broke off into small groups to plan specific activities. I was with Robin Morgan, Kathy Sarachild, Peggy Powell Dobbins, Judith Weston, Joyce Miller, and Susan Silverstein. We planned to auction a giant Miss America puppet and discussed the press release that Robin wrote for the media. Organizationally, NYRW was collaborative and non-hierarchical.

September came and it was time for the Miss America Pageant Protest. We gathered at Union Square on September 7, 1968 to board chartered busses for the trip down to Atlantic City. Some people brought their mothers and grandmothers. I handed out song sheets with parodies I had written, and we all sang on the bus. When we stopped at a rest stop and the line for the restroom seemed endless, Kate Millett, artist and author of the book Sexual Politics, liberated the men's room for the rest of us to use. We cheered!

We brought flyers protesting the mindless-boob-girlie symbol as degrading to women, the racism with roses attitude of the pageant, the use of Miss America as a military mascot for the Vietnam war, the commercial con-game that sees people only as consumers, and the thought-control ritual that tries to bend women's minds.

When we reached Atlantic City, we started picketing on the boardwalk. In addition to the Miss America puppet, we had a live sheep draped in a Miss America sash, and a freedom trash can, into which we threw symbols of oppression—bras, girdles, high heels, *Playboy* magazines, etc. The media referred to us as "bra burners" but there was no truth to that. We had no permit to burn anything on the wooden boardwalk, but somehow the term "bra burners" continues to pop up.

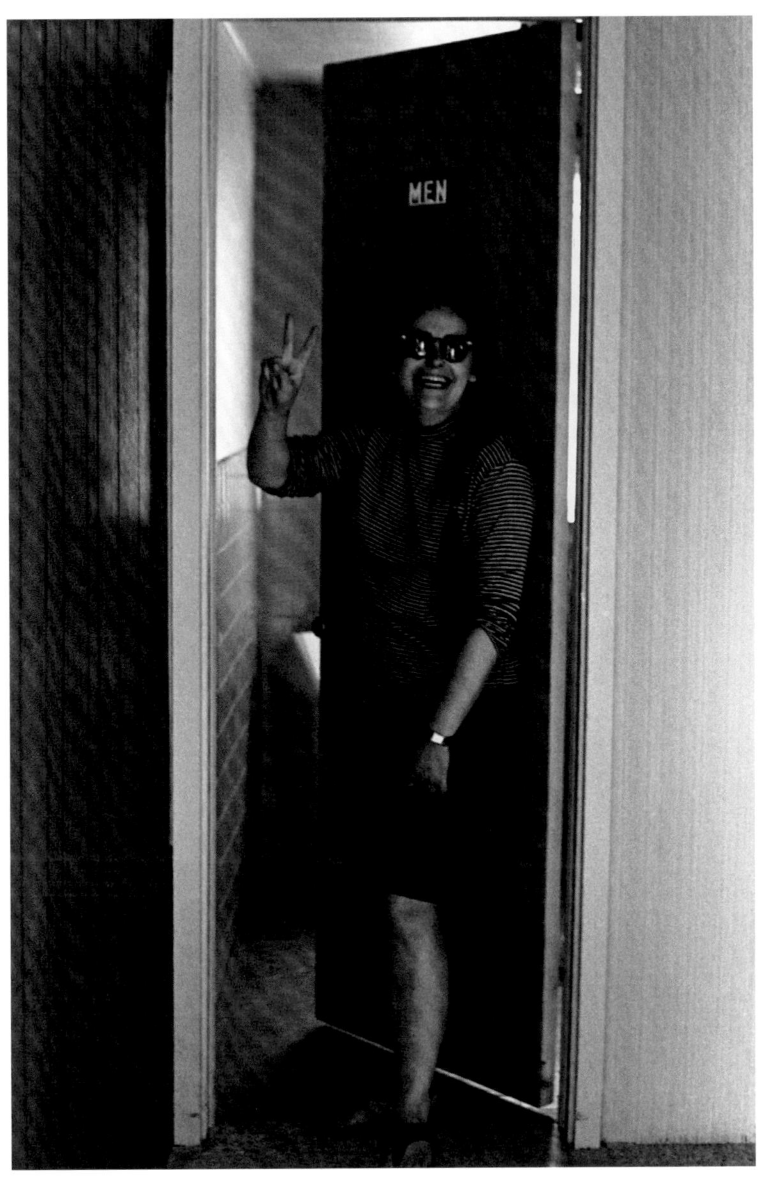

Kate Millett, author of *Sexual Politics*, liberating the rest stop men's room
Miss America Pageant Protest, Atlantic City, New Jersey, September 7, 1968

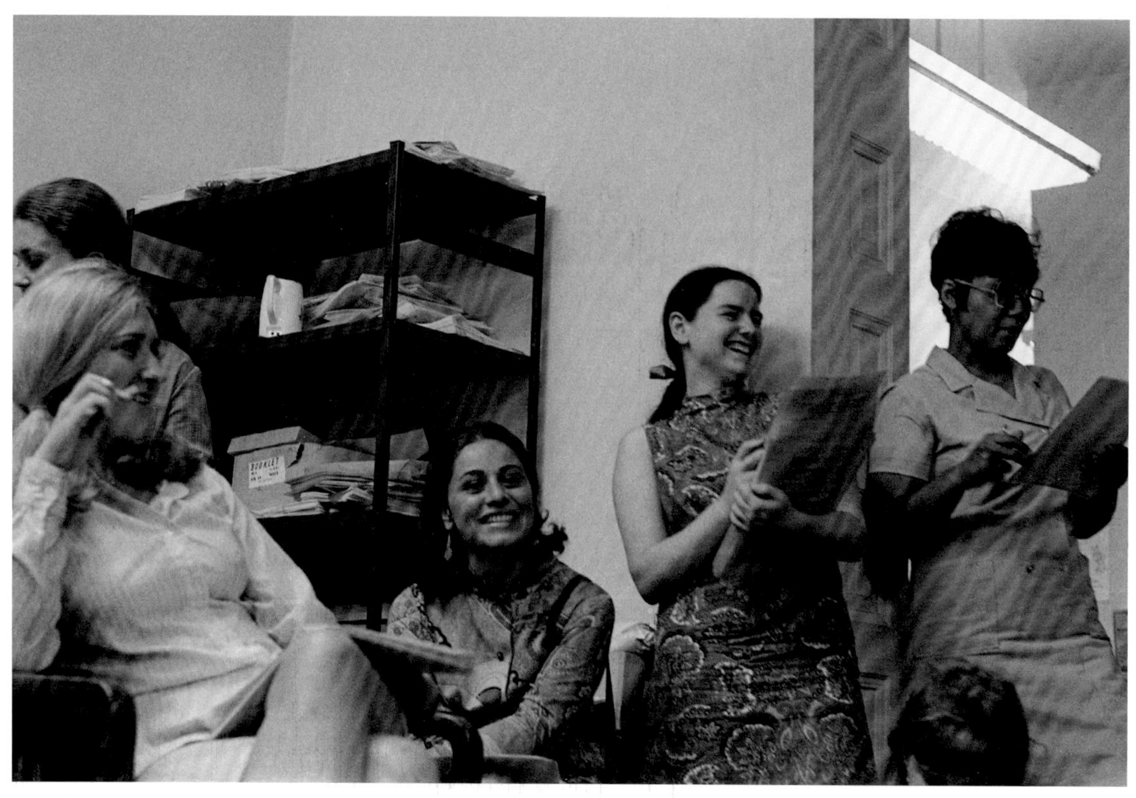

New York Radical Women organizers at a planning meeting, SCEF offices, New York City, Summer 1968

Hecklers had a lot of fun saying things like "They're not beautiful. That's their problem" One guy was waving a George Wallace for president brochure. Wallace was a southern segregationist, former Governor of Alabama, who famously blocked the doors of the University of Alabama to try and prevent desegregation. Peggy Powell Dobbins auctioned off the Miss America puppet in the middle of the boardwalk: *Yesseree folks, step right up. How much am I offered for this prime piece of prime American property. She sings in the kitchen, hums at the typewriter, purrs in bed....You can use her to push you politics, push your products, or push your war. She's the man's best friend as long as he keeps her in her place. And he better, cuz she might be dangerous.*

Several of us went inside the pageant. I had press accreditations and sat right beneath the runway with the mainstream journalists. Karen Liptak, a sister Newsreel member, and Miriam Bokser, from Liberation News Service, also had press access. We watched the women parade up and down the runway and observed the onlookers. We heard Bert Parks sing: "There she is, Miss America." Peggy Powell Dobbins had provided some of us with small plastic atomizer bottles full of Toni home permanent solution (we called them stink bombs) to spray at a strategic moment. Toni was the sponsor of the event. Kathy and Carol sat in the front row of the balcony. When the strategic moment came, Kathy and Carol unfurled a "Women's Liberation" banner over the balcony railing. We pulled out our atomizers, but Miriam accidentally sprayed me with hers, so we left quickly. Peggy was arrested and charged with spraying a noxious odor.

The general feeling of the protest was one of exhilaration. It was a success! It was fun! We got national media attention! We were really proud of ourselves. In retrospect, however, there was almost instant regret for how much emphasis we had placed on blaming the contestants. Our real point had been to attack the pageant as an institution. Even though we made mistakes. Because of the national attention, many women could identify with what we were saying and doing, and find encouragement and a sense of belonging to a movement.

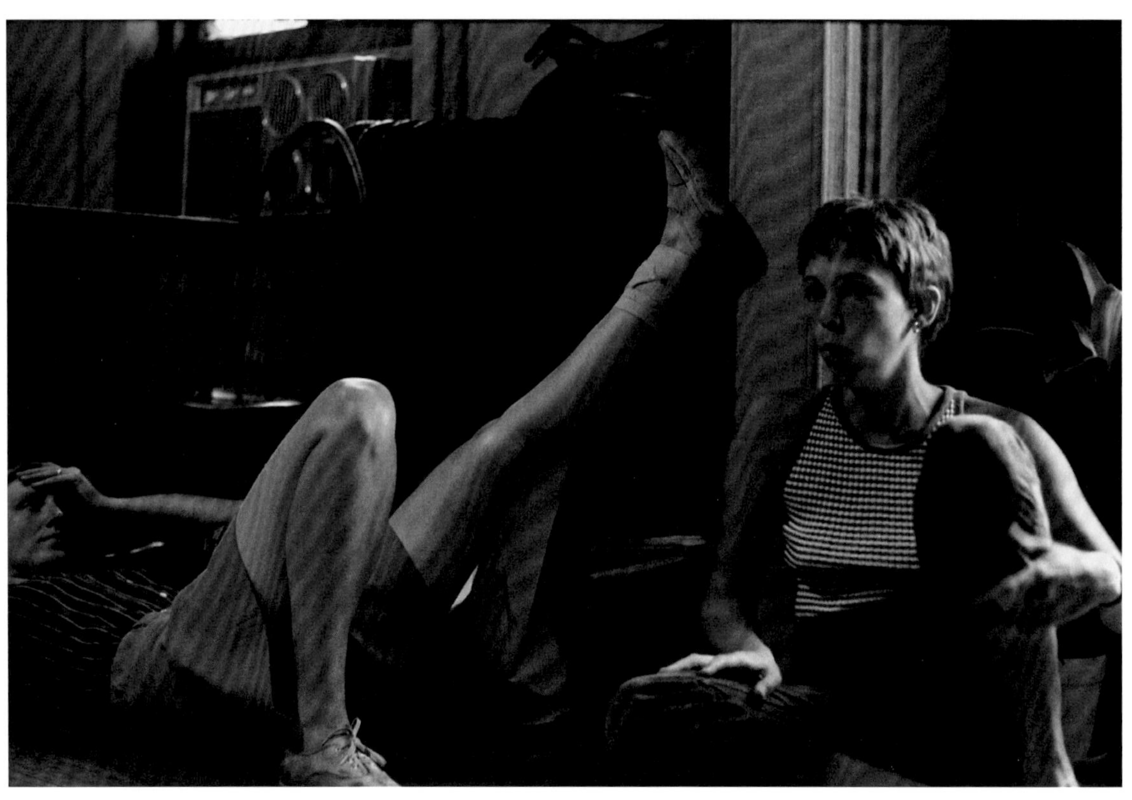

Peggy Powell Dobbins and Kathie Sarachild at a planning meeting, New York City, Summer 1968

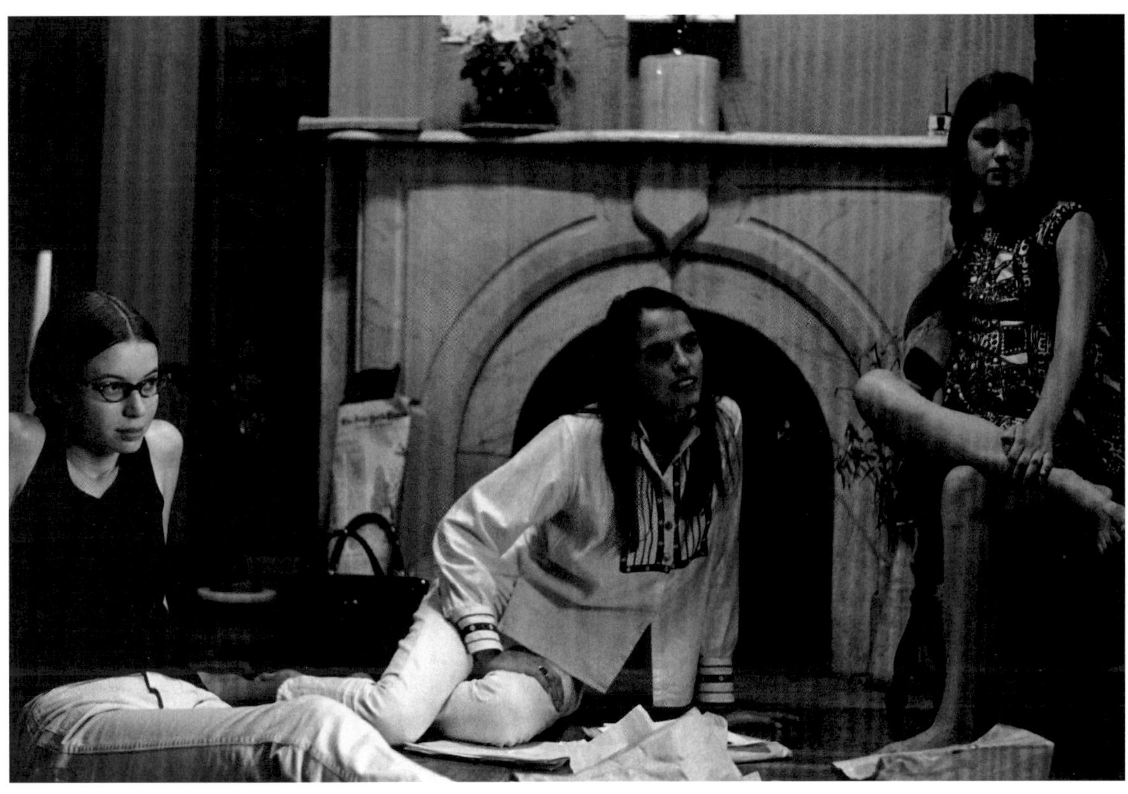

Judith Weston Hoskins, Cynthia Funk, and Joyce Miller at a planning meeting, New York City, Summer 1968

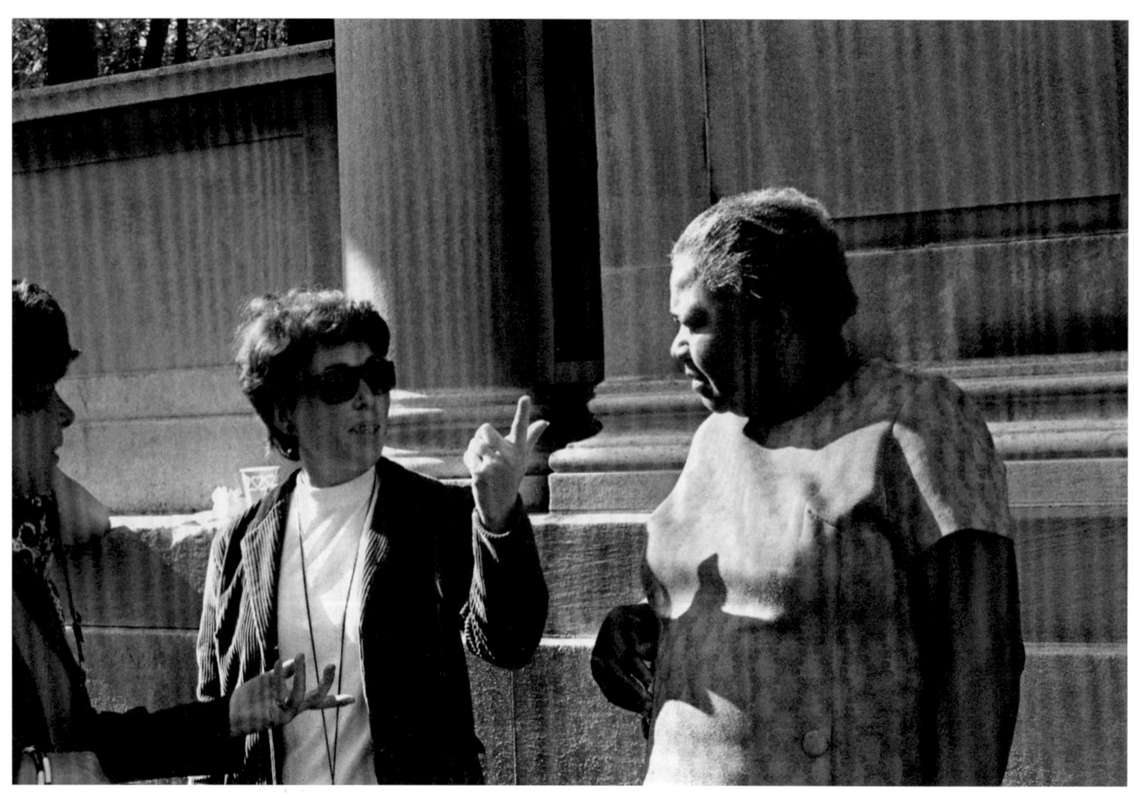

Women waiting to board the charter bus to the Miss America Pageant Protest
New York City, September 7, 1968

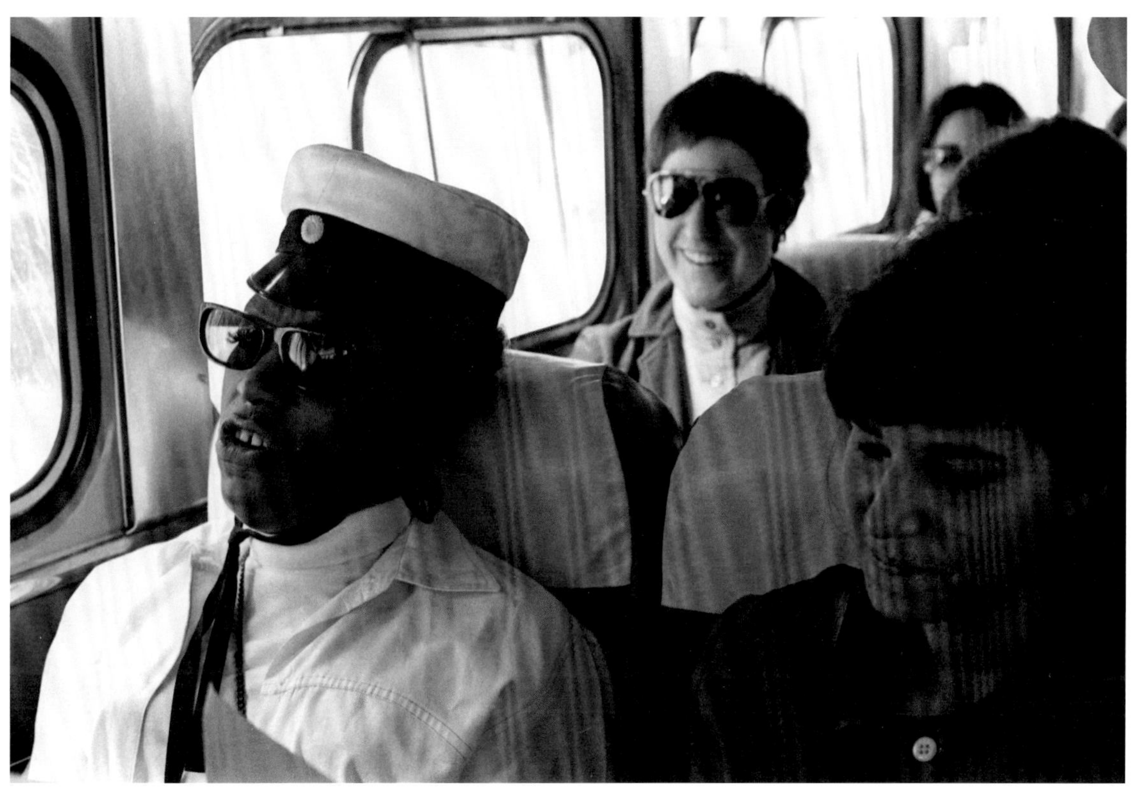

Flo Kennedy and Helen Kritzler on the bus
Miss America Pageant Protest, Atlantic City, New Jersey, September 7, 1968

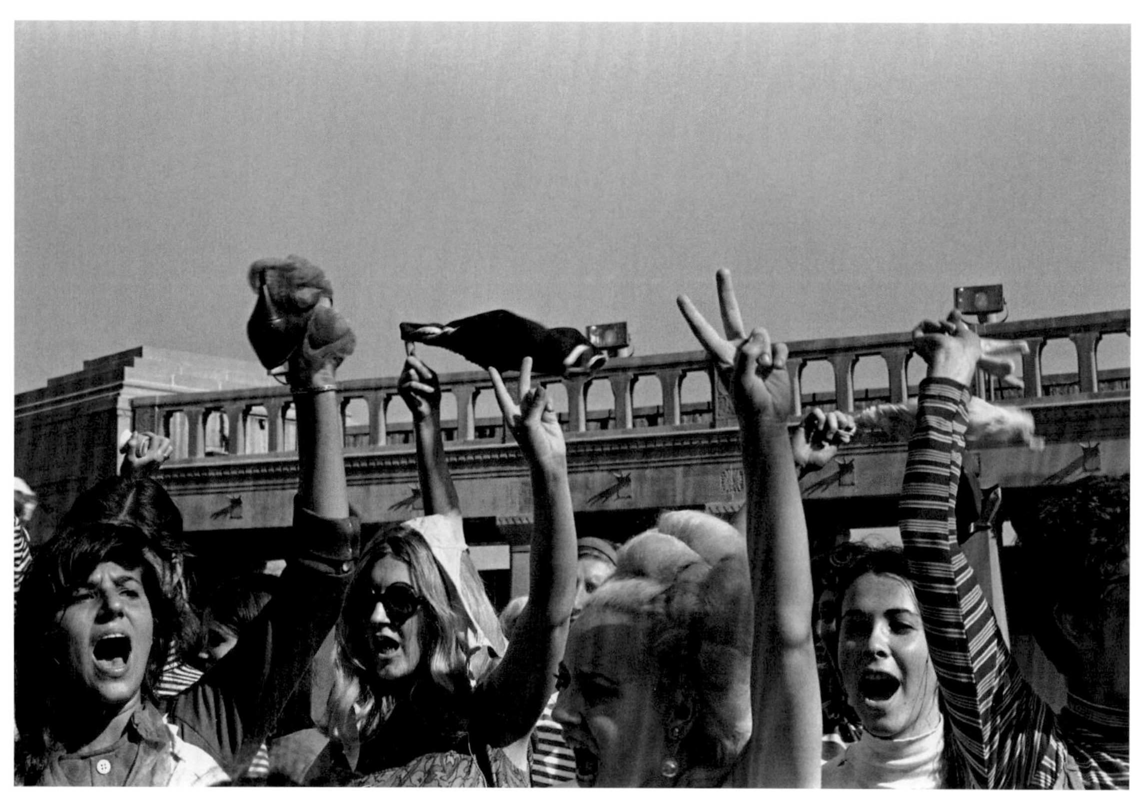

Helen Kritzler and Carol Ann Jones throwing symbols of women's oppression into the freedom trash can
Miss America Pageant Protest, Atlantic City, New Jersey, September 7, 1968

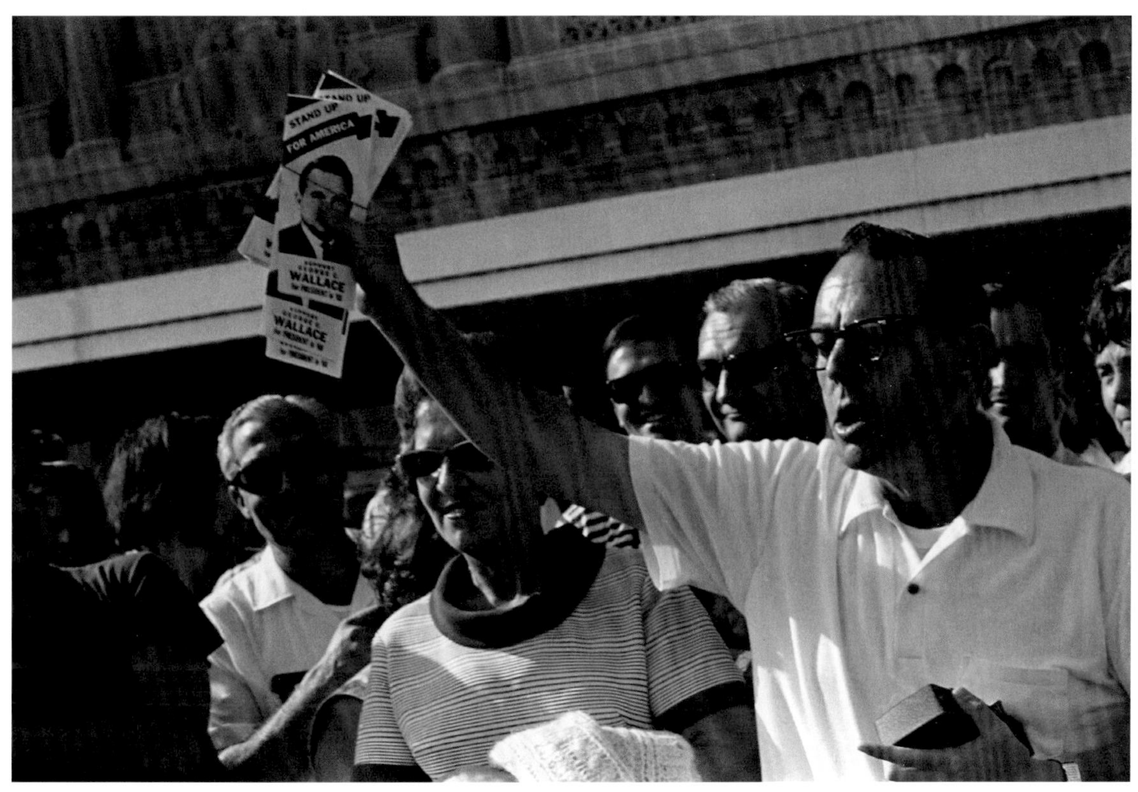

Heckler holding a *Wallace for President* brochure
Miss America Pageant Protest, Atlantic City, New Jersey, September 7, 1968

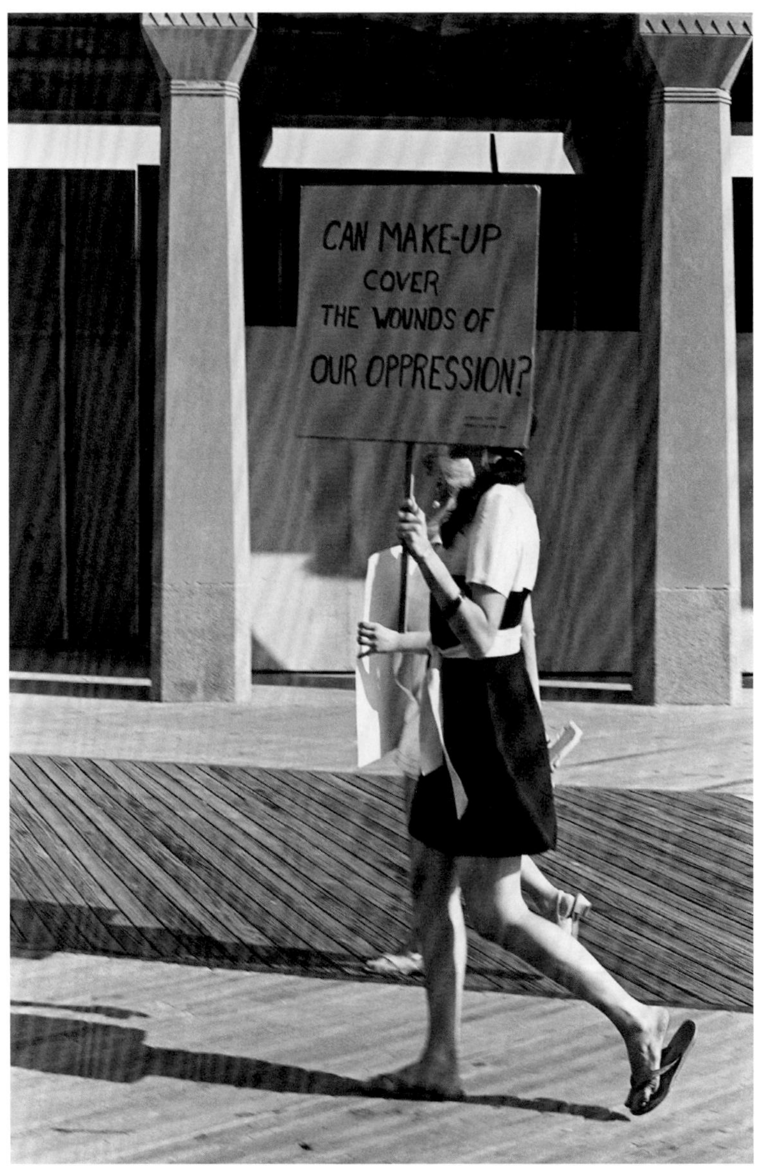

Miss America Pageant Protest, Atlantic City, New Jersey, September 7, 1968

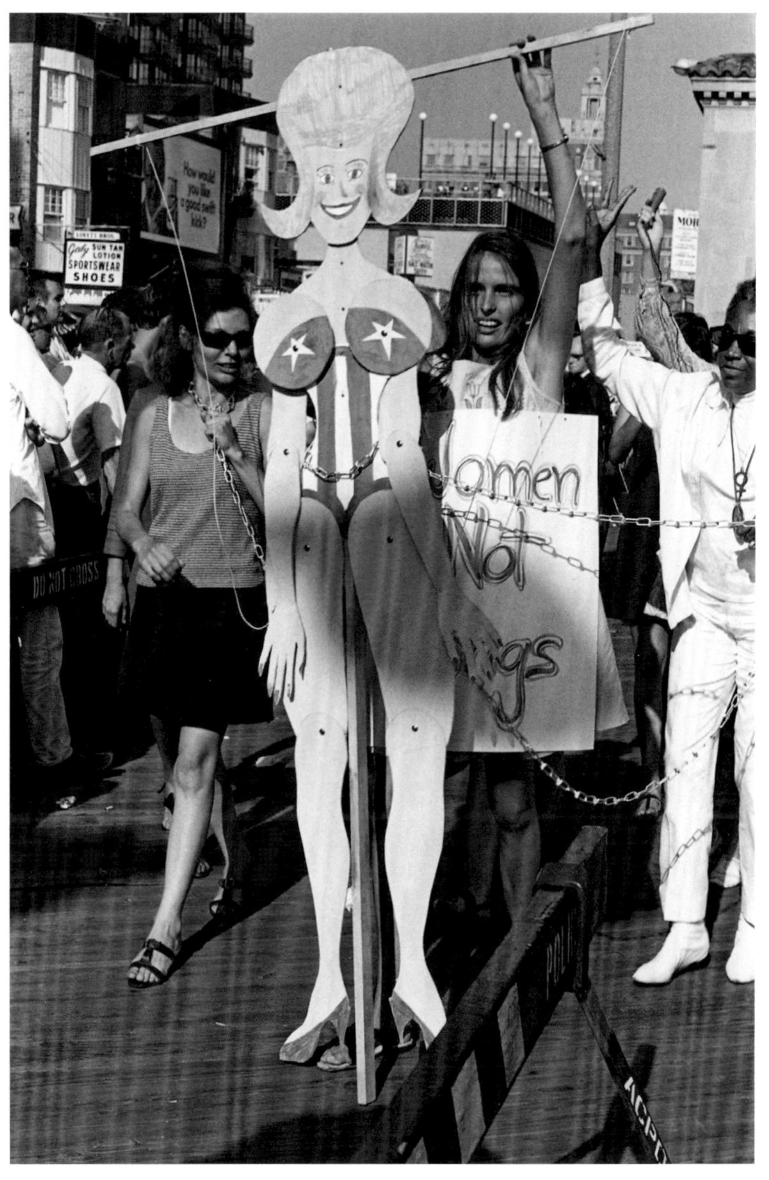

Florika Remetier, Cynthia Funk, and Flo Kennedy
Miss America Pageant Protest, Atlantic City, New Jersey, September 7, 1968

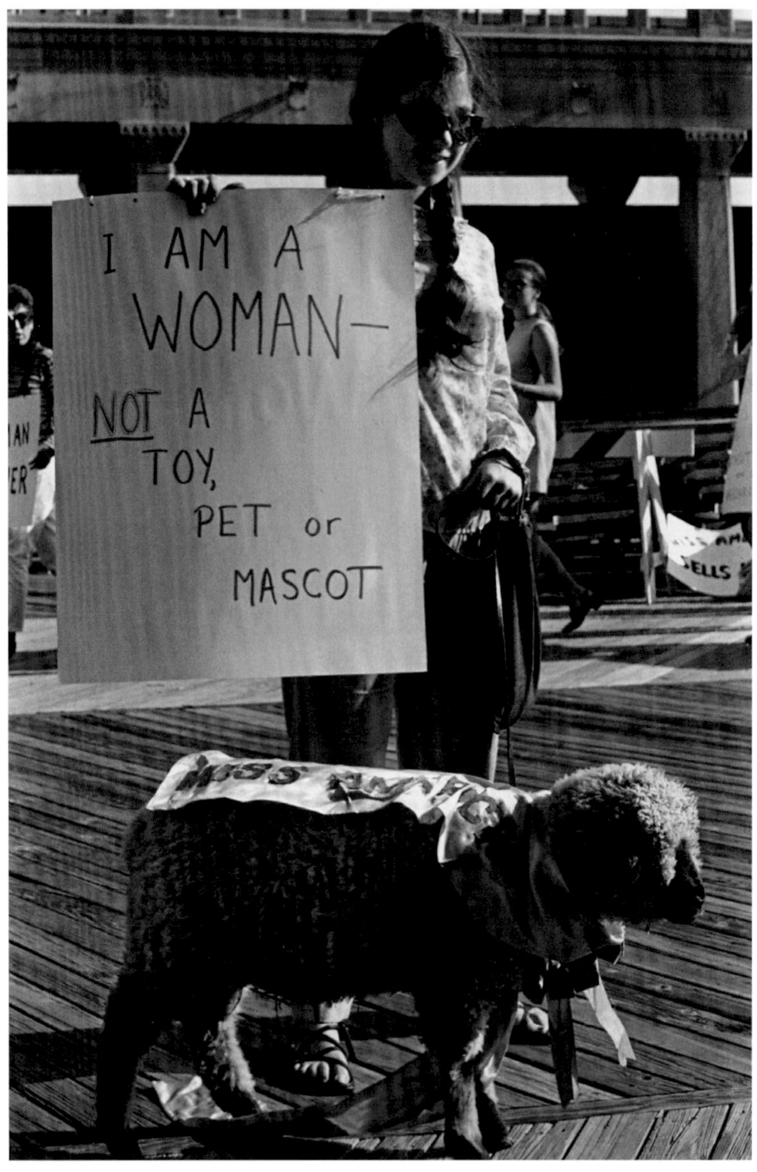

Miss America Pageant Protest, Atlantic City, New Jersey, September 7, 1968

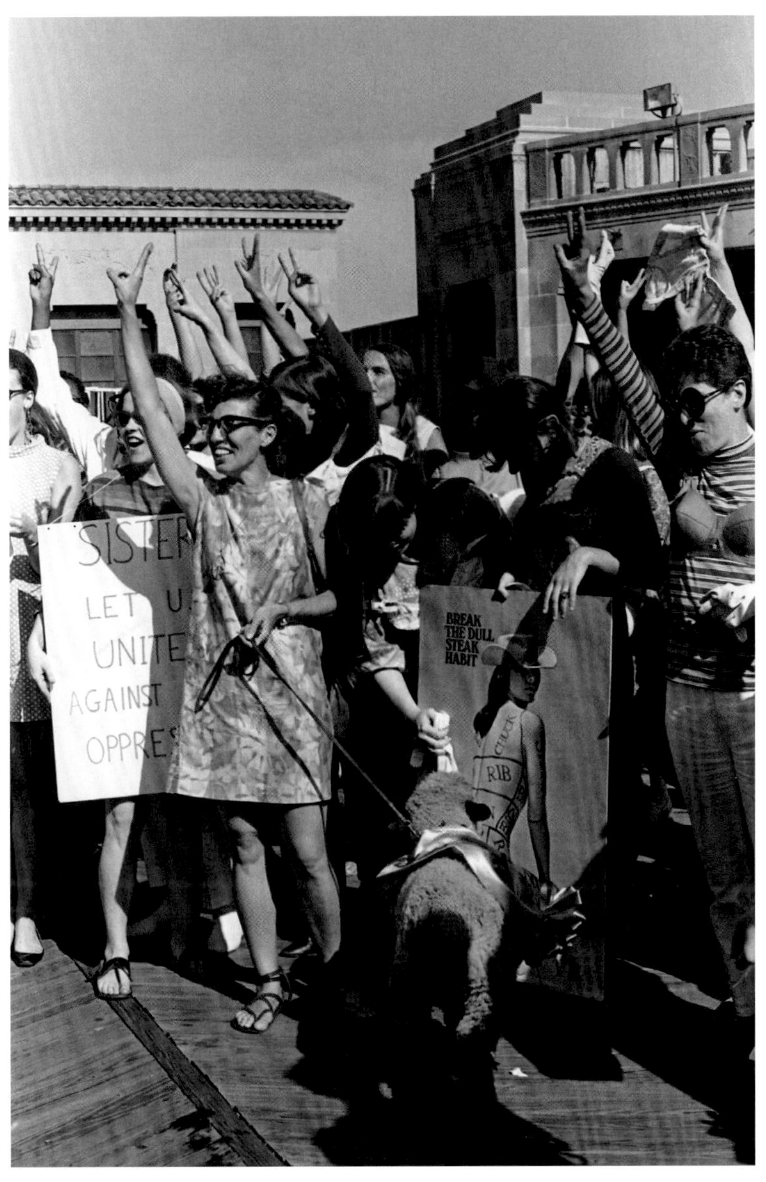

Carol Hanisch and Lynn Laredo from New York Radical Women
Miss America Pageant Protest, Atlantic City, New Jersey, September 7, 1968

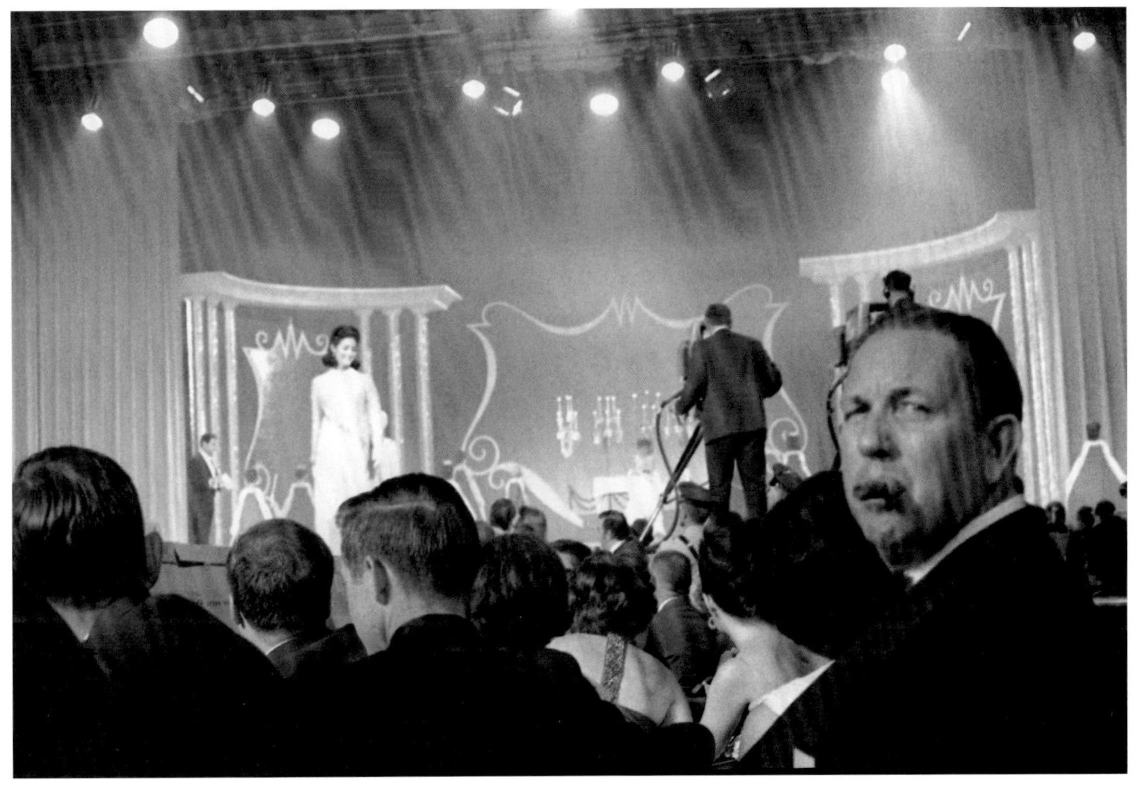

Inside Convention Hall
Miss America Pageant Protest, Atlantic City, New Jersey, September 7, 1968

Following spread
Miss America Pageant Protest, Atlantic City, New Jersey, September 7, 1968

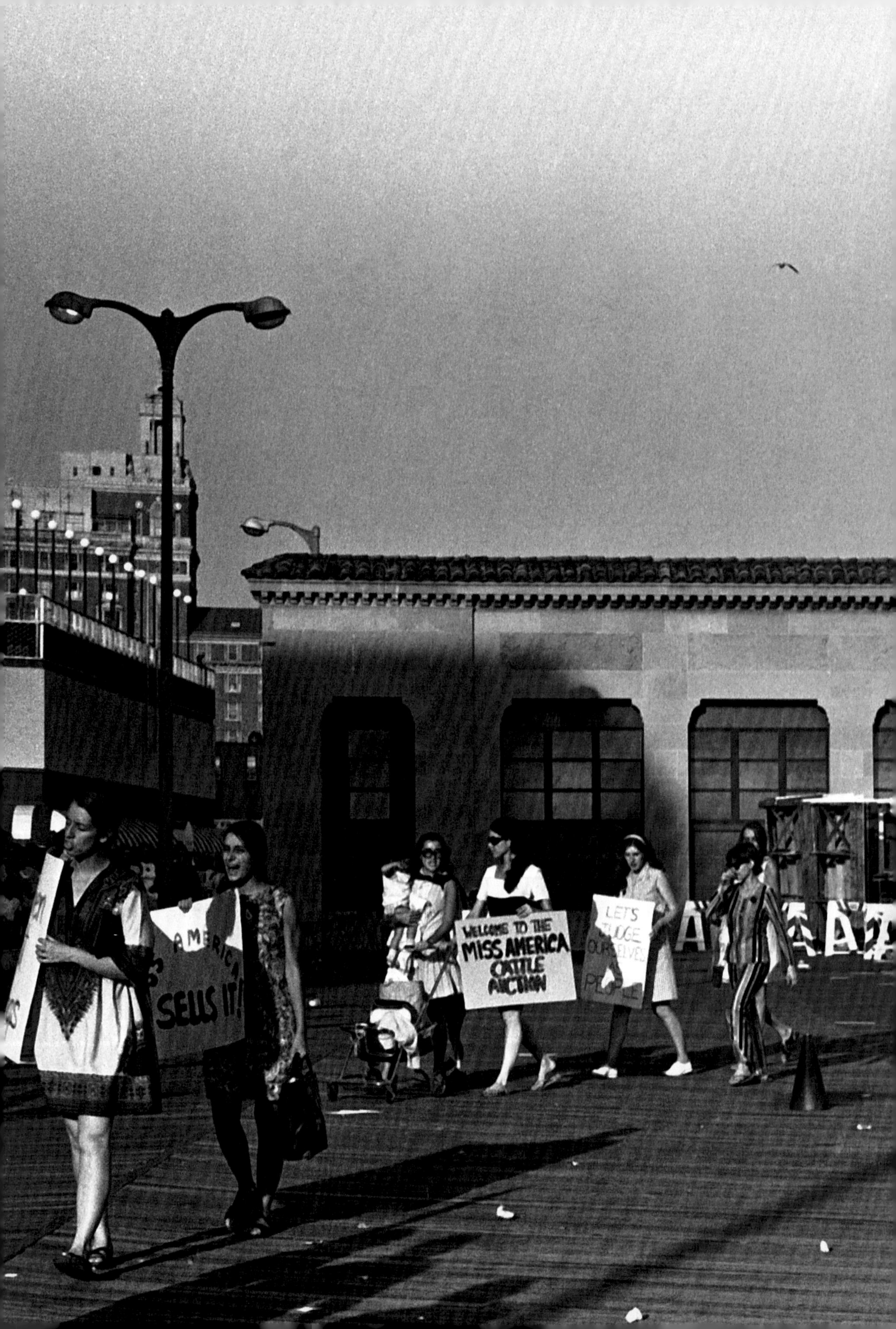
AMERICA
SELLS IT!
WELCOME TO THE
MISS AMERICA
CATTLE AUCTION
LET'S
JUDGE
OURSELVES
PEOPLE

NO!
MISS AMERICA IS NOT
MY IDEAL!
THE WORLD
EVERY
IS
BEAUTI

Fillmore East Takeover
East Village, New York

On the night of October 22, 1968, The East Village rock music venue Fillmore East hosted an overnight benefit for the legal defense fund for Columbia University students who had been arrested during the student strike at Columbia in April. The benefit had been organized by Julian Beck and Judith Malina of the Living Theatre, with Leonardo Shapiro's New York Free Theater and Joe Chaikin's Open Theater among those scheduled to perform. After the first scene of the Living Theatre's audience-participation piece Paradise Now, Up Against the Wall Motherfuckers, an East Village radical anarchist hippie group, seized the stage (with the consent of the Living Theatre). The Motherfuckers ran a storefront serving free food and patrolled St. Marks Place, wearing black armbands, to protect people from police harassment. Ben Morea, who was one of the spokespersons, went head to head with rock music promoter and Fillmore East owner, Bill Graham, over the issue of community involvement, calling it a clash between the grassroots and those who exploit them. Given the money the Fillmore East was making off the community, Morea said, they should give something back, and so the Motherfuckers demanded the free use of the theater on Thursday nights for the community, threatening to burn the theater if Graham did not agree. The stage was occupied and it was chaotic; dope was smoked and food passed around, and musicians and theater people performed. Eventually Graham gave in and gave them three more free Thursday nights before he terminated the arrangement and called the police. It was a total happening.

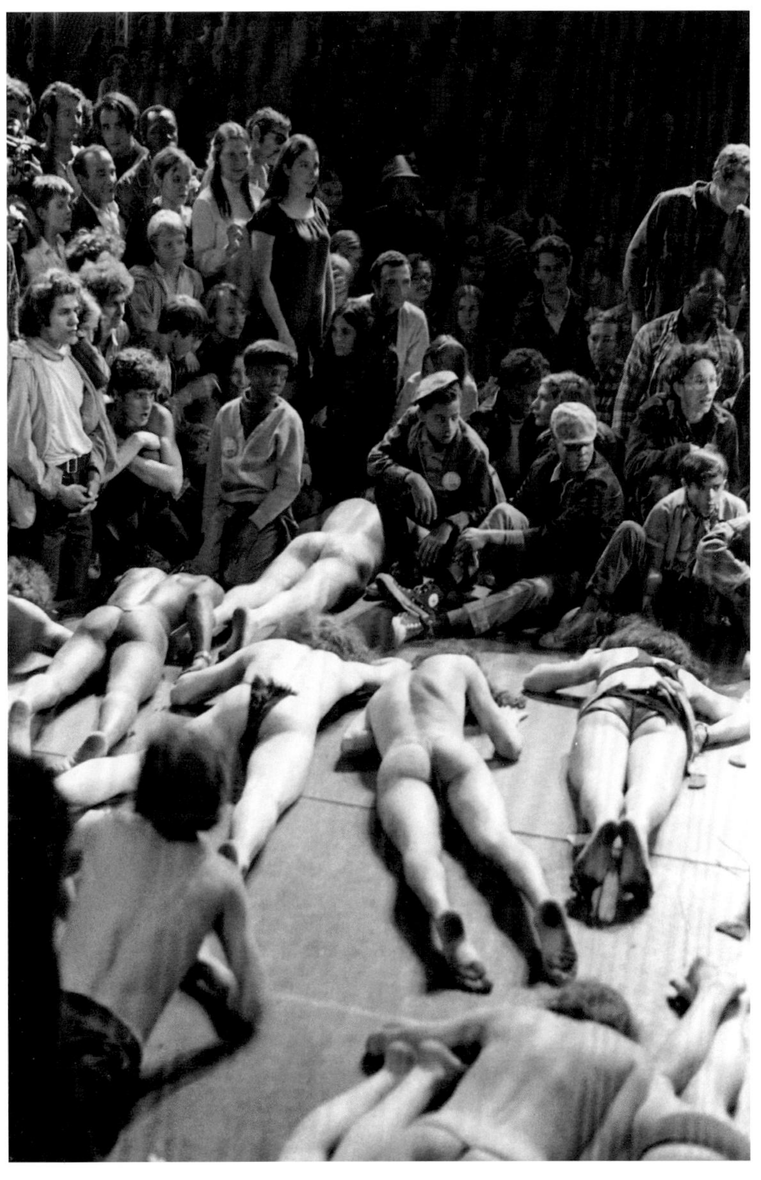

The Living Theatre performing *Paradise Now*
Fillmore East Takeover, East Village, New York, October 22, 1968

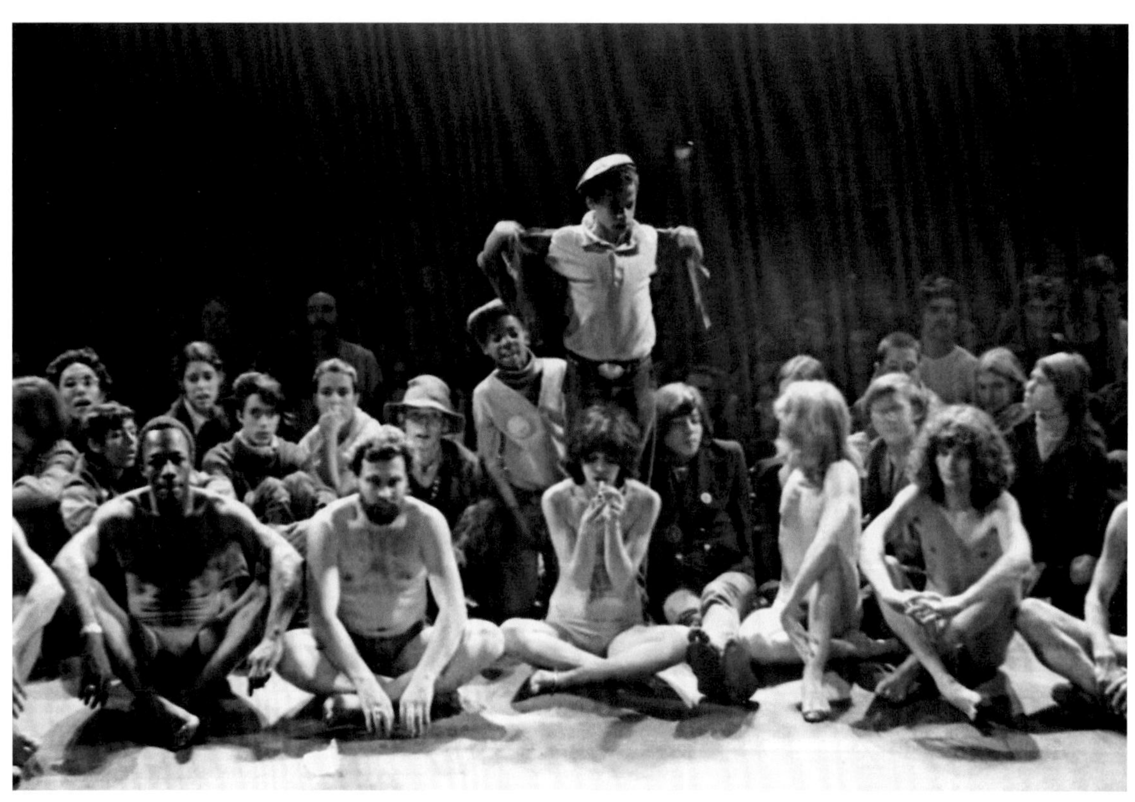

The Living Theatre performing *Paradise Now*
Fillmore East Takeover, East Village, New York, October 22, 1968

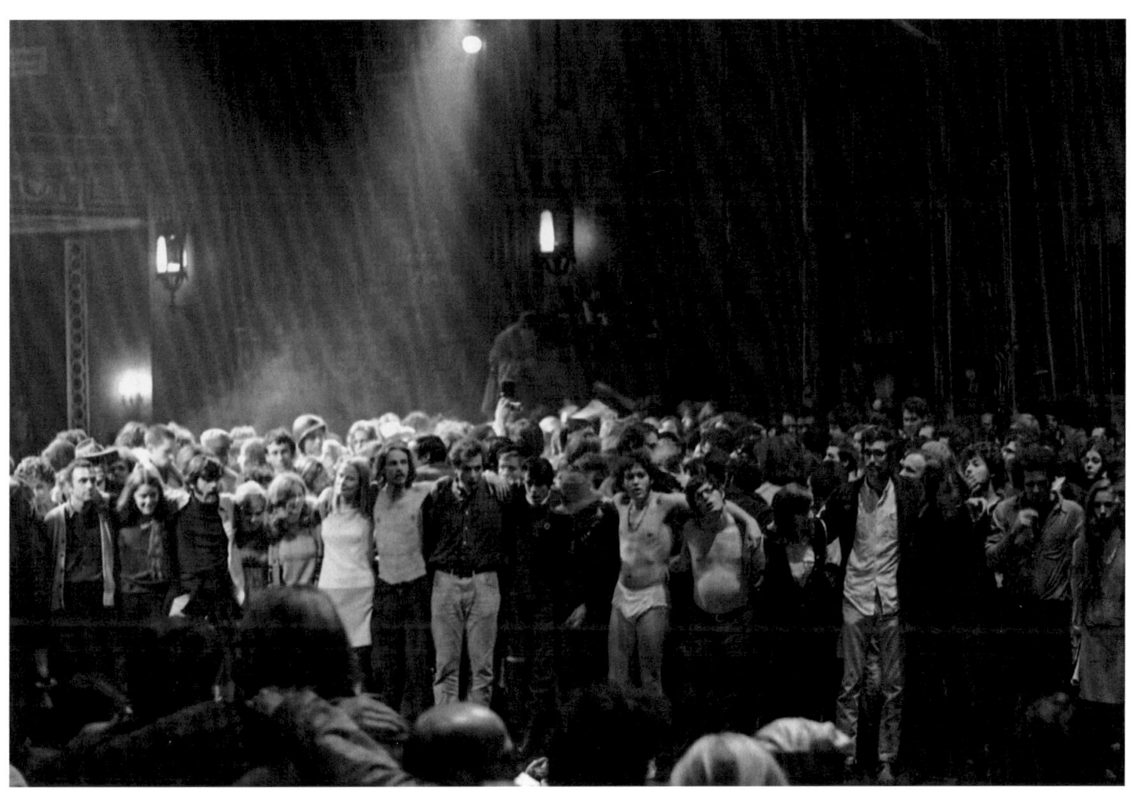

Fillmore East Takeover, East Village, New York, October 22, 1968

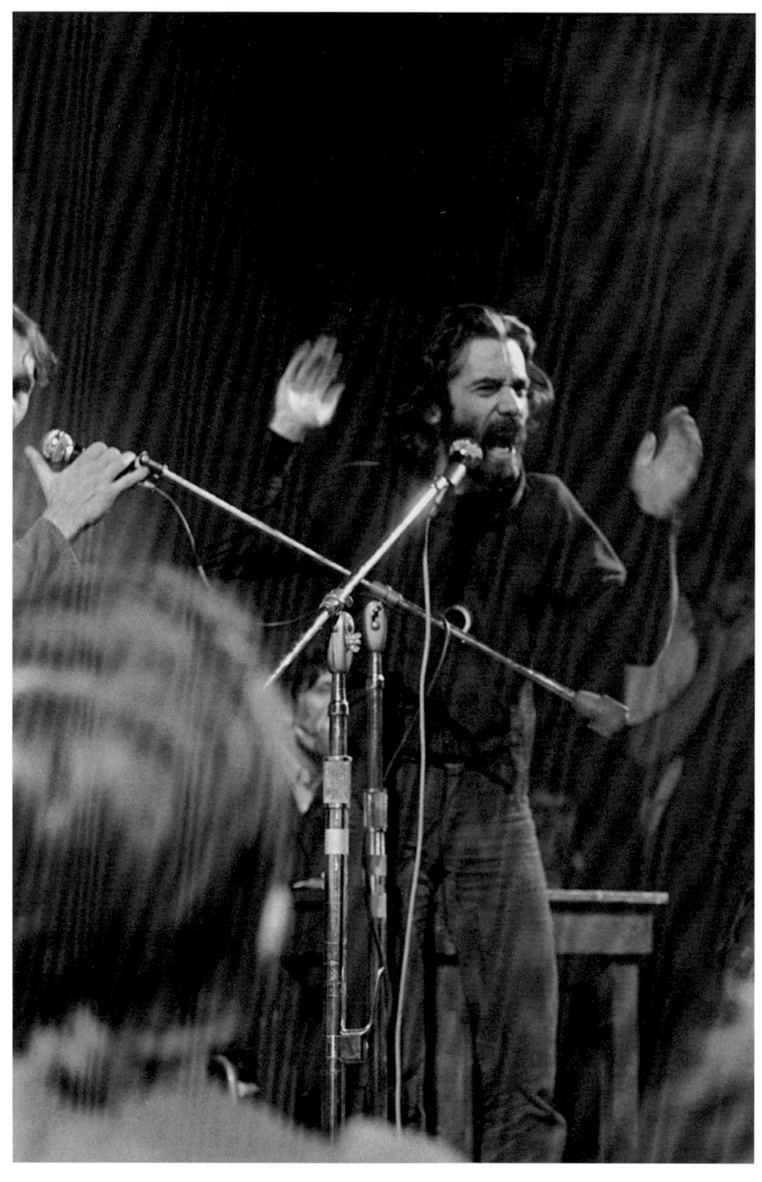

Ben Morea from the Motherfuckers
Fillmore East Takeover, East Village, New York, October 22, 1968

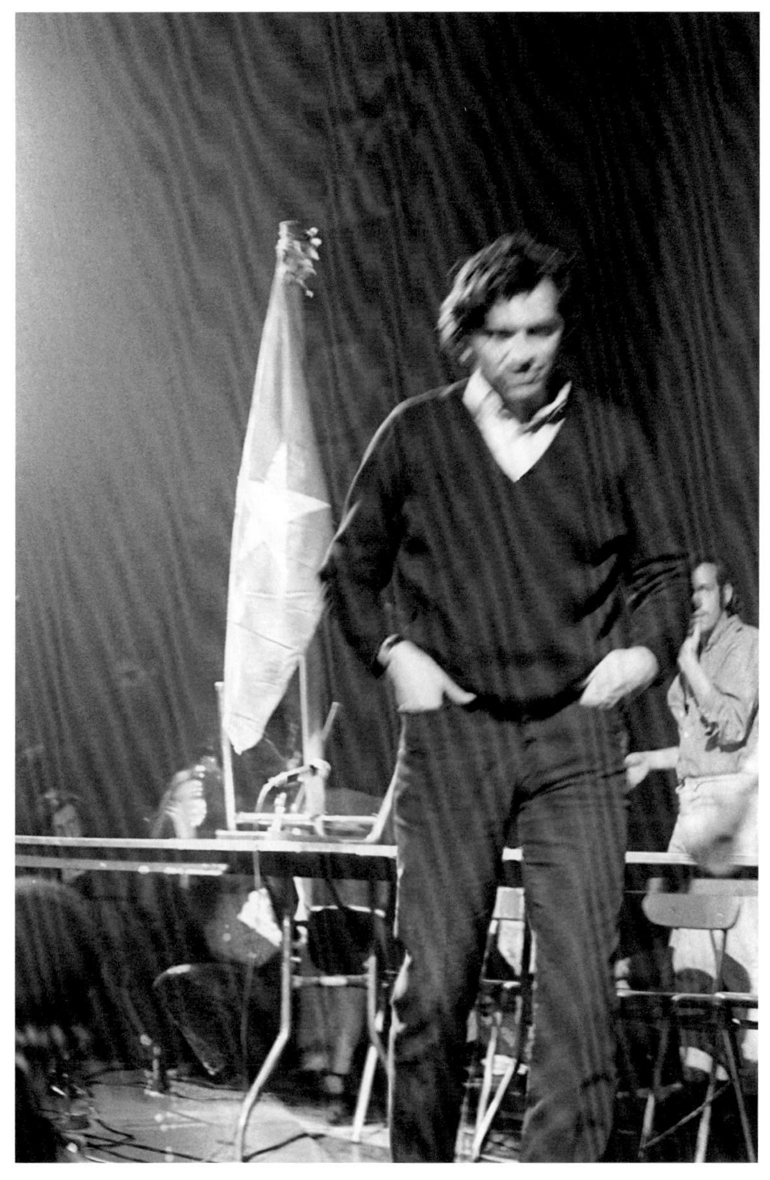

Bill Graham, owner of the Fillmore East
Fillmore East Takeover, East Village, New York, October 22, 1968

Following spread
Fillmore East Takeover, East Village, New York, October 22, 1968

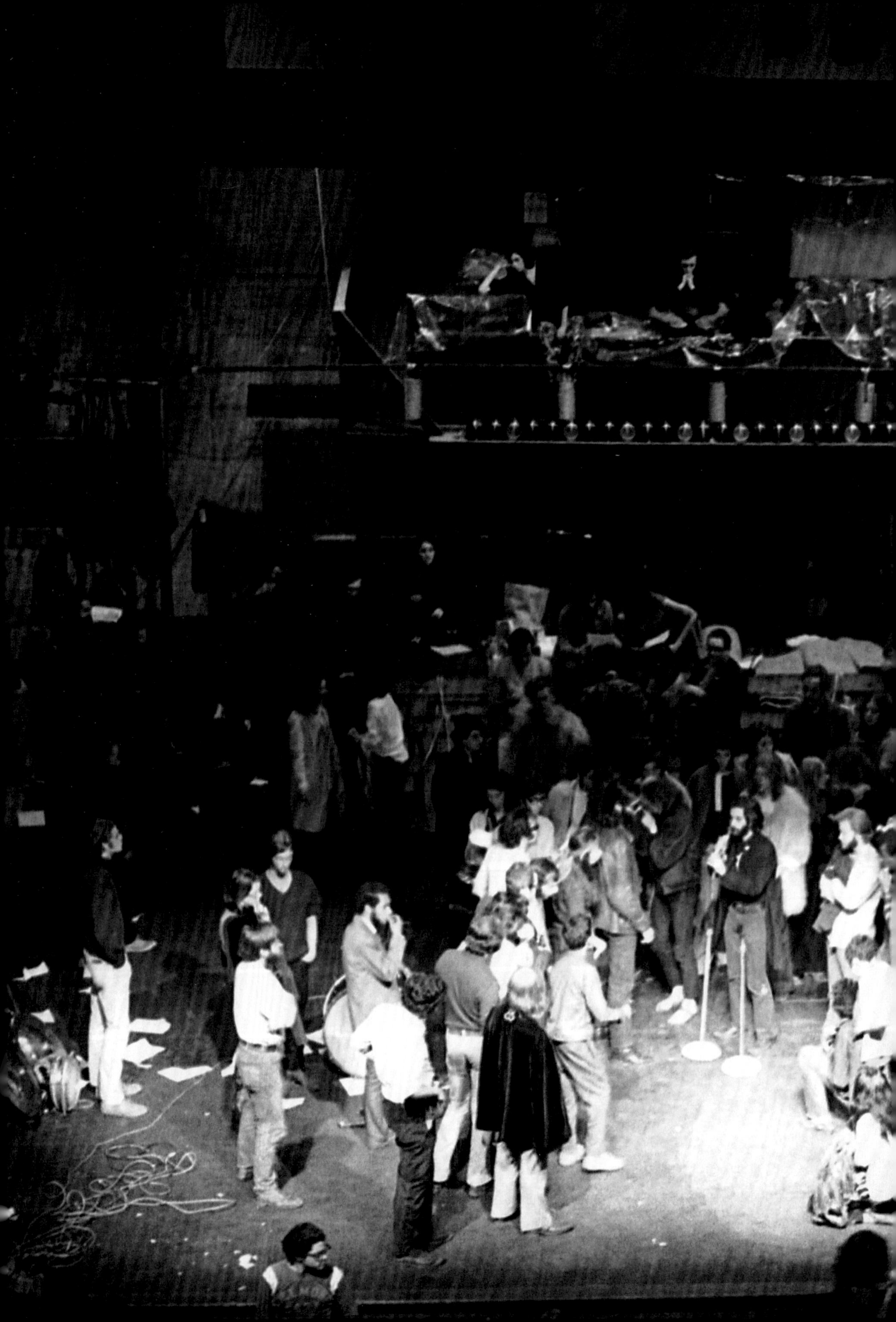

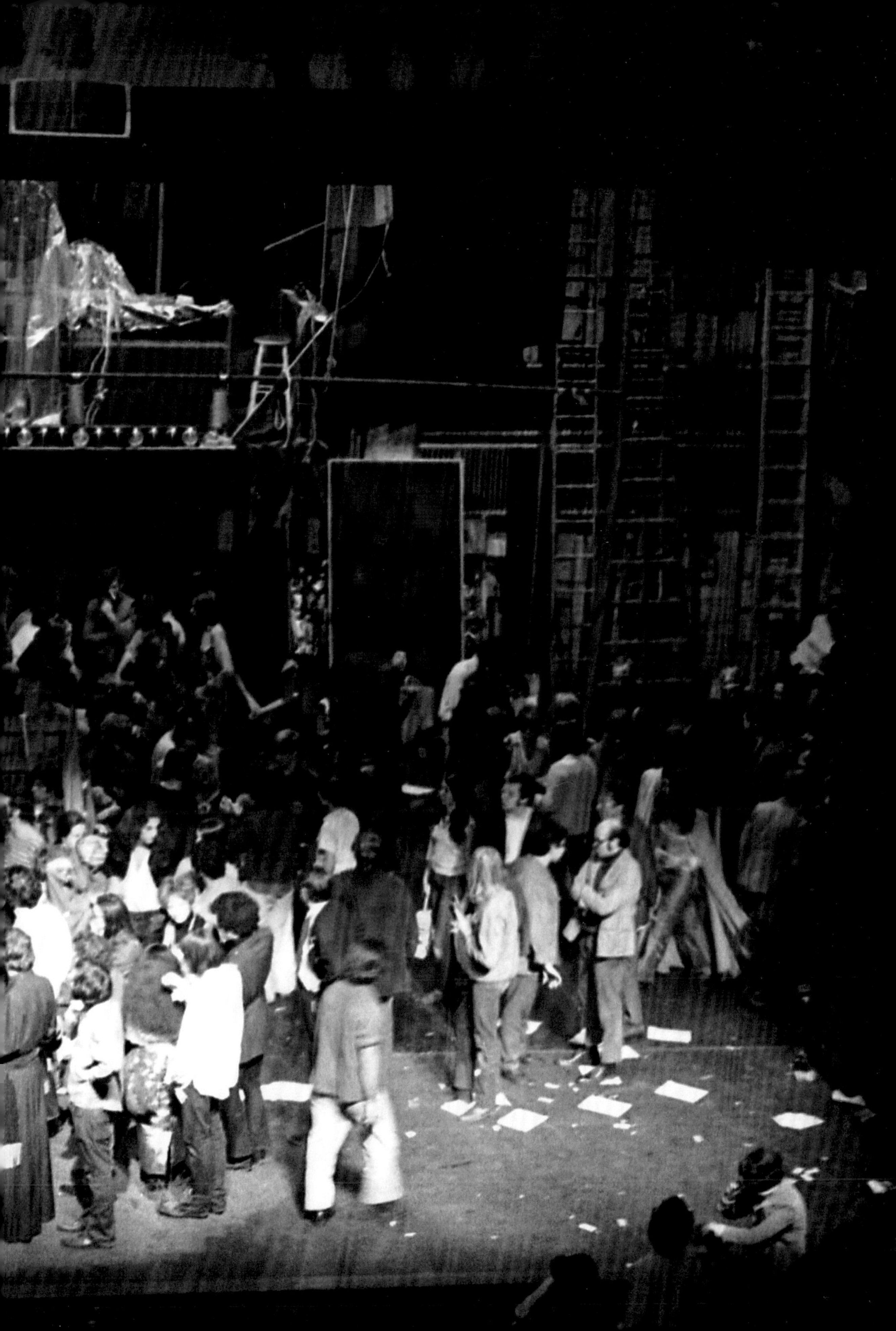

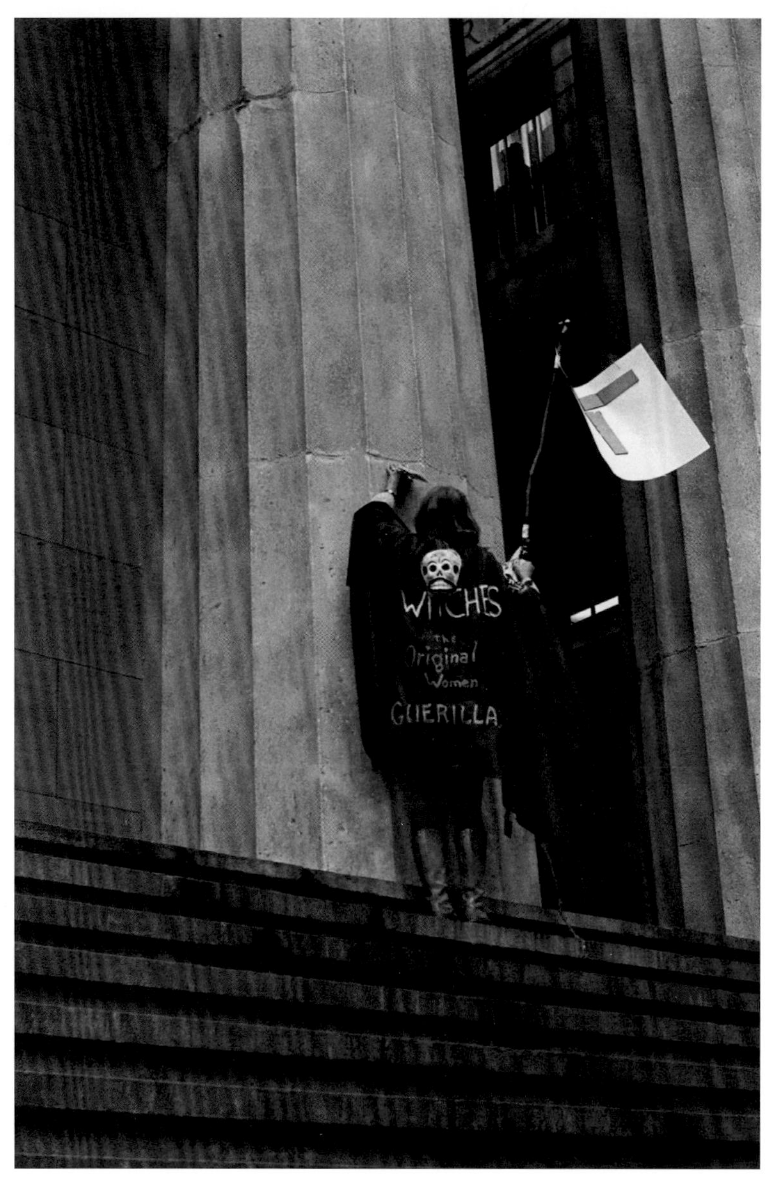

Ros Baxandall in front of Federal Hall
W.I.T.C.H. Hex on Wall Street, New York City, October 31, 1968

October 31, 1968

W.I.T.C.H. Hex on Wall Street
New York City

On Halloween 1968, I photographed the W.I.T.C.H. Hex on Wall Street. When Peggy Powell Dobbins had to return to Atlantic City for trial on her noxious odor charge, she travelled with a woman named Marsha Seavey, who likened what New York Radical Women were doing to the witches of old—the independent women, the midwives, the soothsayers, the healers, who were burned at the stake. Peggy ran with it and started Women's International Terrorist Conspiracy from Hell or W.I.T.C.H. We used guerrilla theater as a political tool to get our message across. We decided, as our first action, to hex Wall Street, pointing out it's complicity with the patriarchy, the war in Vietnam, and the oppression of working people. Most of this took place on the steps of Federal Hall, located directly across the street from the Stock Exchange. It afforded us, and the people who gathered round, a perfect theatrical space. It was lunch time, and the onlookers didn't know what to make of us. We chanted: *Wall Street, Wall Street, mightiest wall of all street, trick or treat, corporate elite, up against the Wall Street. Wall Street, Wall Street, mightiest wall of all street, stock exchange, foreign exchange, student exchange, wife exchange, up against the Wall Street.*

From there, we moved on to Chase Manhattan Bank, where we huddled and chanted, handed out leaflets, and tried to talk to people who worked or banked there. We got kicked out pretty quickly but felt energized by our action. W.I.T.C.H. covens were sprouting up all over the country, independent of each other, but sharing in the general purpose of stirring the pot, making some noise, pointing the finger at patriarchy, raising consciousness about women's rights, and having some fun.

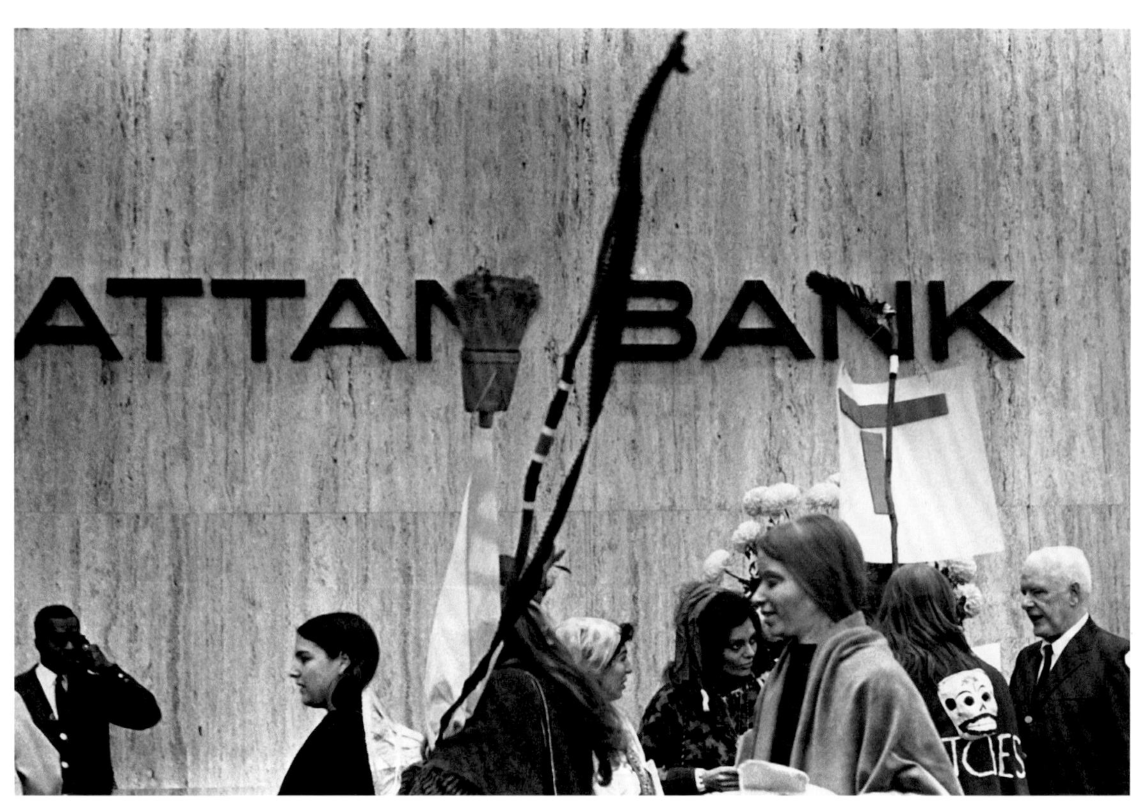

Susan Silverman, Florika Remetier, and Judith Weston Hoskins in Chase Manhattan Bank
W.I.T.C.H. Hex on Wall Street, New York City, October 31, 1968

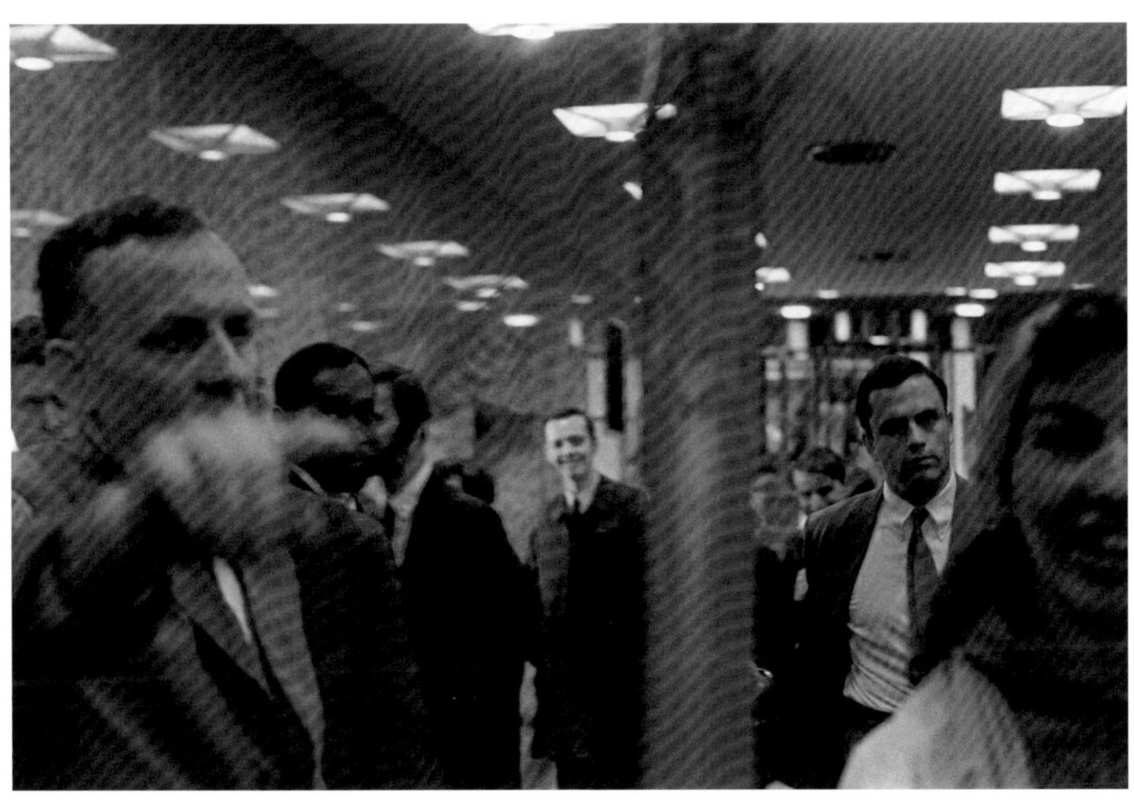

Lynn Laredo in Chase Manhattan Bank
W.I.T.C.H. Hex on Wall Street, New York City, October 31, 1968

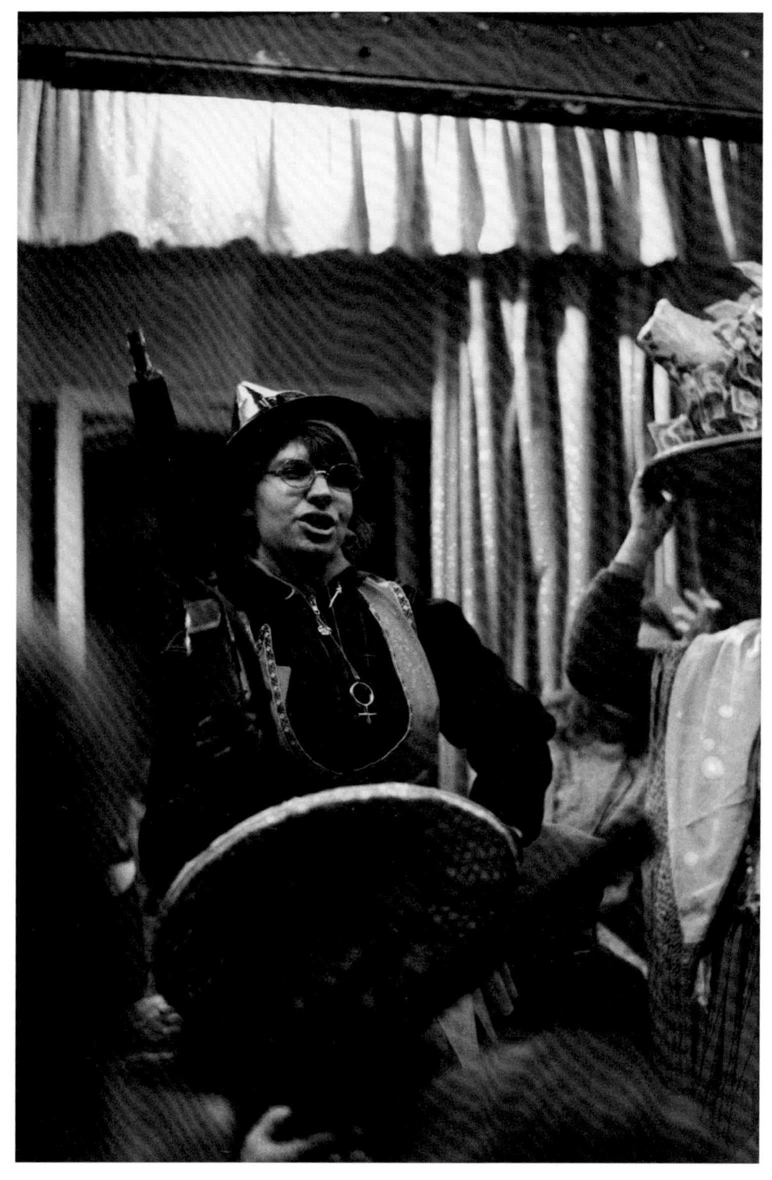

Robin Morgan protesting McSorley's *Men only* policy
W.I.T.C.H. Hex on Wall Street, New York City, October 31, 1968

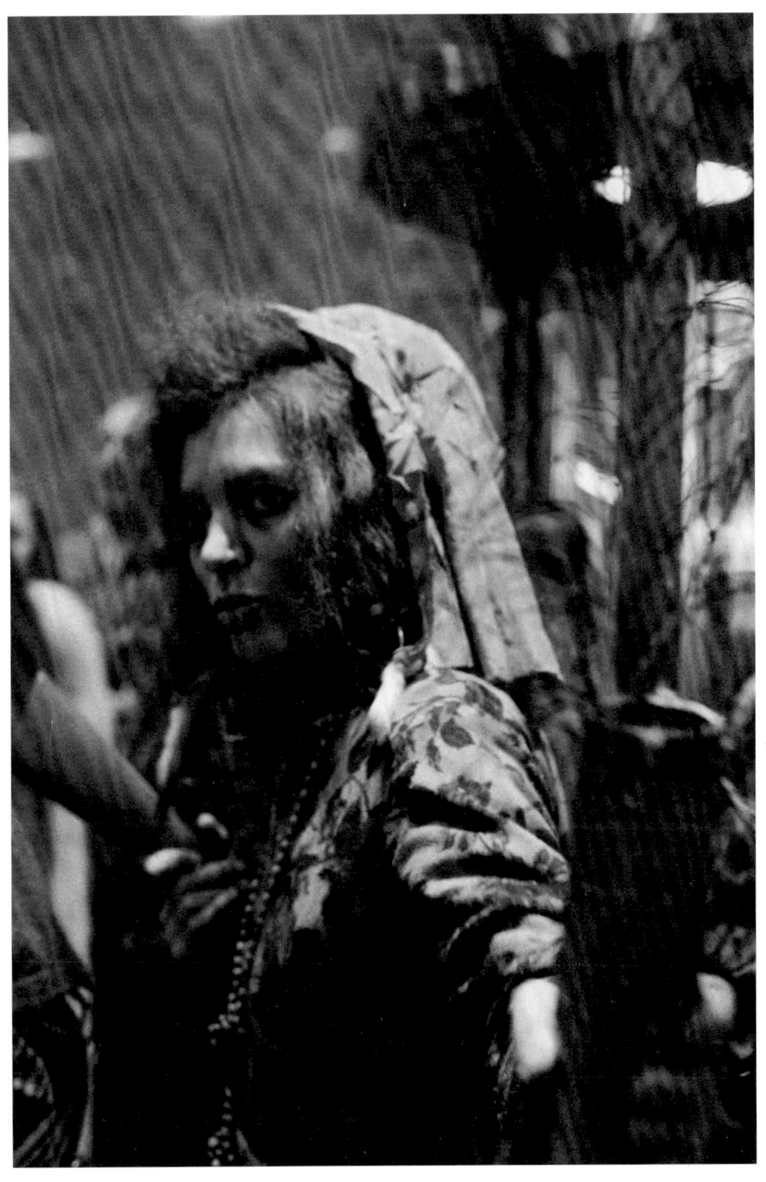

Florika Remetier in Chase Manhattan Bank
W.I.T.C.H. Hex on Wall Street, New York City, October 31, 1968

Following spread
W.I.T.C.H. Hex on Wall Street, New York City, October 31, 1968

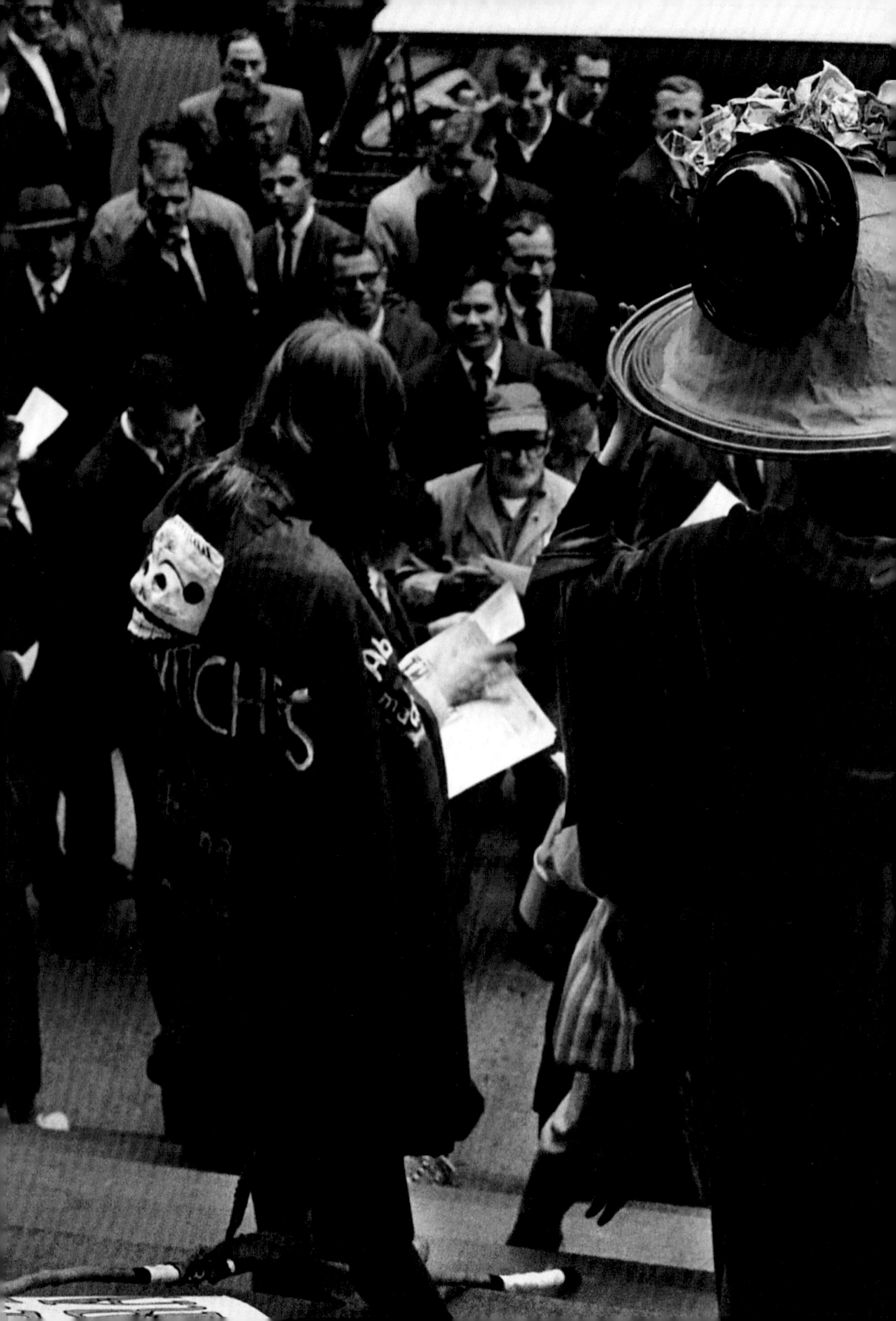

ITCHES

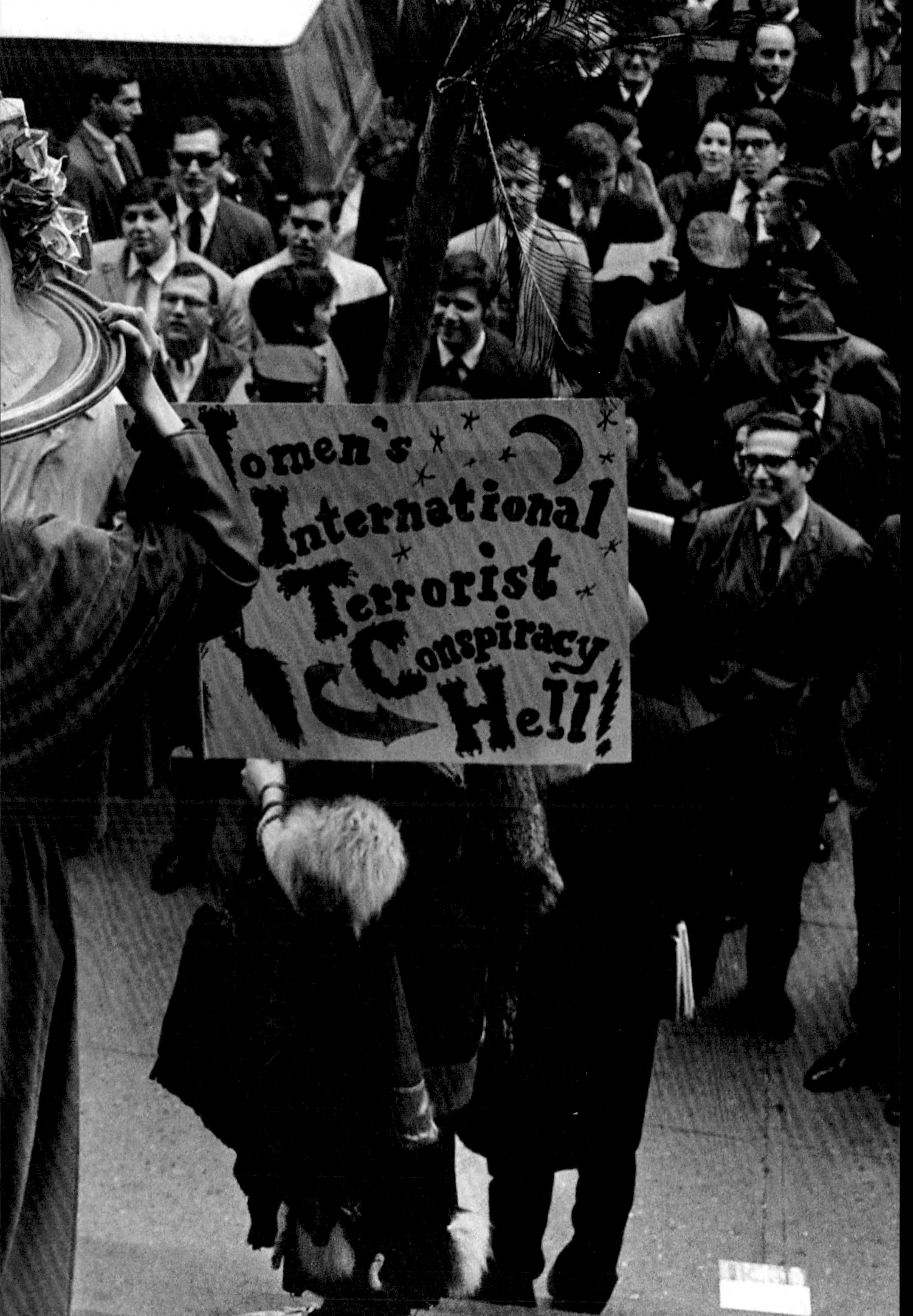

omen's
International
Terrorist
Conspiracy
Hell!

Tenth Anniversary of the Cuban Revolution
Cuba

I had been in Newsreel for about a year when we were invited by the Cuban government to send a representative to the Tenth Anniversary of the Cuban Revolution as part of a delegation of alternative media people from around the United States.

It was a life-changing experience for me. Our first event was on January 2, 1969 in Revolution Square, where Fidel Castro spoke for hours to the thousands of people who had gathered. Our delegation was seated near the podium from which Fidel spoke. I had free access to whatever I wanted to photograph.

We all stayed at the Hotel Nacional in Havana. On our floor was a group of cultural workers from different Latin American countries who I got to know and jam with. The Cubans lent me a guitar to use while I was there, and I wrote a song or two.

We toured the island, visiting farms and schools. The first thing the Cuban revolutionaries did when they took power was to launch a literacy campaign with particular emphasis on rural areas, where people had the least opportunity for education. I was particularly struck by a small school in the countryside run by a former businessman who became a teacher after the revolution. When you entered his one-room school house, the first thing you saw was a long table, almost the length of the room, with chess sets lined up and children sitting across from each other playing. It was charming, and I could tell the children were happy and bright with the light of learning in their eyes. It was evident that they adored their teacher, and he them. We went to Santiago, where the Moncada Barracks had been turned into a museum. This had been the site of the July 26, 1953 attack on the Batista regime, considered the beginning of the Cuban revolution. We visited cane plantations and sugar production facilities, small towns and the countryside. The only dissent we encountered was in Havana from formerly middle-class and wealthy people, who were not happy with the new government's policy of sharing the wealth.

We returned home by freighter boat to Nova Scotia. What was normally a five-day trip, took us thirteen days because of stormy weather, which meant we had to spend most of our time with the crew below deck. We were all fine with that, because it gave us a chance to play chess and dominoes with working-class Cubans. We interviewed one young crew member who expressed gratitude for the revolution, because it provided an education and a job enabling him to take care of his family.

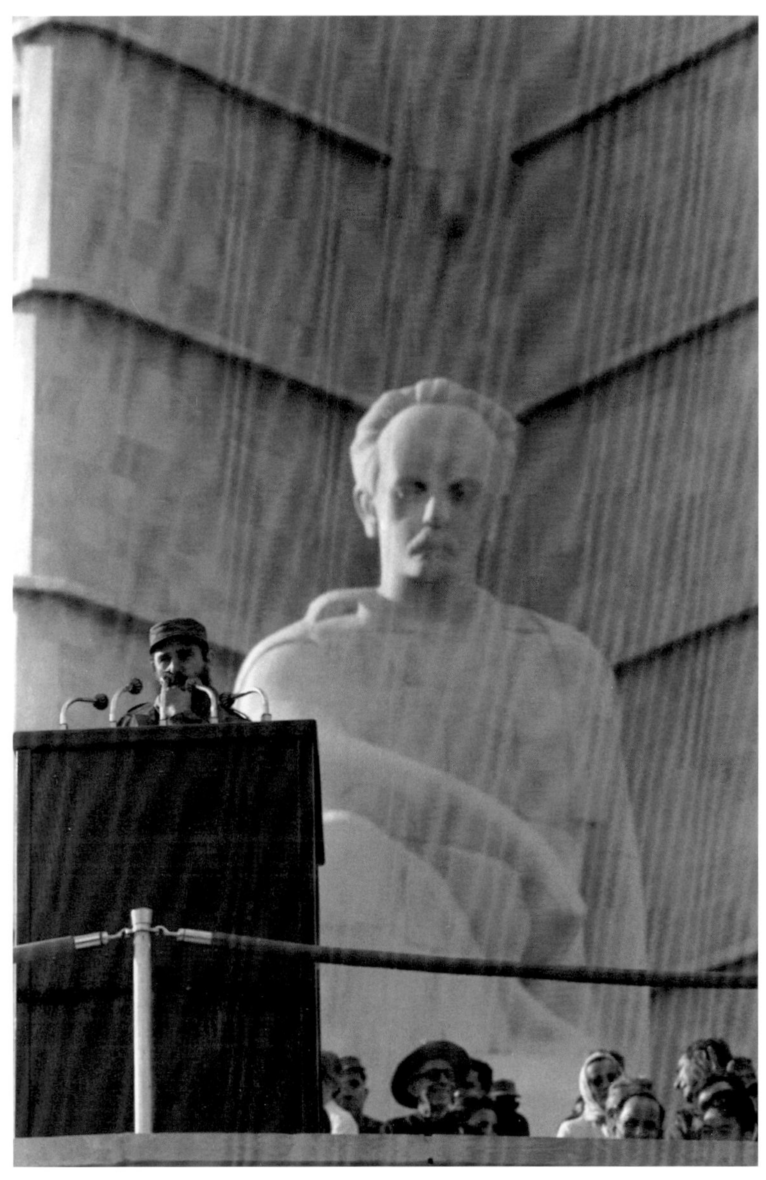

Fidel Castro speaking under the watchful eye of Jose Martí on January 2, 1969
Tenth Anniversary of the Cuban Revolution, Cuba, January 1969

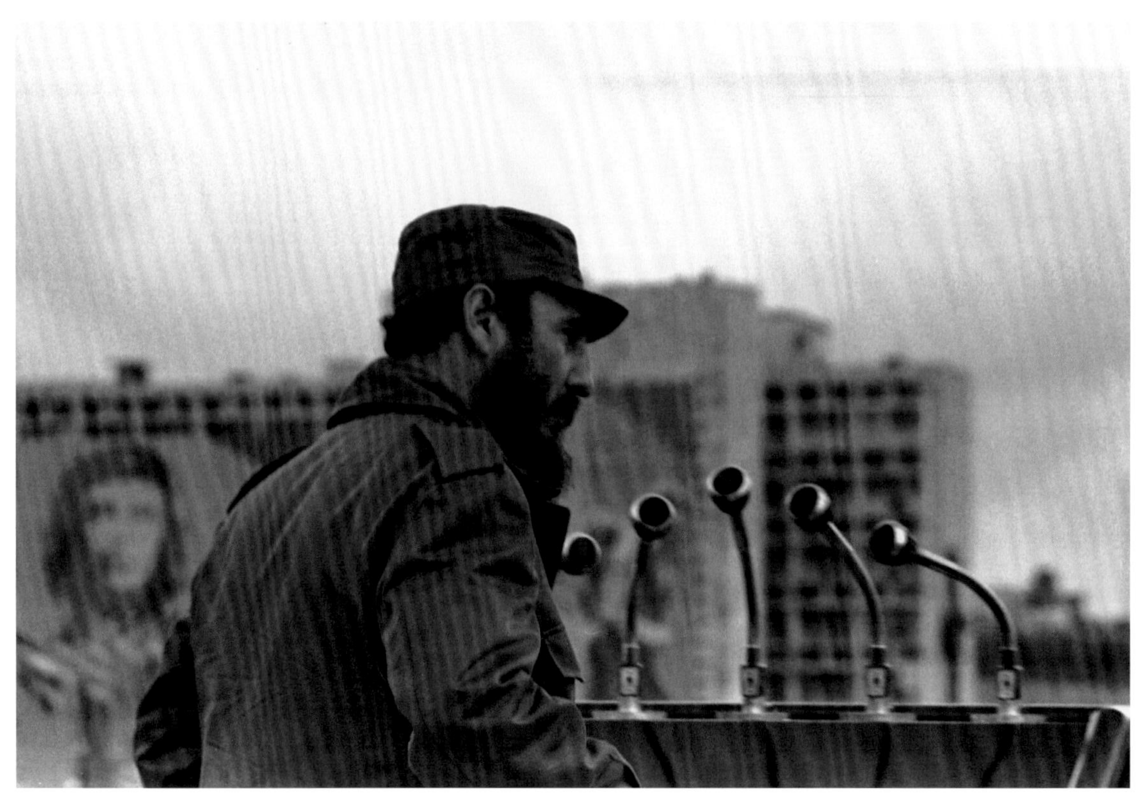

Fidel Castro speaking in Revolution Square on January 2, 1969
Tenth Anniversary of the Cuban Revolution, Cuba, January 1969

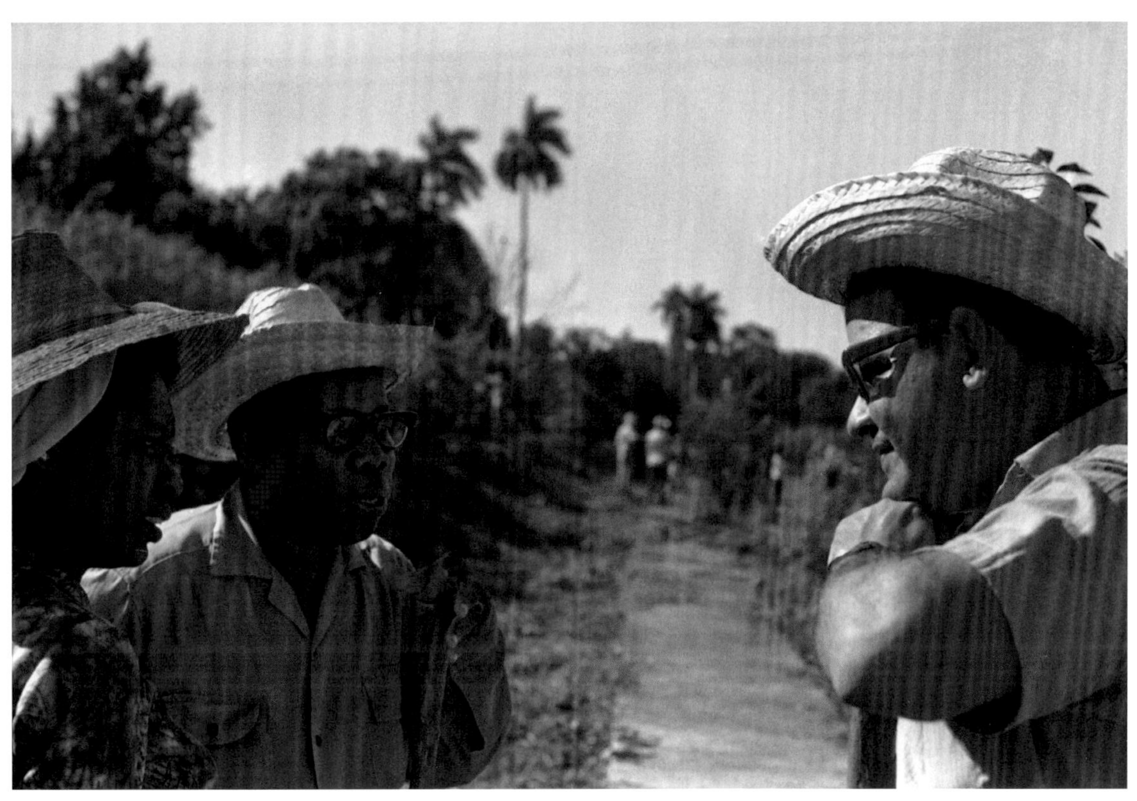

Agricultural workers in the countryside
Tenth Anniversary of the Cuban Revolution, Cuba, January 1969

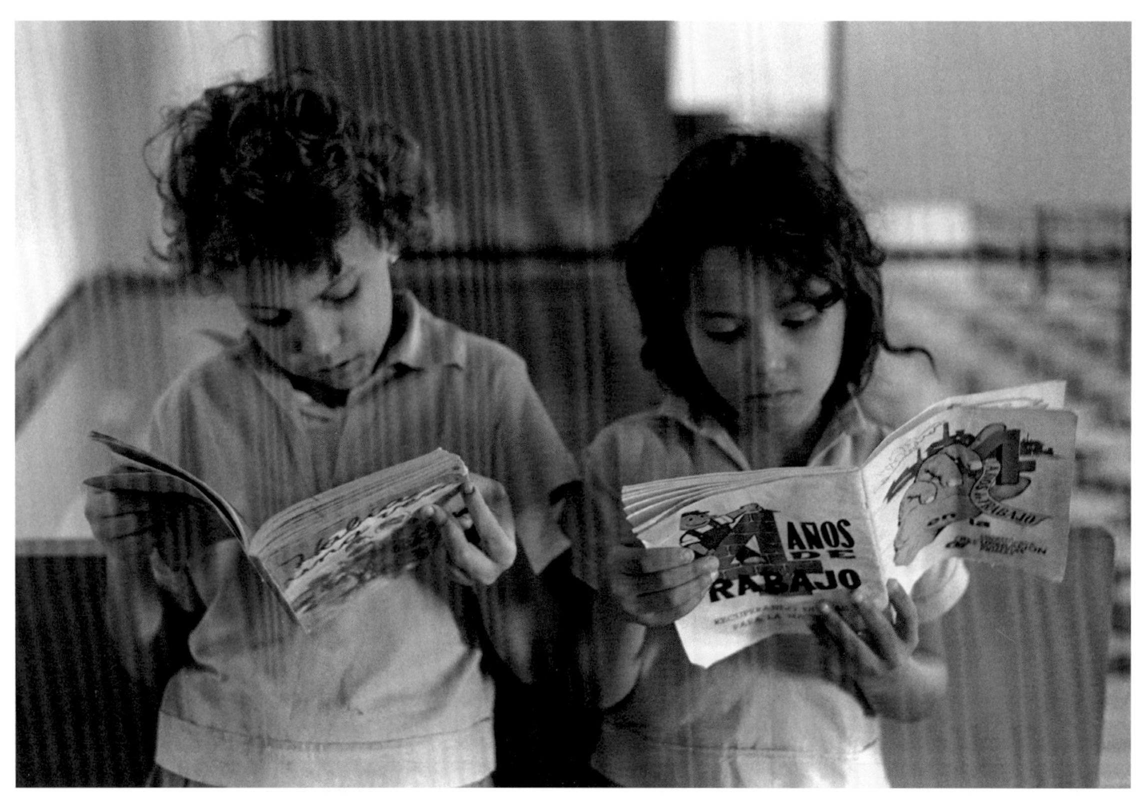

Children at the Moncada museum, Santiago
Tenth Anniversary of the Cuban Revolution, Cuba, January 1969

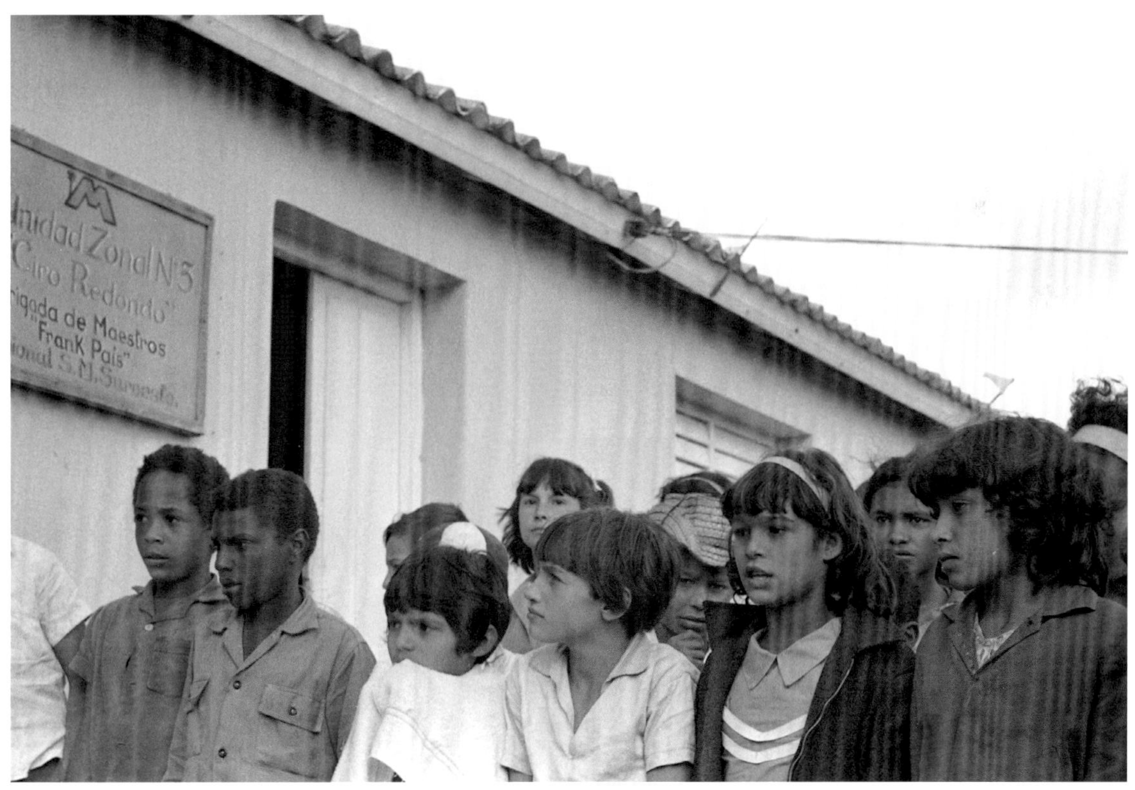

Children outside their one-room schoolhouse in the countryside
Tenth Anniversary of the Cuban Revolution, Cuba, January 1969

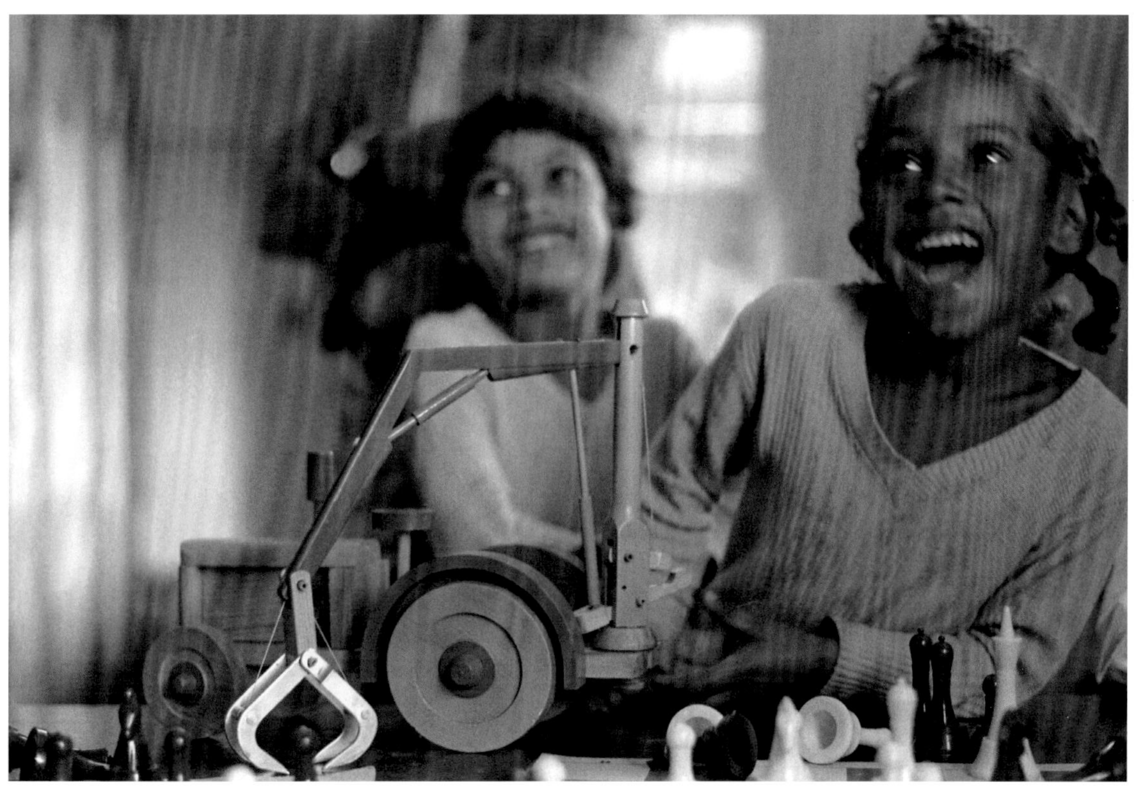

Children inside their one-room schoolhouse in the countryside
Tenth Anniversary of the Cuban Revolution, Cuba, January 1969

Following spread
Cubans listening to Fidel Castro, January 2, 1969
Tenth Anniversary of the Cuban Revolution, Cuba, January 1969

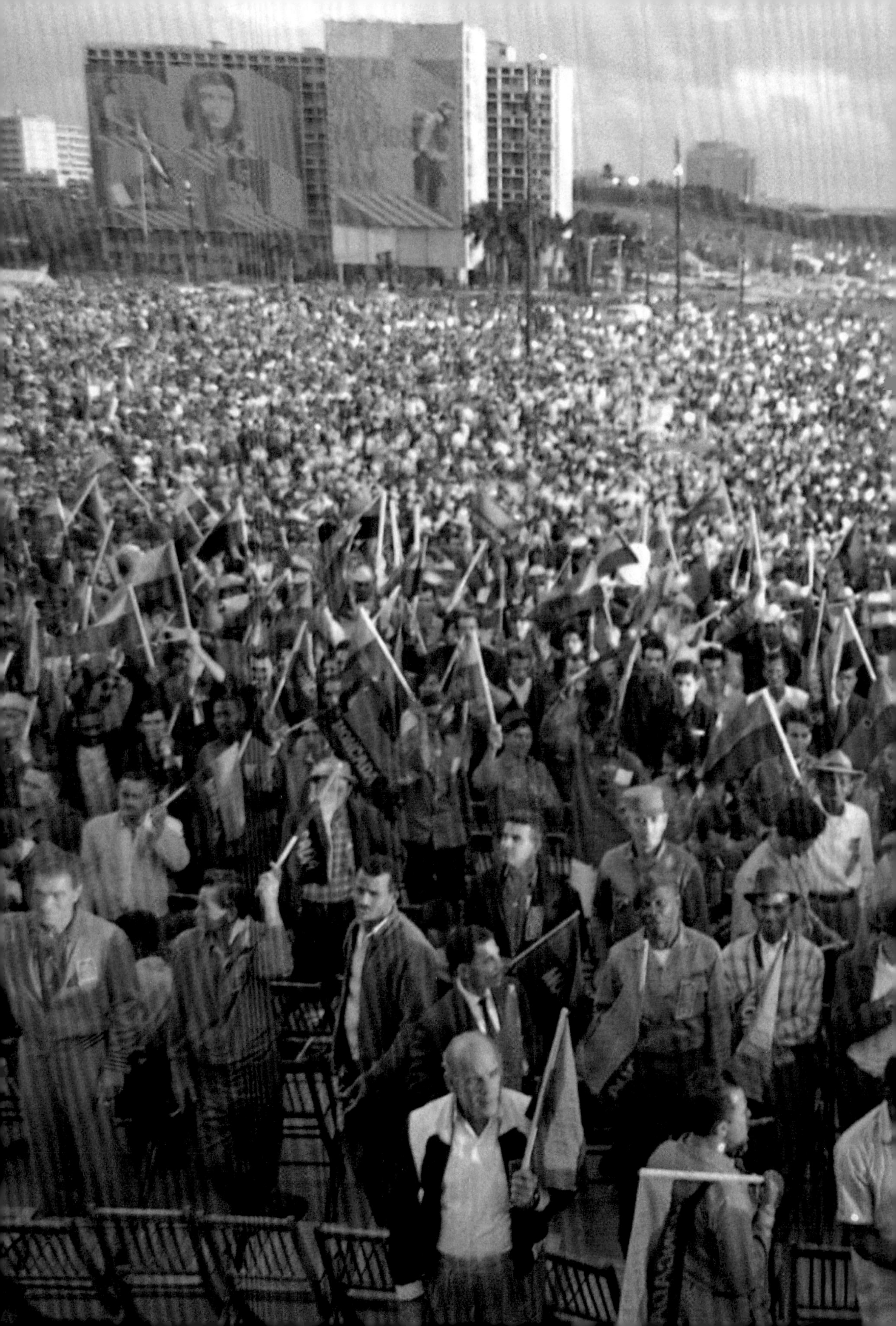

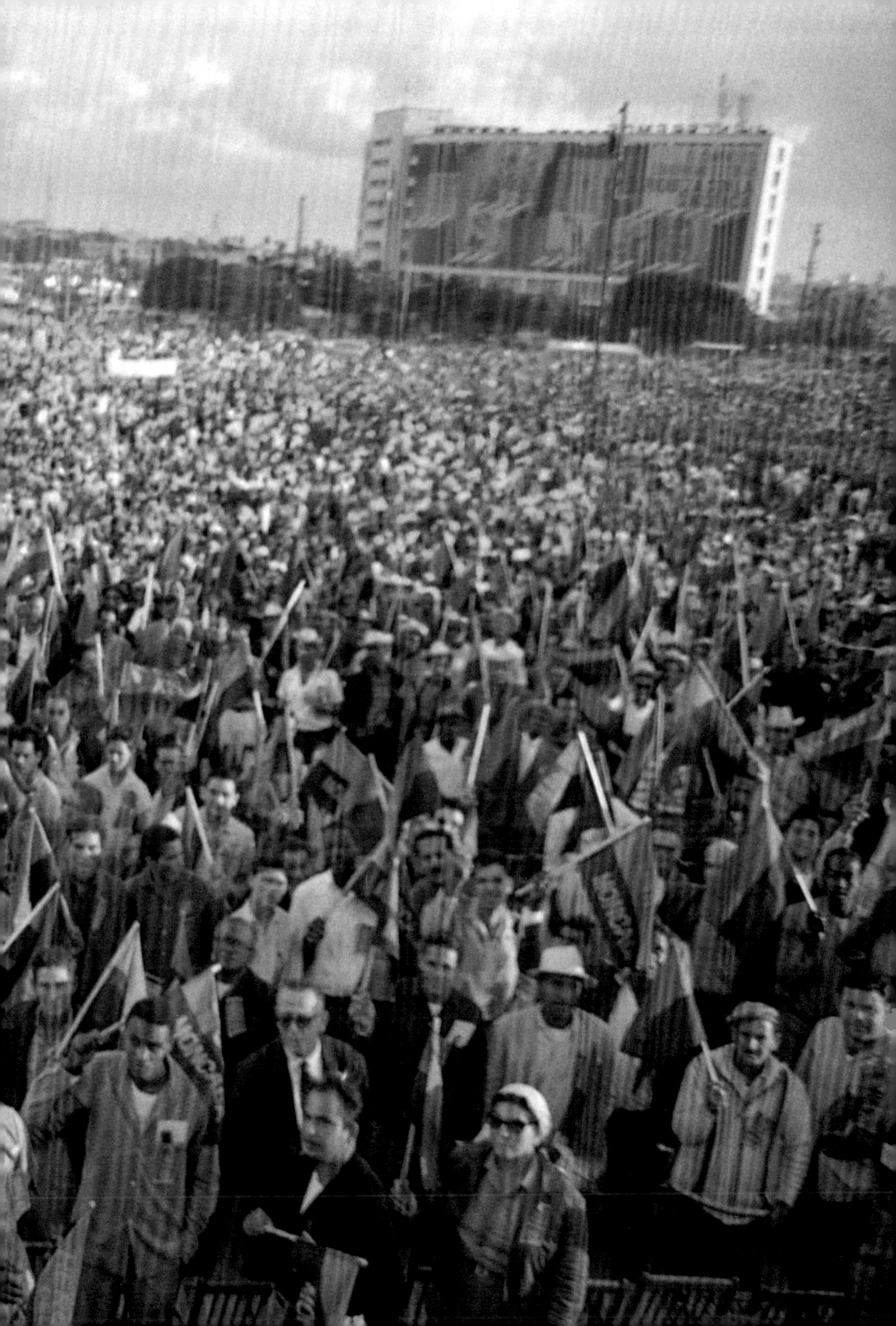

Black Panther Party Free Breakfast Program
Harlem, New York

My image of the Black Panther Party in New York City was based on the organizing they did in the community: the free breakfast and liberation school programs, community health clinics, and free clothing drives, which rarely got covered in the mainstream media. This was the everyday work of the Black Panther Party, responding to the needs of their community. Unfortunately, J. Edgar Hoover didn't see it that way; he saw them as a primary threat. In 1956, as head of the FBI, Hoover had unleashed a counter-intelligence program called COINTELPRO, aimed at surveilling, infiltrating, discrediting, and disrupting domestic political organizations. While the Panthers were opening offices around the country, COINTELPRO was infiltrating, spreading misinformation, and acting as provocateurs by sowing dissent within the ranks and egging people on to commit violent acts.

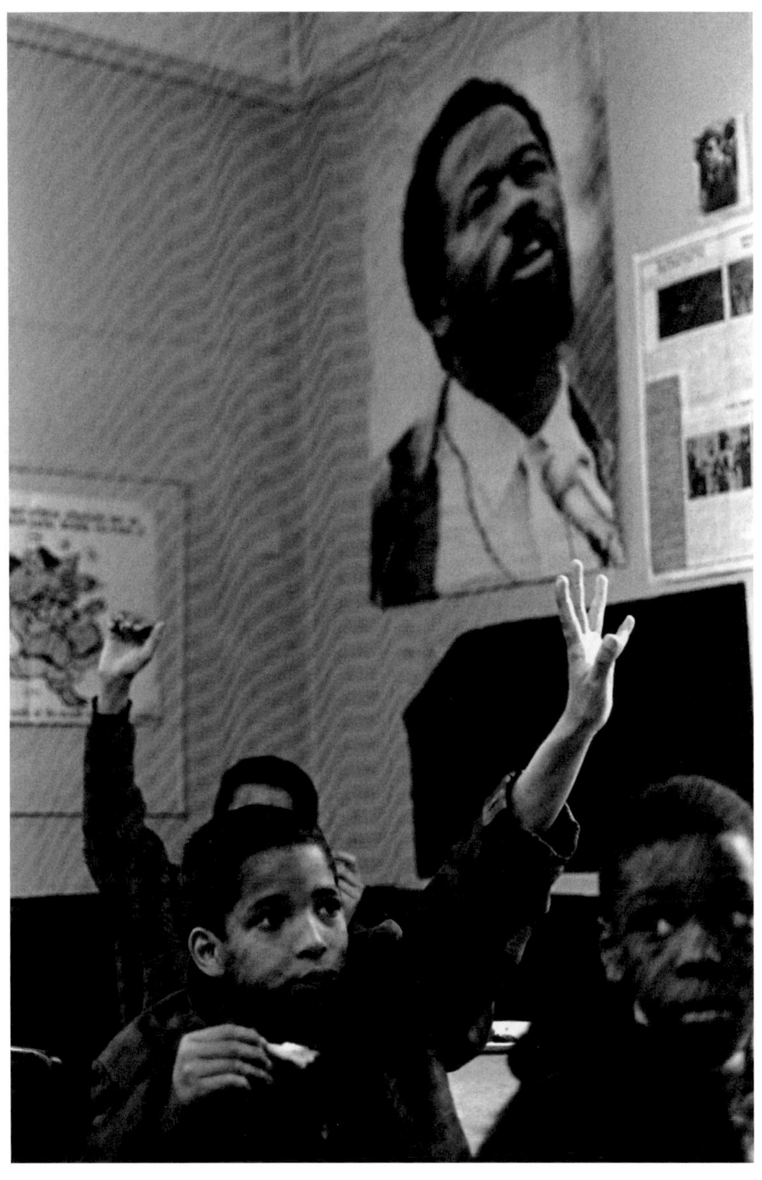

Liberation school, All Saints Catholic Church
Black Panther Party Free Breakfast Program, Harlem, New York, Spring 1969

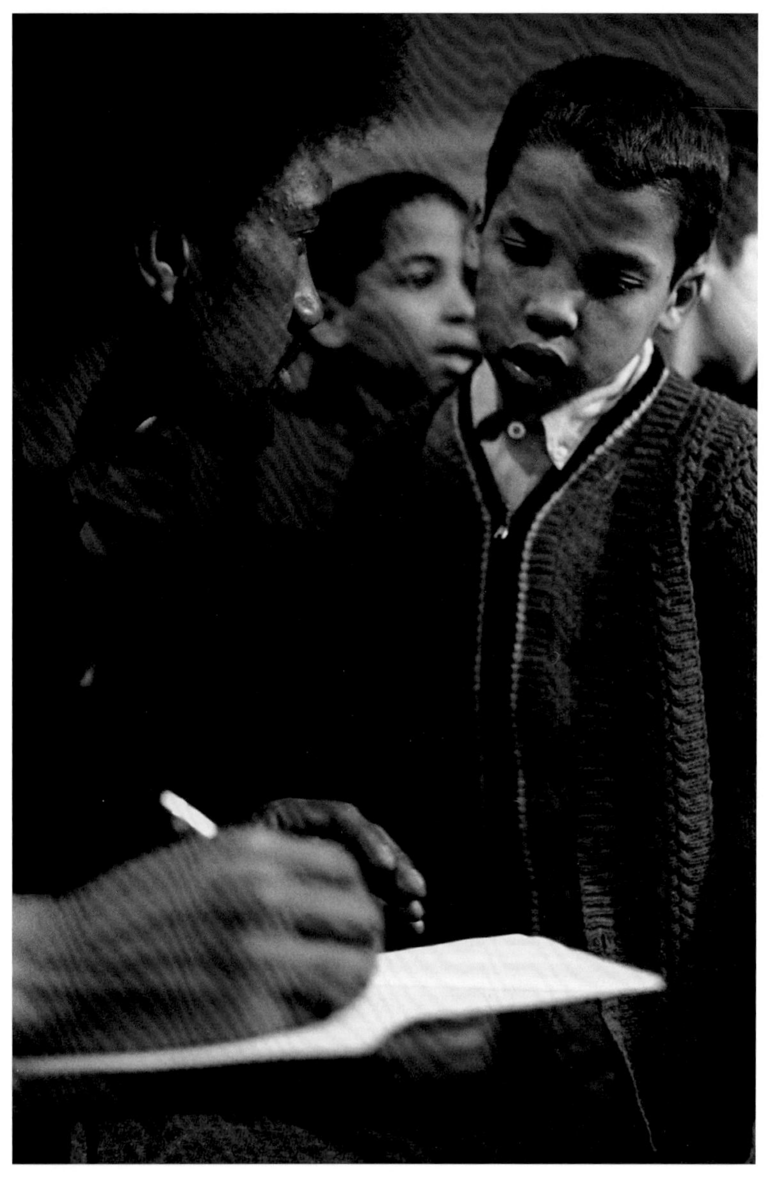

Liberation school, All Saints Catholic Church
Black Panther Party Free Breakfast Program, Harlem, New York, Spring 1969

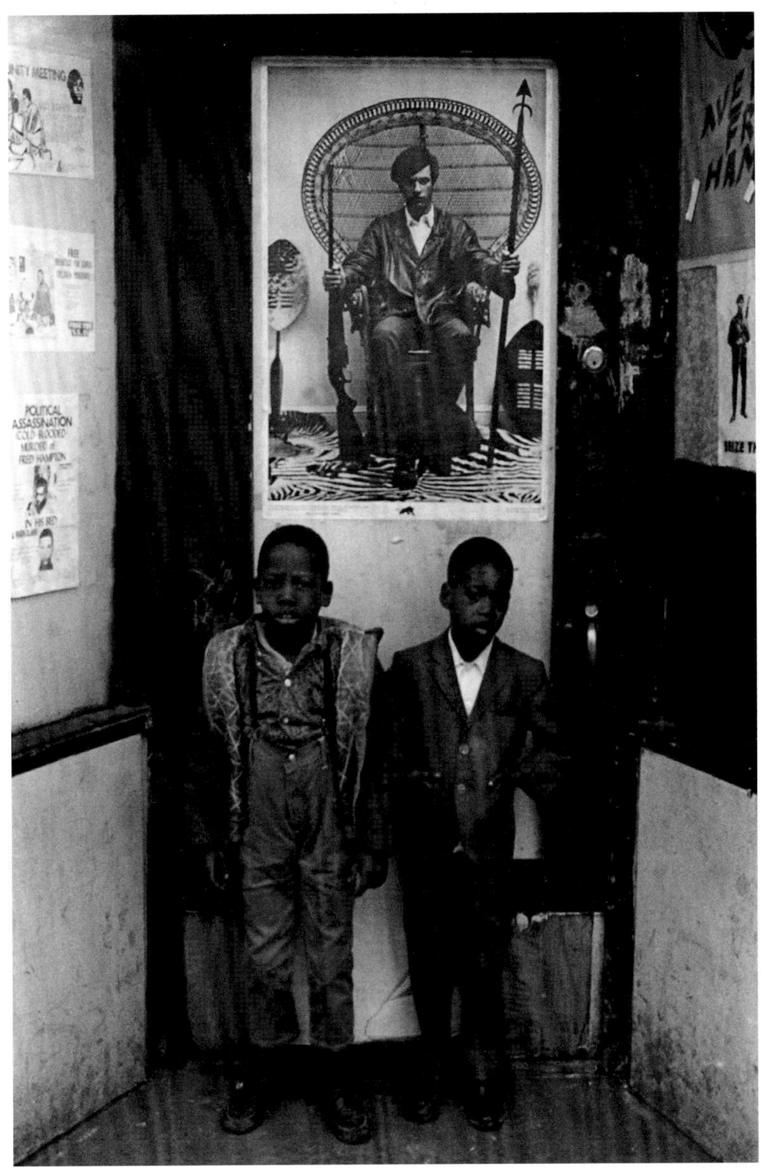

Black Panther Party Free Breakfast Program, Harlem, New York, Spring 1969

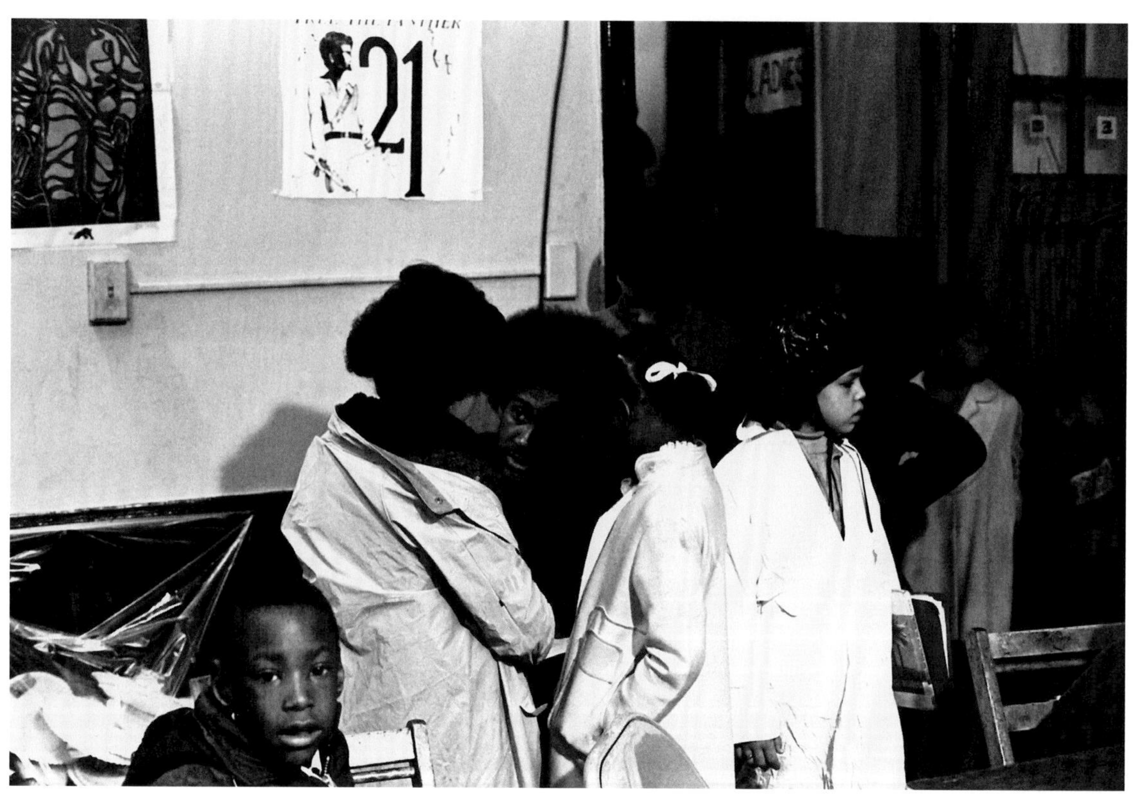

Liberation school, All Saints Catholic Church
Black Panther Party Free Breakfast Program, Harlem, New York, Spring 1969

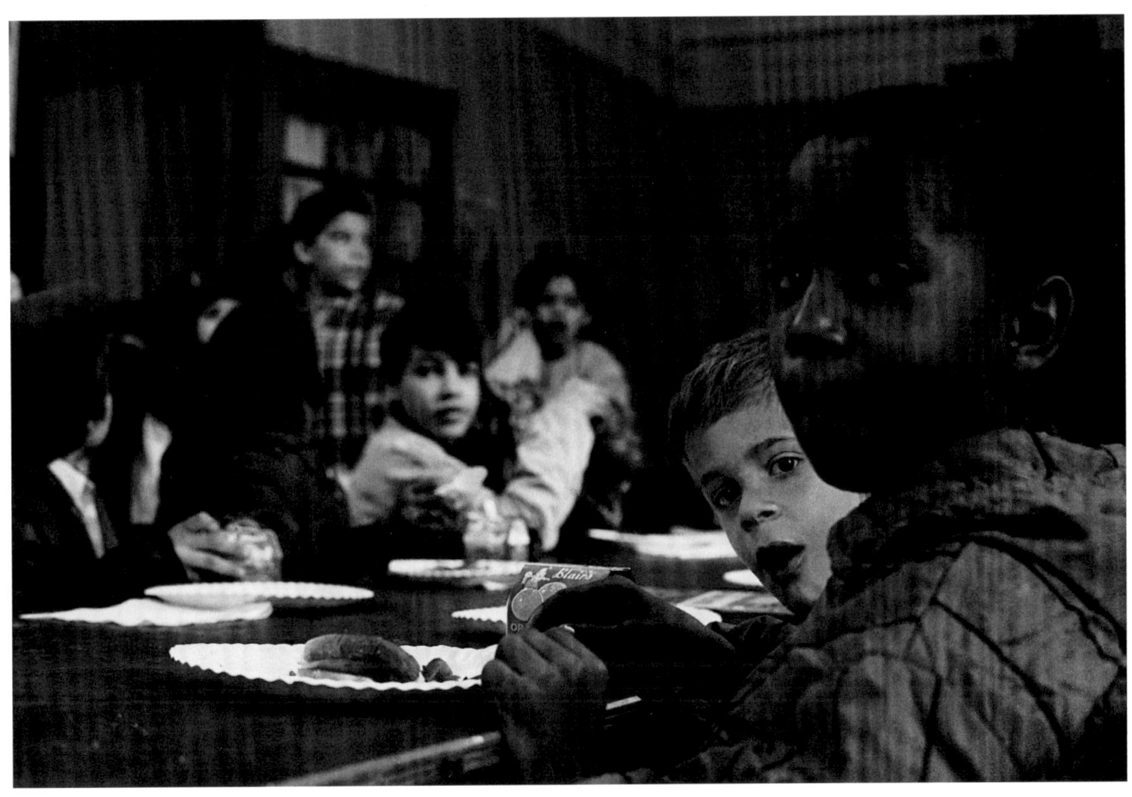

Free breakfast program, All Saints Catholic Church
Black Panther Party Free Breakfast Program, Harlem, New York, Spring 1969

Following spread
Black Panther Party Free Breakfast Program, Harlem, New York, Spring 1969

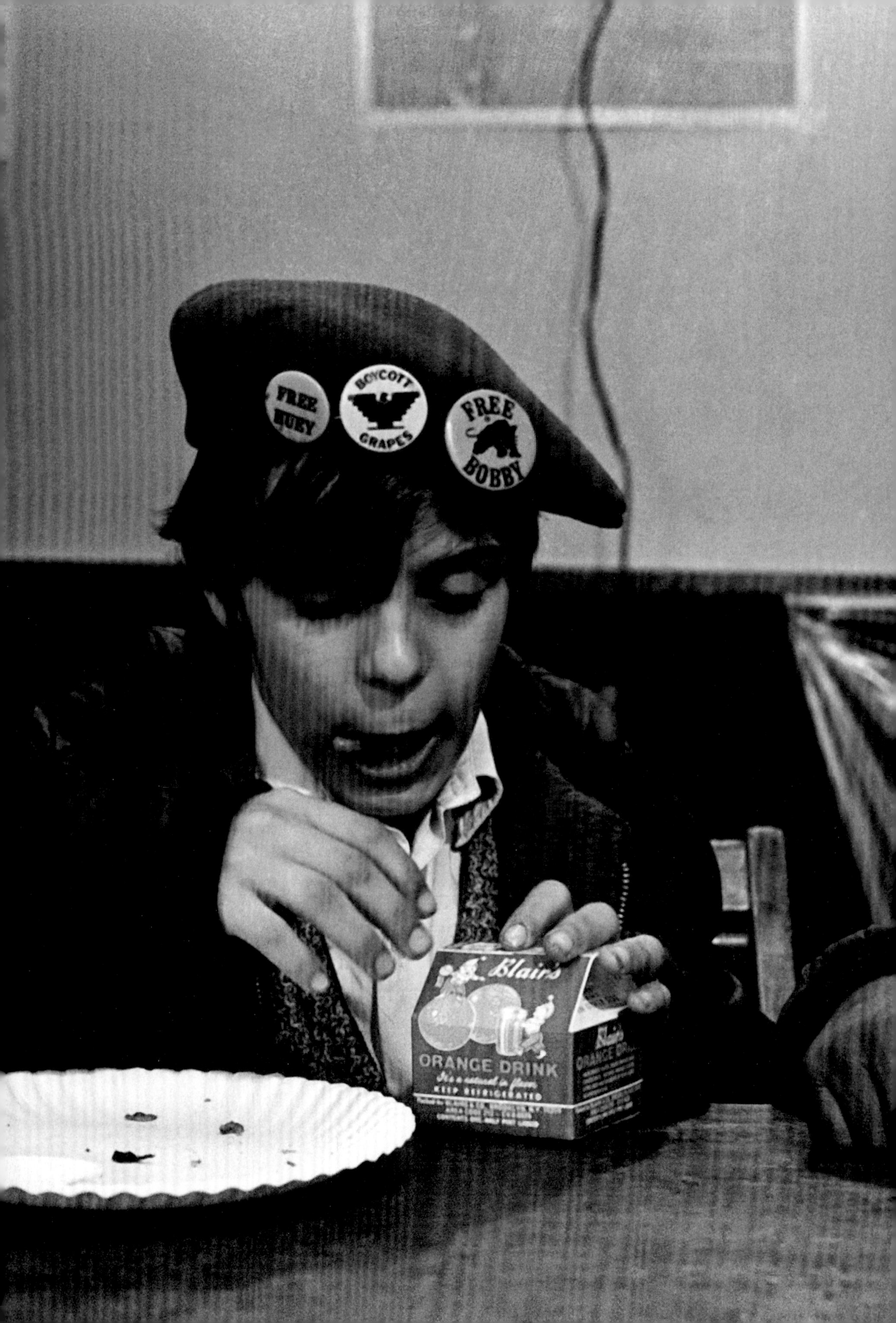

FREE HUEY
BOYCOTT GRAPES
FREE BOBBY
Blairs
ORANGE DRINK
KEEP REFRIGERATED

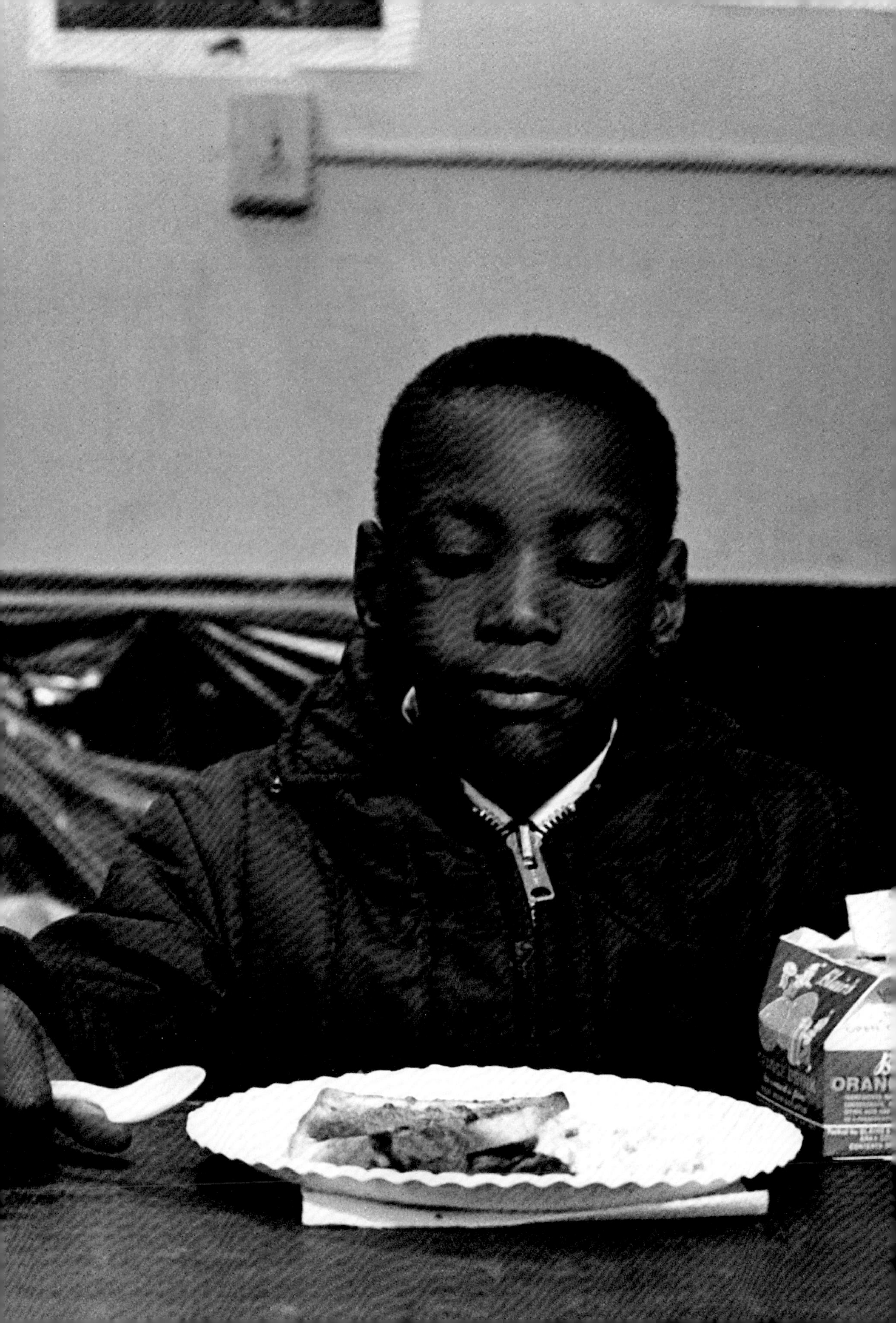

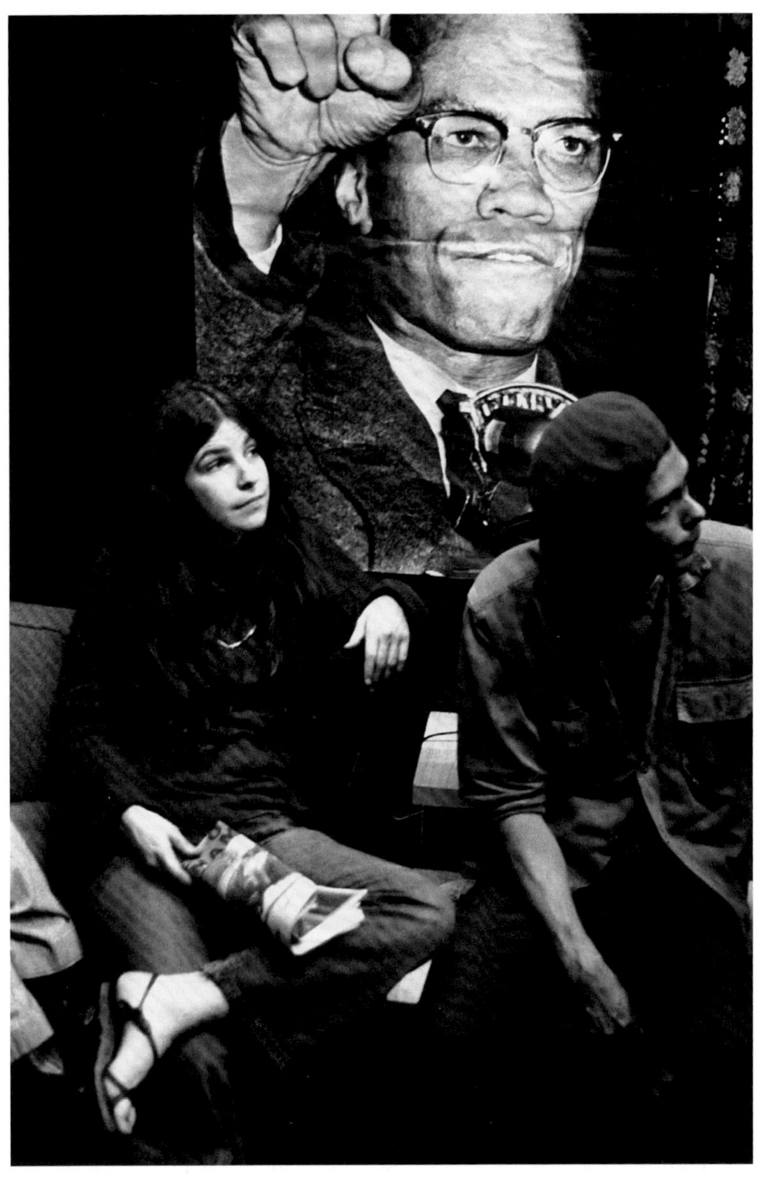

Bev Grant and Young Lords Deputy Minister of Defense, Juan González
Young Lords offices, East Harlem, New York, Summer 1969
Photographer unknown

Young Lords Rainbow Coalition
East Harlem, New York

In mid 1969, I met members of the Young Lords Organization, which later broke away from its Chicago affiliation and changed their name to the Young Lords Party. I was part of a subgroup in Newsreel called the Third World Cadre. Our job was to reach out to organizers in communities of color to let them know about our films and to find out how we could be of service as filmmakers. The Lords were very welcoming to us and embraced our willingness. Pablo Yoruba Guzmán, their Minister of Information, was media savvy and helped open the door for us. It resulted in a strong and lasting relationship and a film called *El Pueblo Se Levanta*. I was part of the three-member crew that worked on the film.

After they established an office in El Barrio (East Harlem) on July 25, 1969, I began taking my first photos of the Young Lords. The Lords were trying to organize a Rainbow Coalition based on the Chicago model that Fred Hampton, head of the Chicago Black Panther Party, had initiated. It brought together the Panthers, the Chicago Young Lords, and the Young Patriots, a white group that represented poor Southern whites in Chicago. I think this was the only Rainbow Coalition meeting that was held in New York, because the Young Patriots did not have a poor white base in New York like they had in Chicago, and those involved were experiencing harassment and arrest from the FBI and the NYPD.

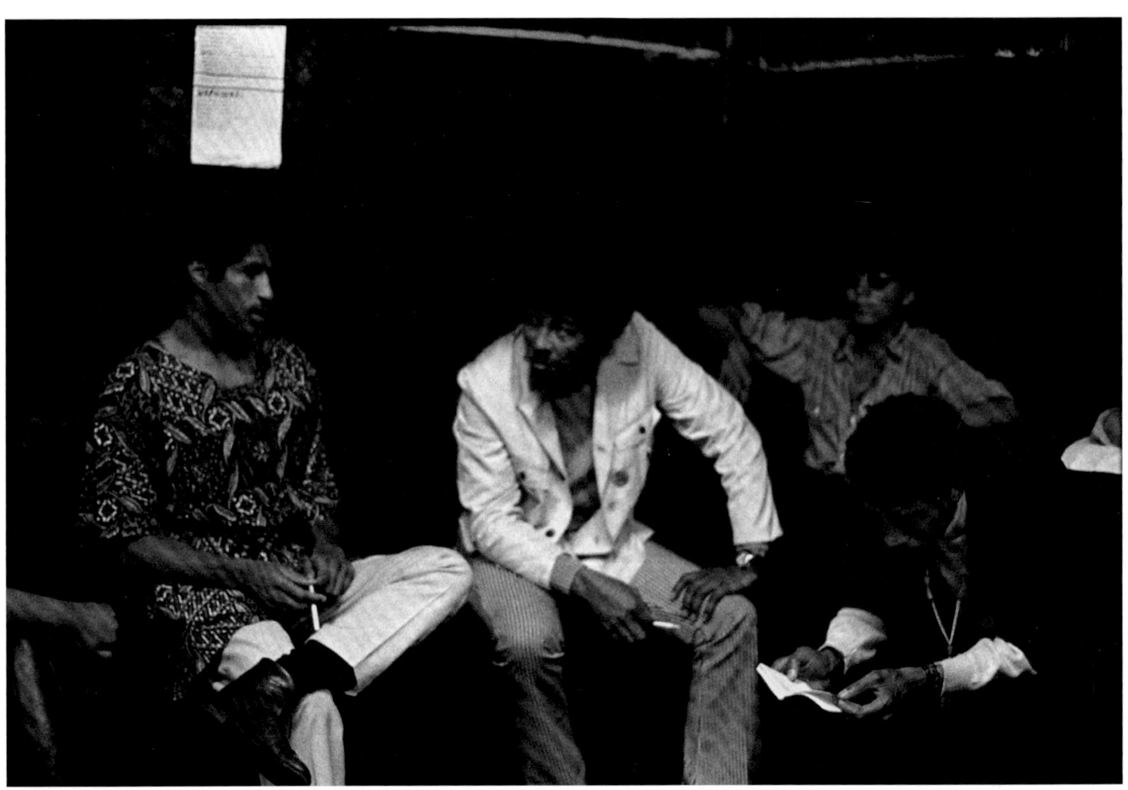

Felipe Luciano, Young Lords Regional Chairman; Donald "DC" Cox, Black Panther Party Field Marshall; Pablo Yoruba
Guzmán, Young Lords Minister of Information; and Sam Napier, Black Panther Party Circulation Manager
Young Lords Rainbow Coalition, East Harlem, New York, Summer 1969

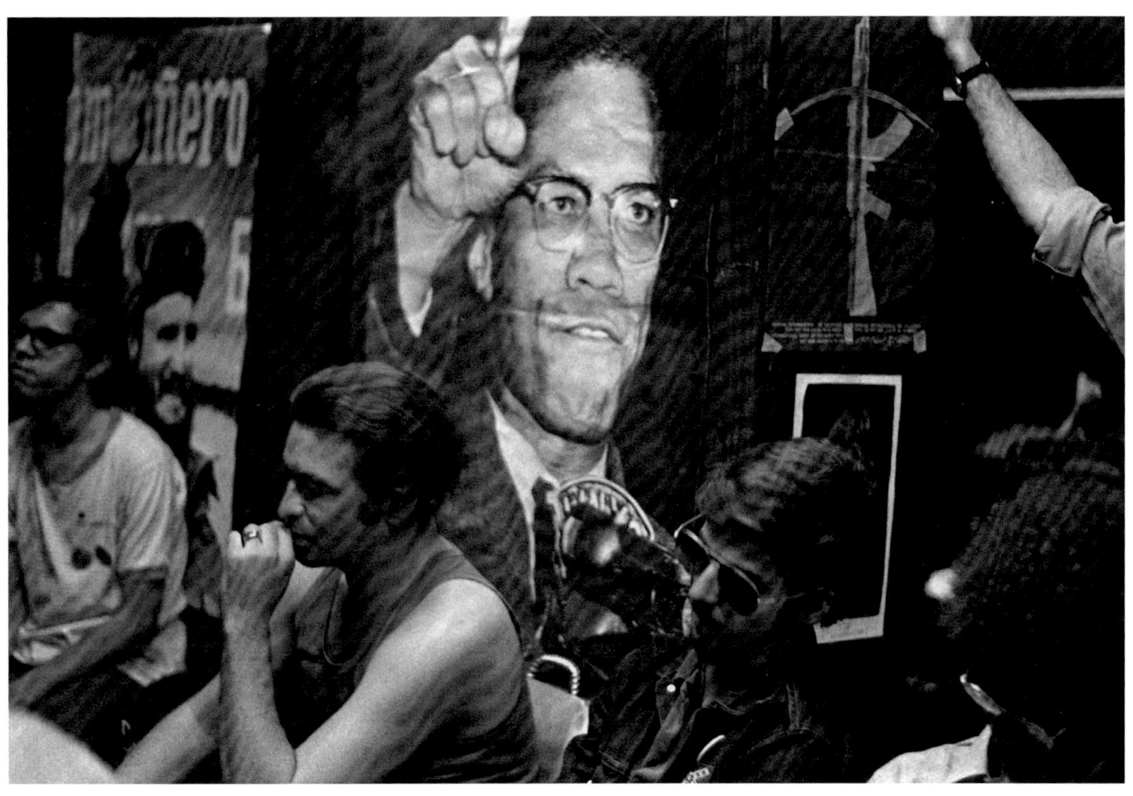

William "Preacherman" Fesperman, Chicago Young Patriots Chairman, with Young Lords and Black Panthers
Young Lords Rainbow Coalition, East Harlem, New York, Summer 1969

Following spread
Pablo Yoruba Guzmán, Young Lords Minister of Information
Young Lords Rainbow Coalition, East Harlem, New York, Summer 1969

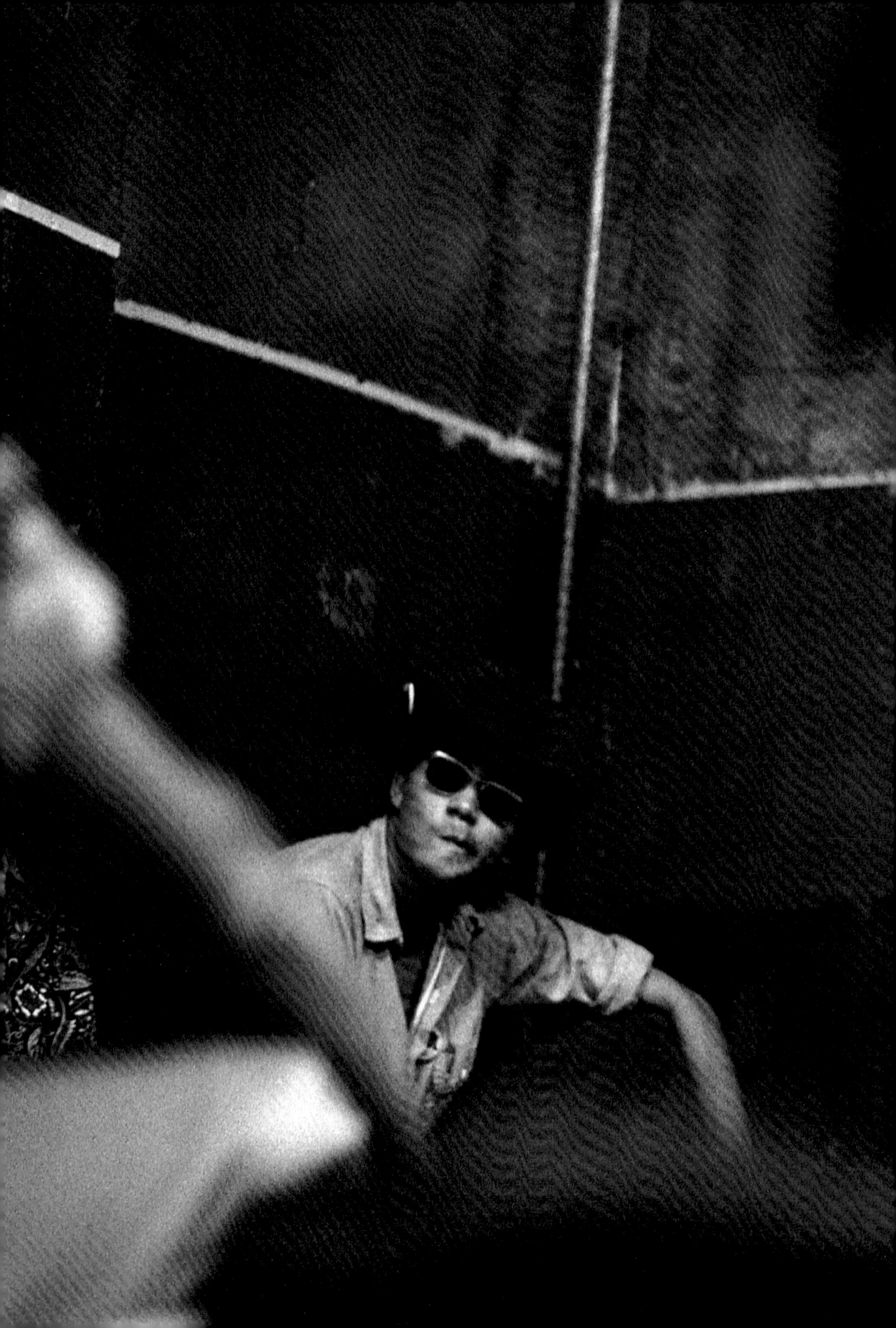

Garbage Offensive
East Harlem, New York

From the start, the Young Lords canvassed the community and held meetings to learn about peoples' needs. They were surprised at the response. They had expected the main concern to be police brutality and repression. What they found out was that the community considered their biggest problem to be sanitation—poor garbage pickup, closely followed by health and housing.

On August 17, 1969, the Young Lords organized their first action, the Garbage Offensive. They organized to clean the streets, sweeping and clearing away garbage from the buildings where it was stacked up. They placed the garbage at the intersection of 110th Street and Third Avenue, totally closing off the street from traffic. Everybody pitched in. It was a high-spirited, good natured and industrious event that motivated people to join. It was also successful, because the Young Lords managed to get the city's attention. The Sanitation Department began crossing 96th Street and picking up the garbage in El Barrio.

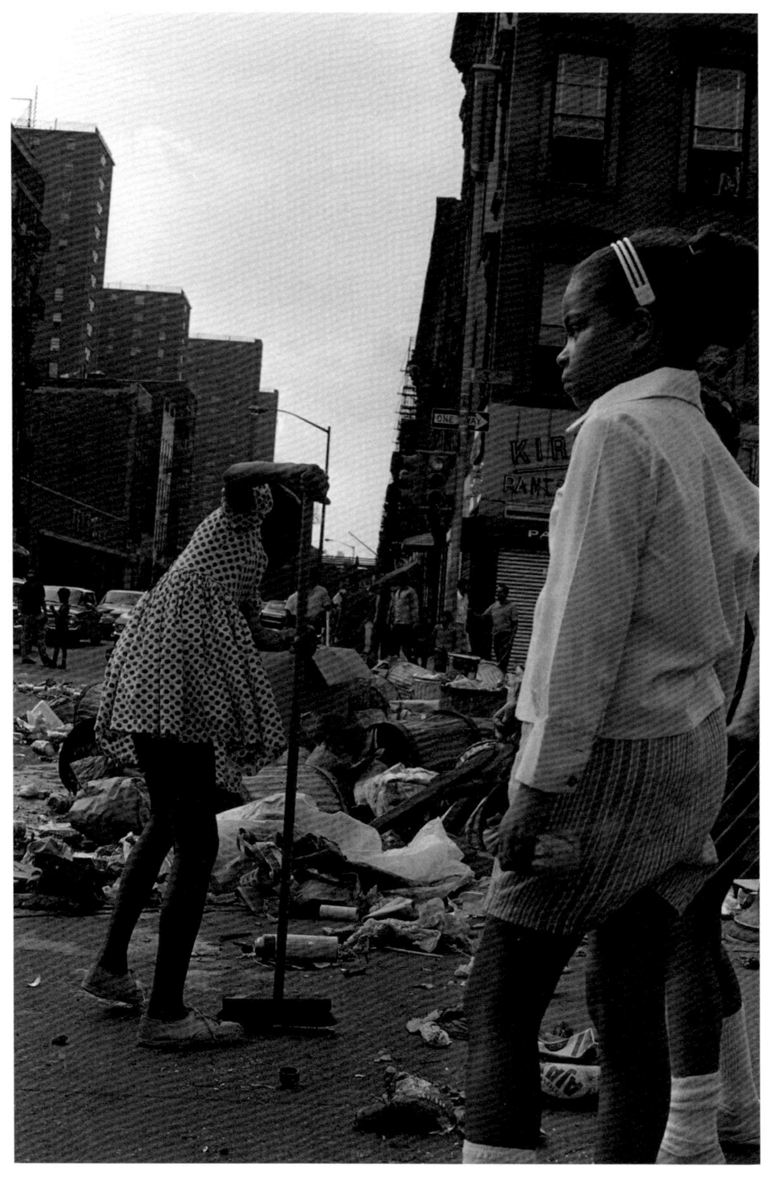

Young girls clean the streets
Garbage Offensive, East Harlem, New York, August 17, 1969

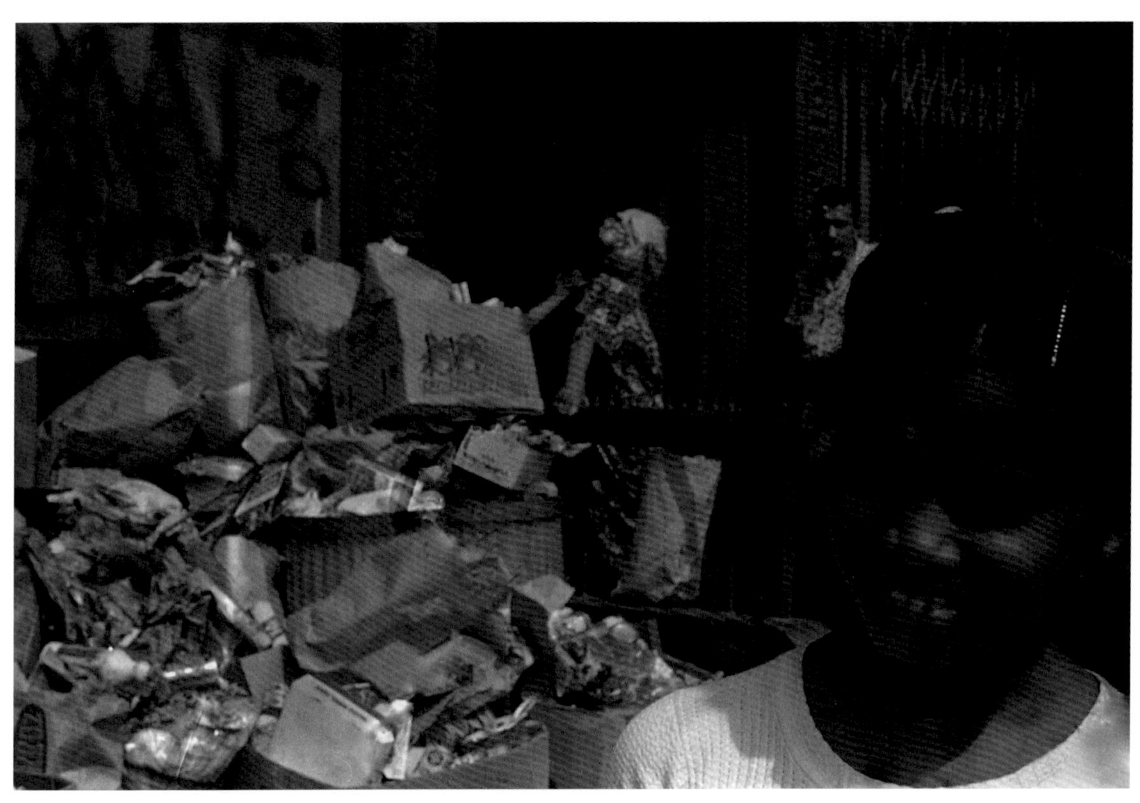

Garbage Offensive, East Harlem, New York, August 17, 1969

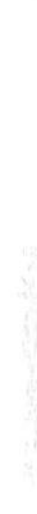
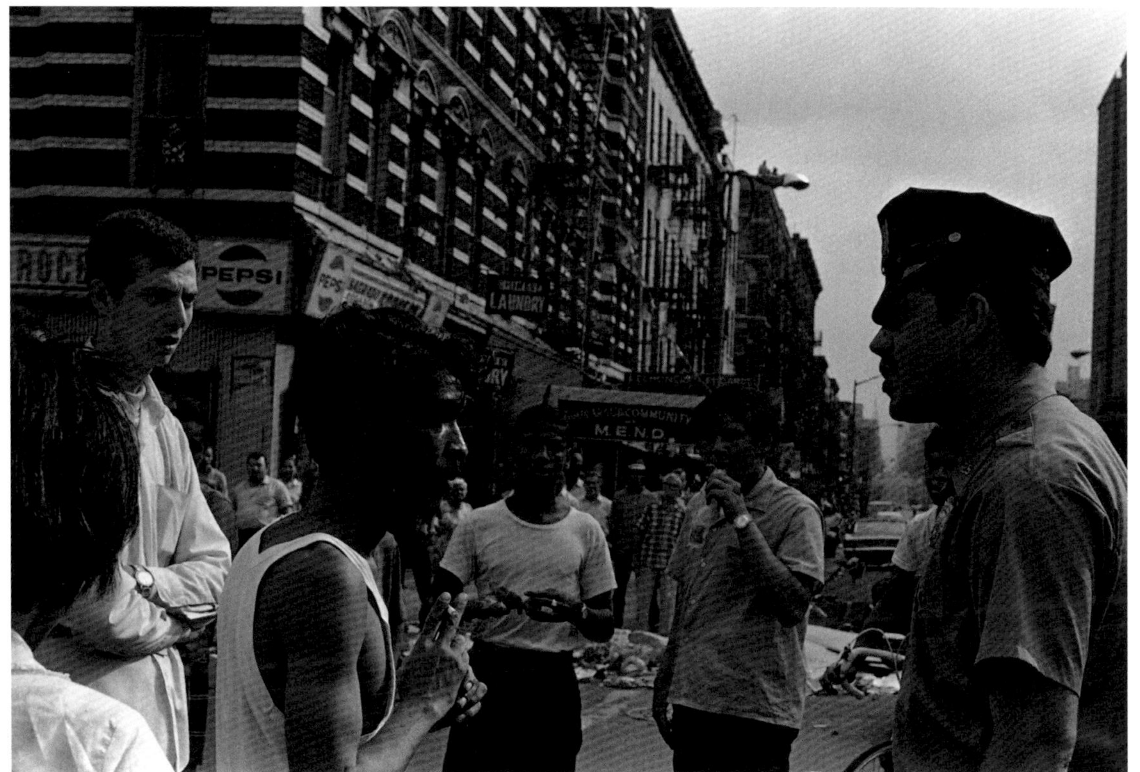

Young Lords talk with a police officer
Garbage Offensive, East Harlem, New York, August 17, 1969

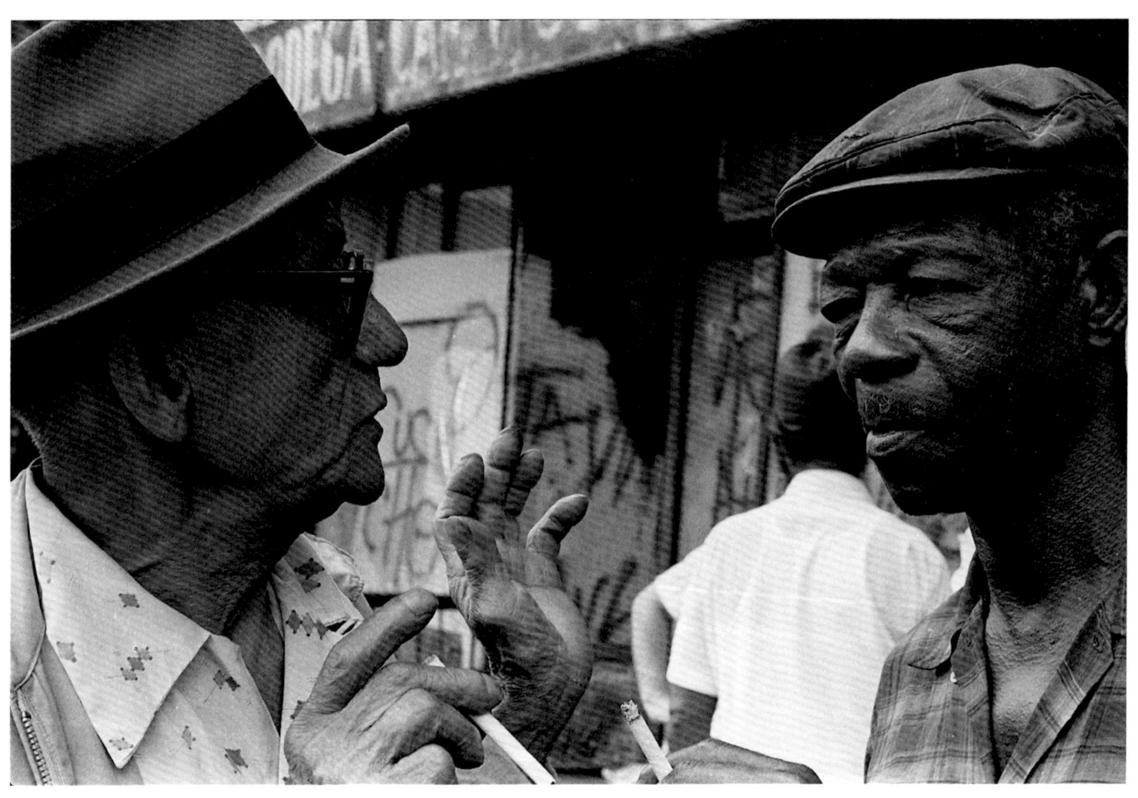

Garbage Offensive, East Harlem, New York, August 17, 1969

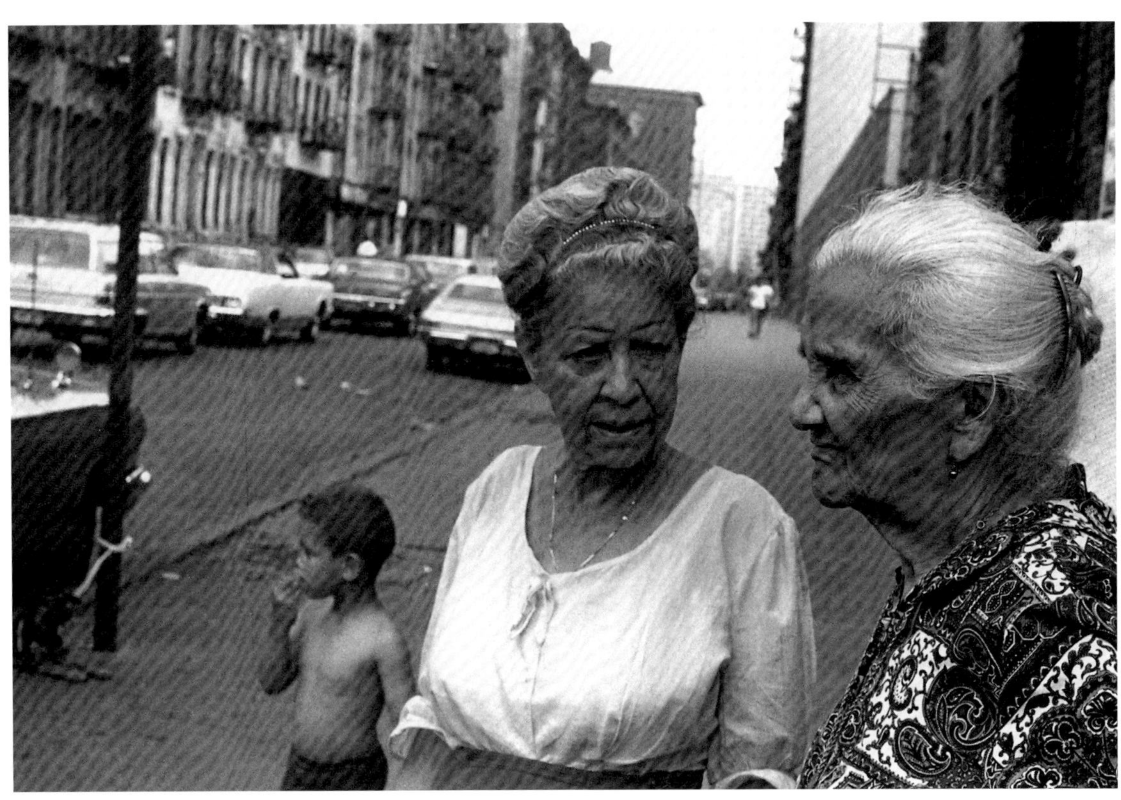

Garbage Offensive, East Harlem, New York, August 17, 1969

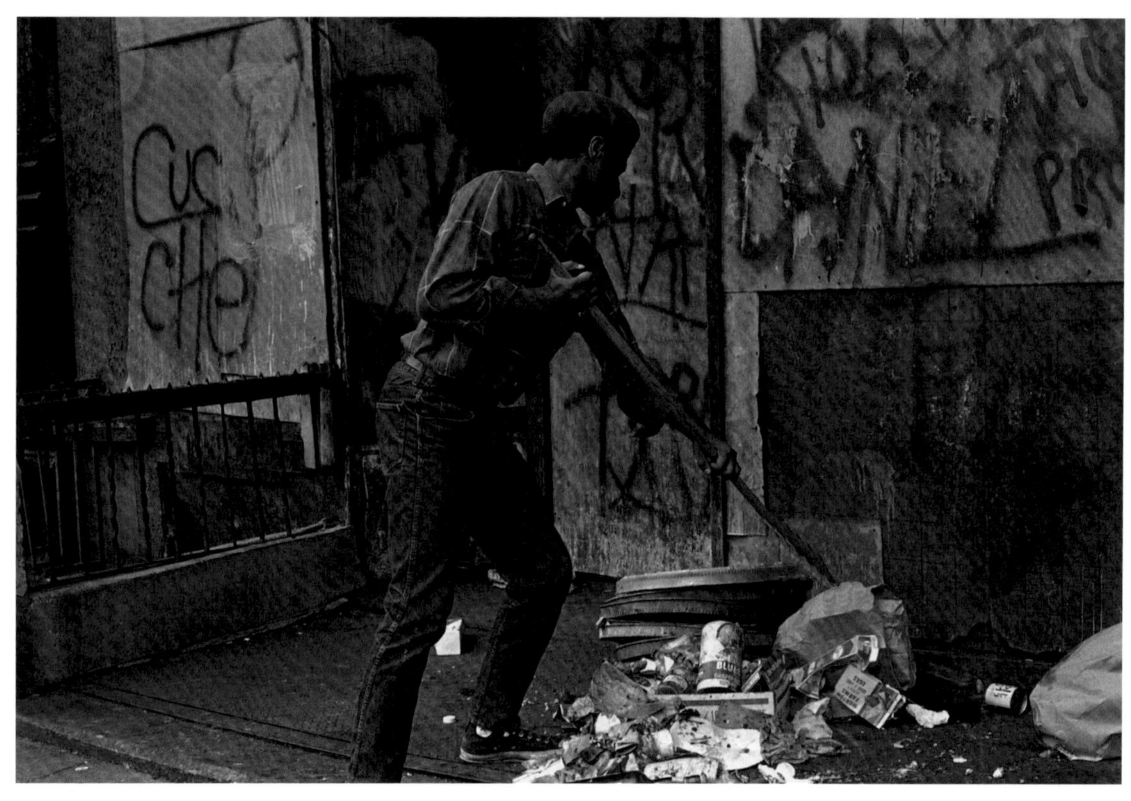

Felipe Luciano, Young Lords Regional Chairman
Garbage Offensive, East Harlem, New York, August 17, 1969

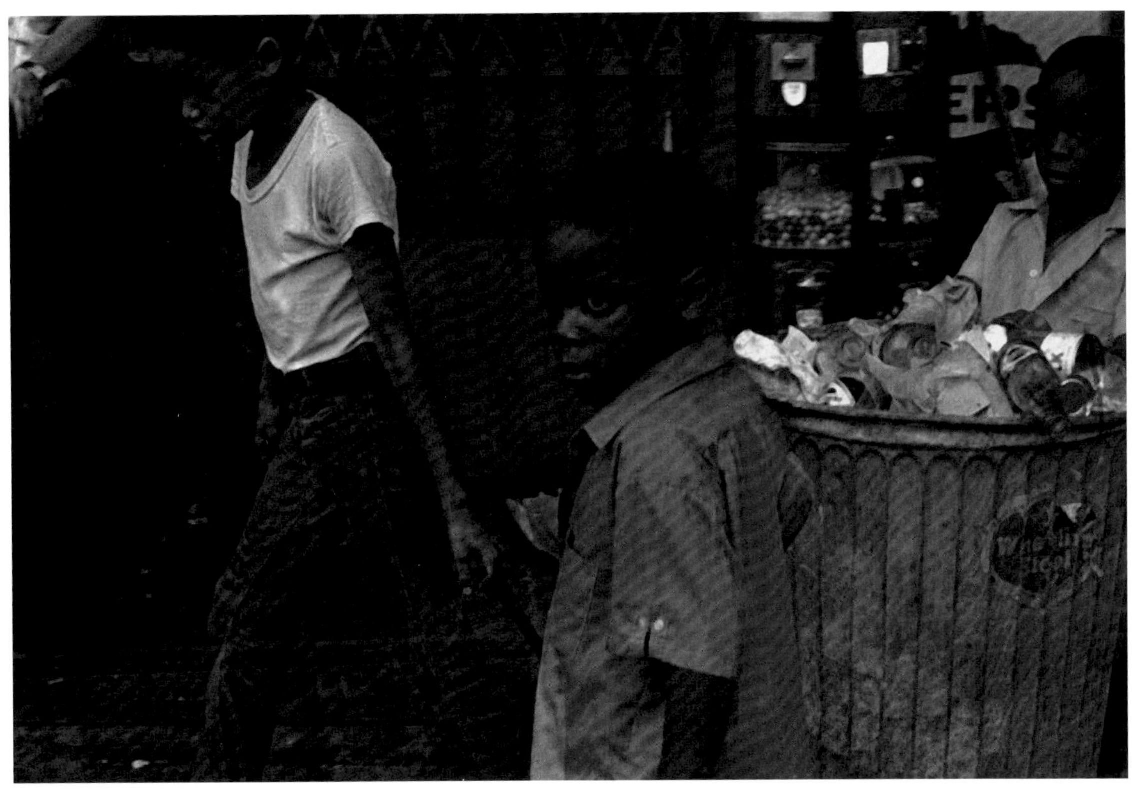

Garbage Offensive, East Harlem, New York, August 17, 1969

Following spread
Garbage on 110th Street and Third Avenue
Garbage Offensive, East Harlem, New York, August 17, 1969

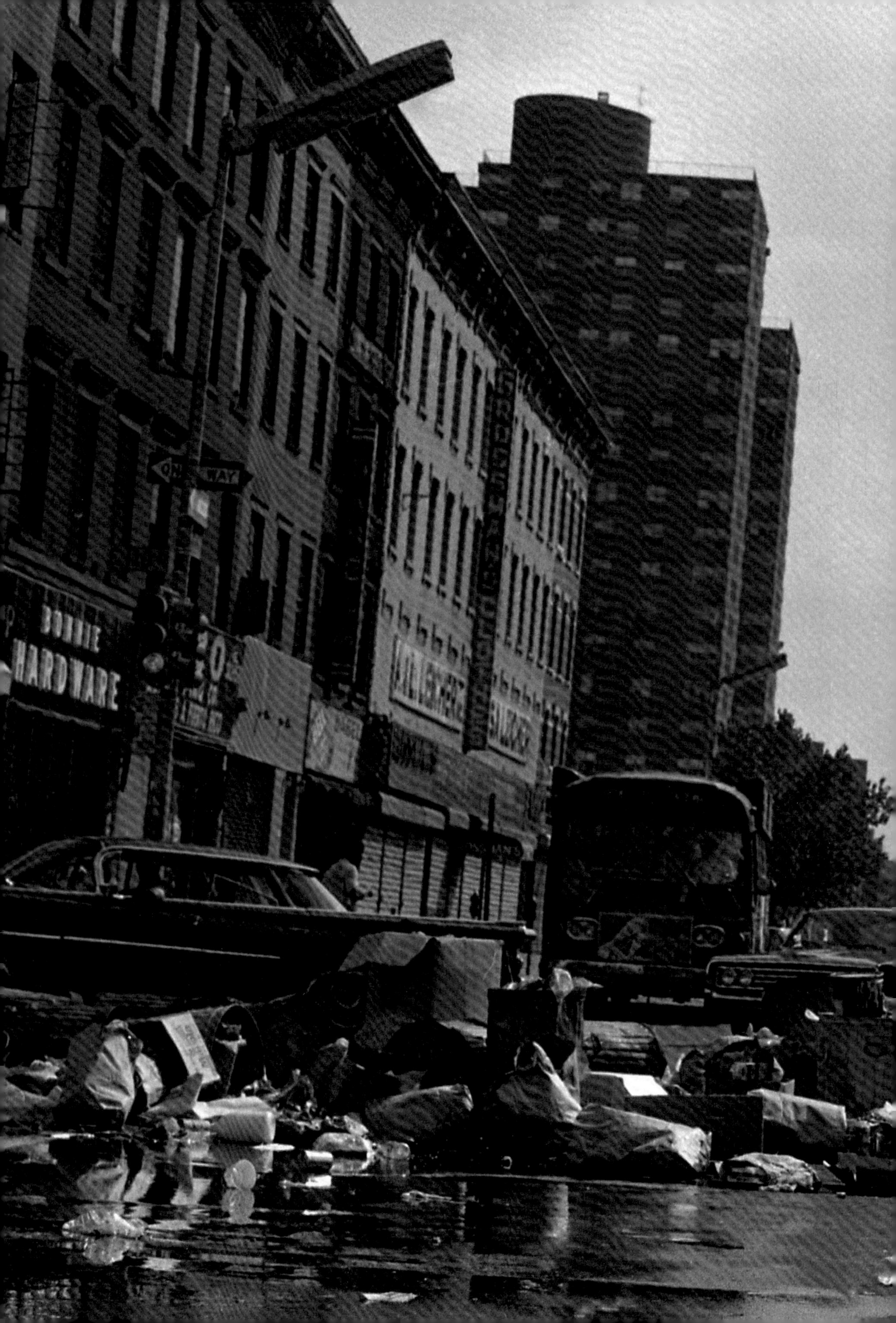

ONE WAY
BONNIE
HARDWARE

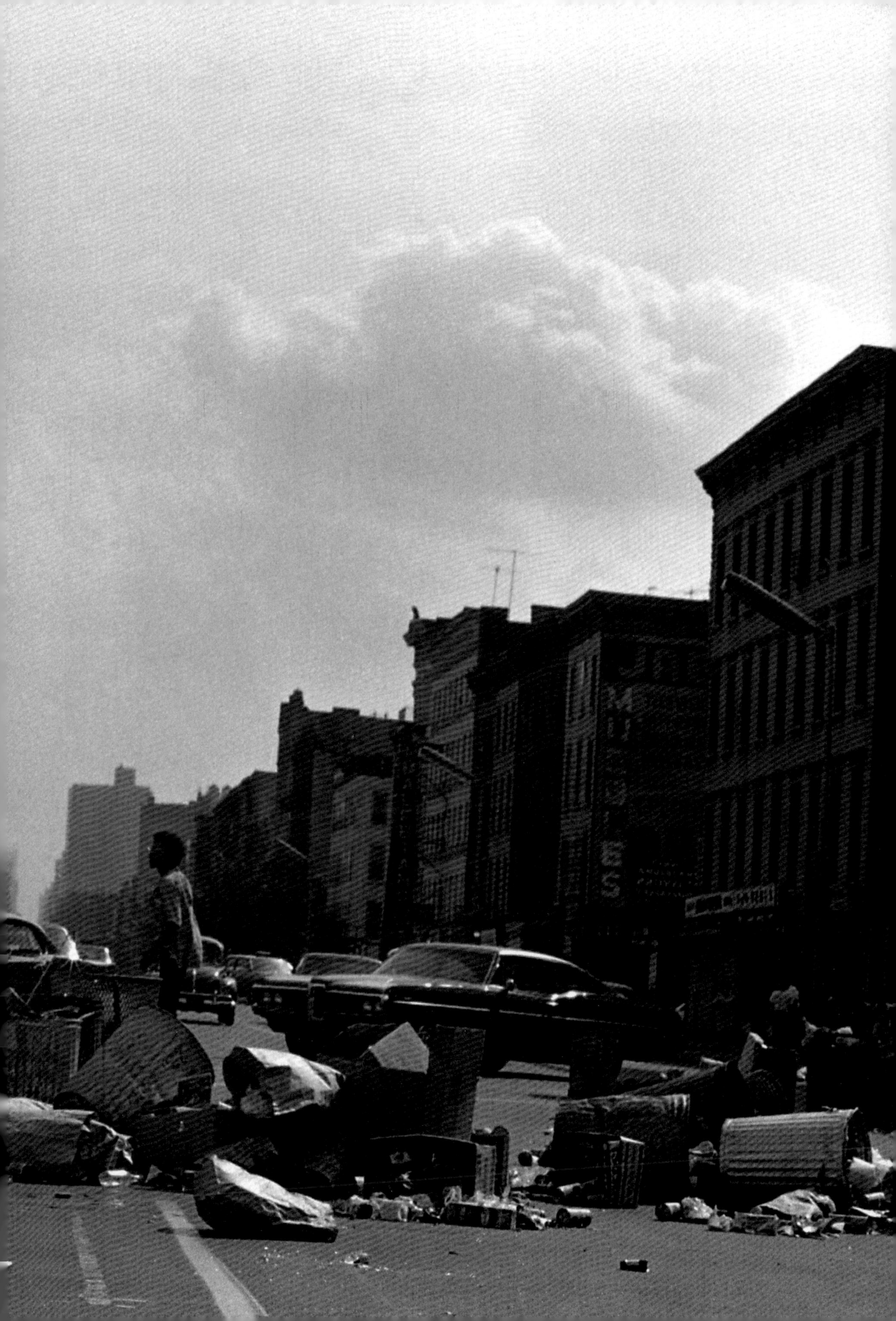

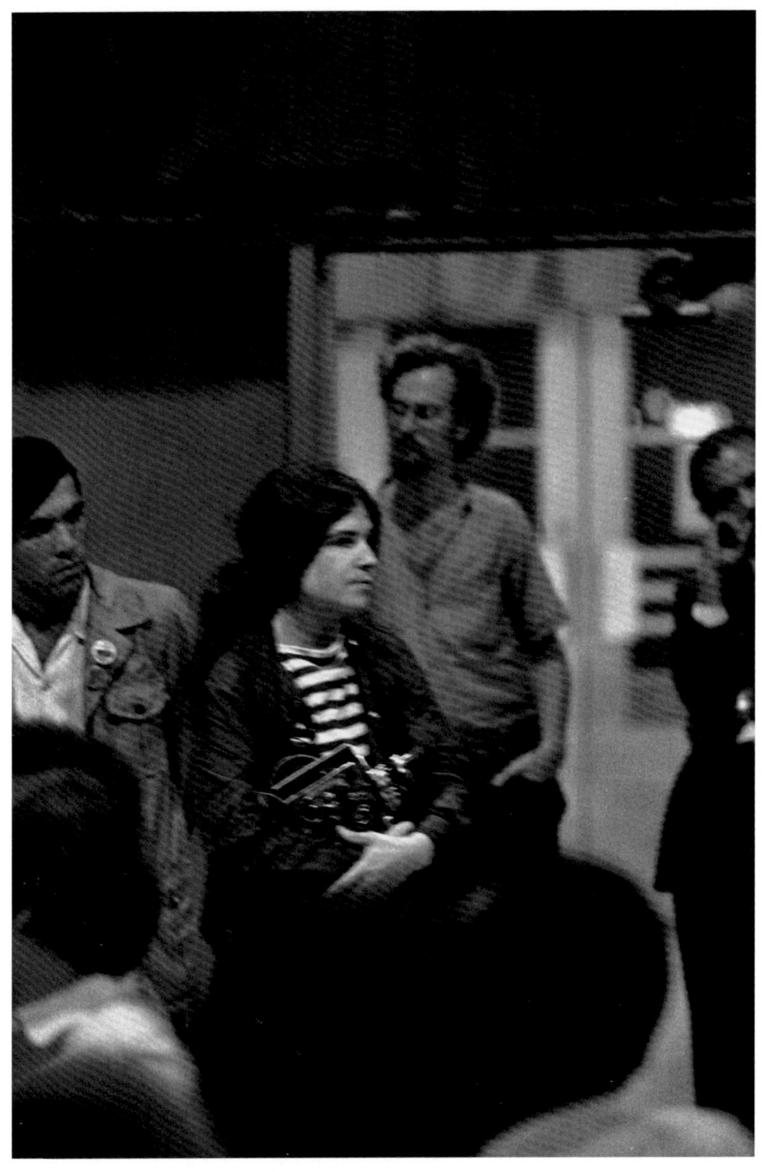

Bev Grant with Bolex 16mm camera
Young Lords Community Outreach, East Harlem, New York, Fall 1969
Photographer unknown

Young Lords Community Outreach
East Harlem, New York

After their Garbage Offensive, the Young Lords continued with community outreach and meetings, modeled after the Black Panther Party's community programs. The Young Lords offered free breakfast for children and held joint free clothing drives with the Panthers. They developed and sold a newspaper called *Palante* and often spoke in the streets to keep the community advised on what was going on.

In the fall of 1969, the Young Lords held a meeting at the Theater Arts Community Center, in the Clinton Houses on 110th Street in East Harlem. Juan González, one of the founders of the Young Lords, recalls: "If my memory serves me right, the meeting preceded our sit-in at the Metropolitan Hospital and was geared around issues of community health care, specifically lead poisoning."

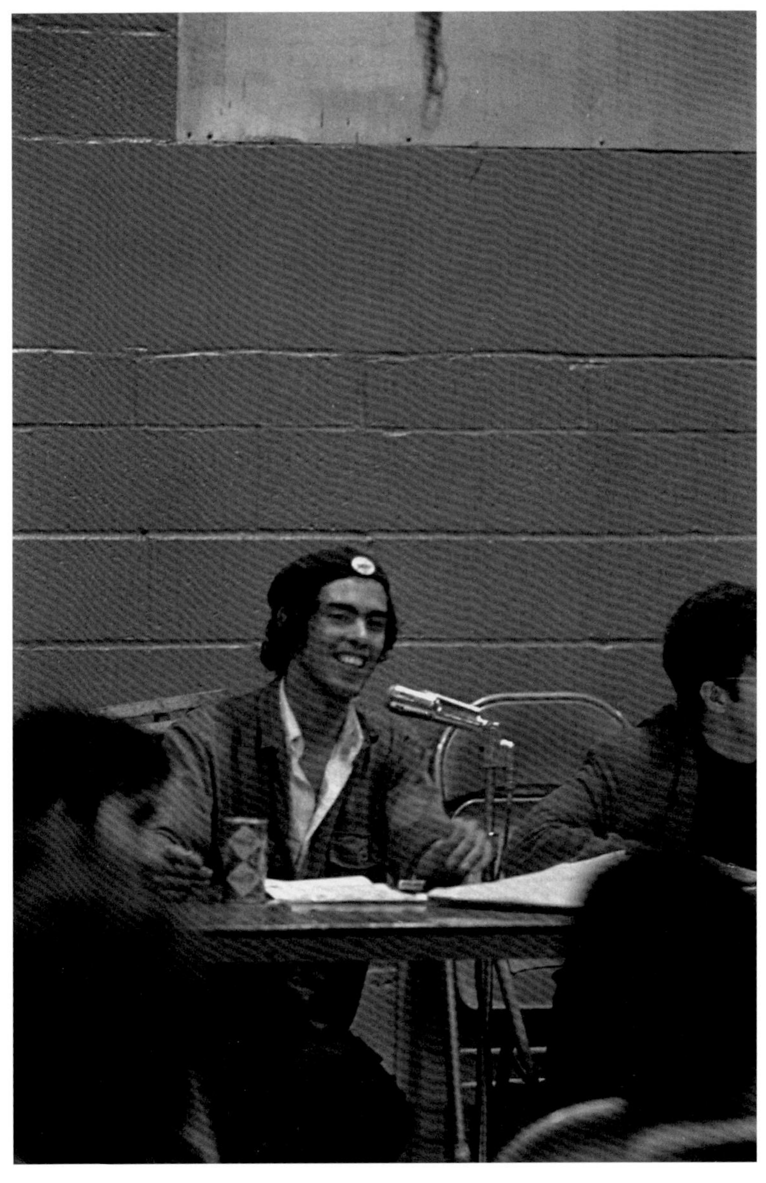

Juan González, Young Lords Minister of Education
Young Lords Community Outreach, East Harlem, New York, Fall 1969

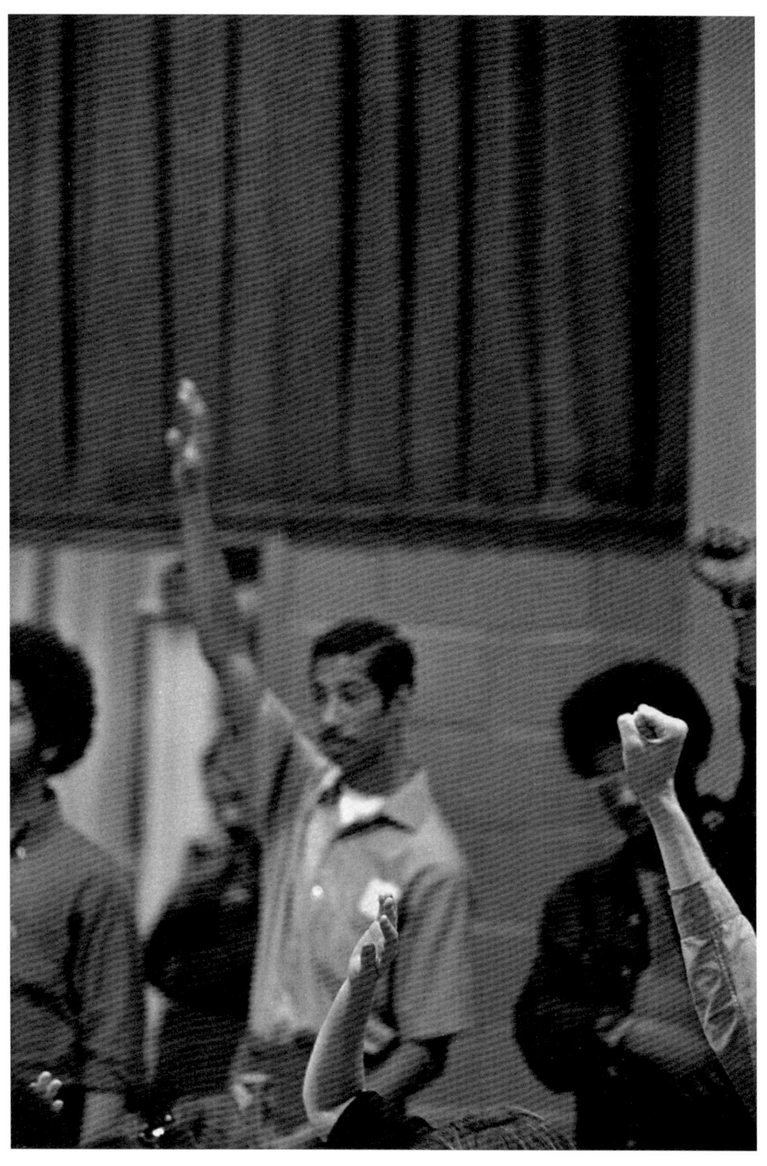

Young Lords Community Outreach, East Harlem, New York, Fall 1969

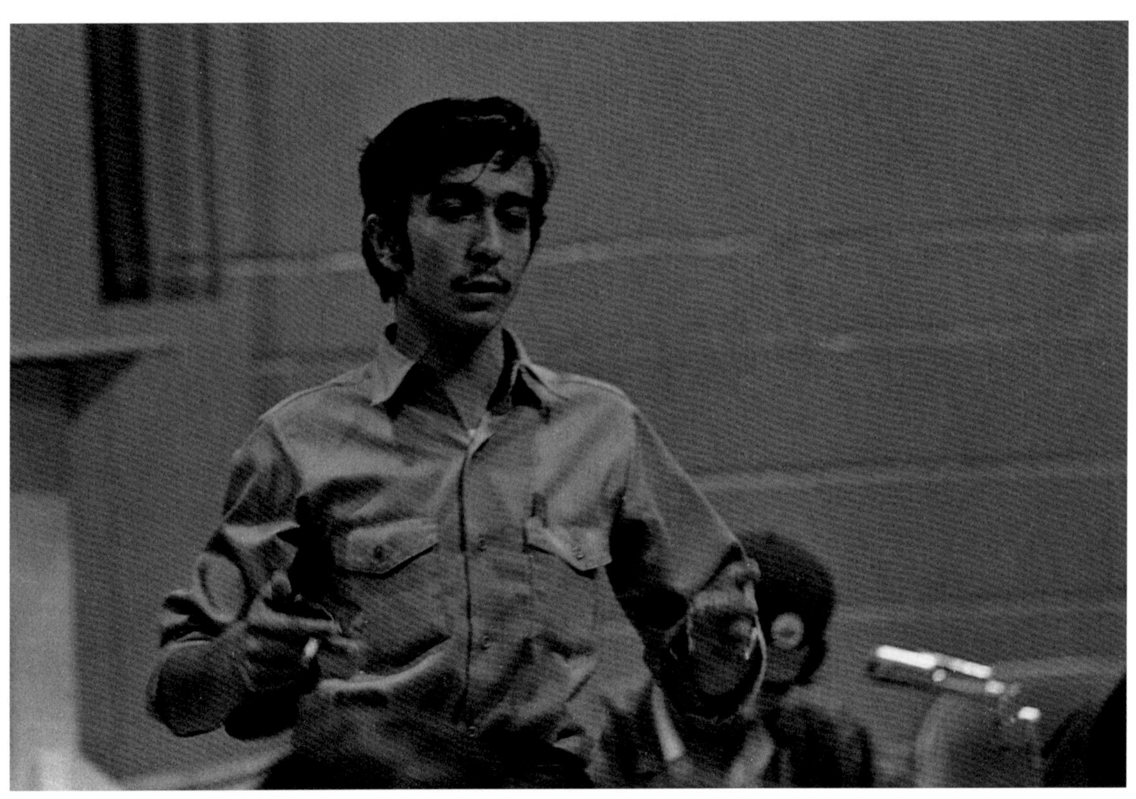

David Perez, Young Lords Minister of Defense
Young Lords Community Outreach, East Harlem, New York, Fall 1969

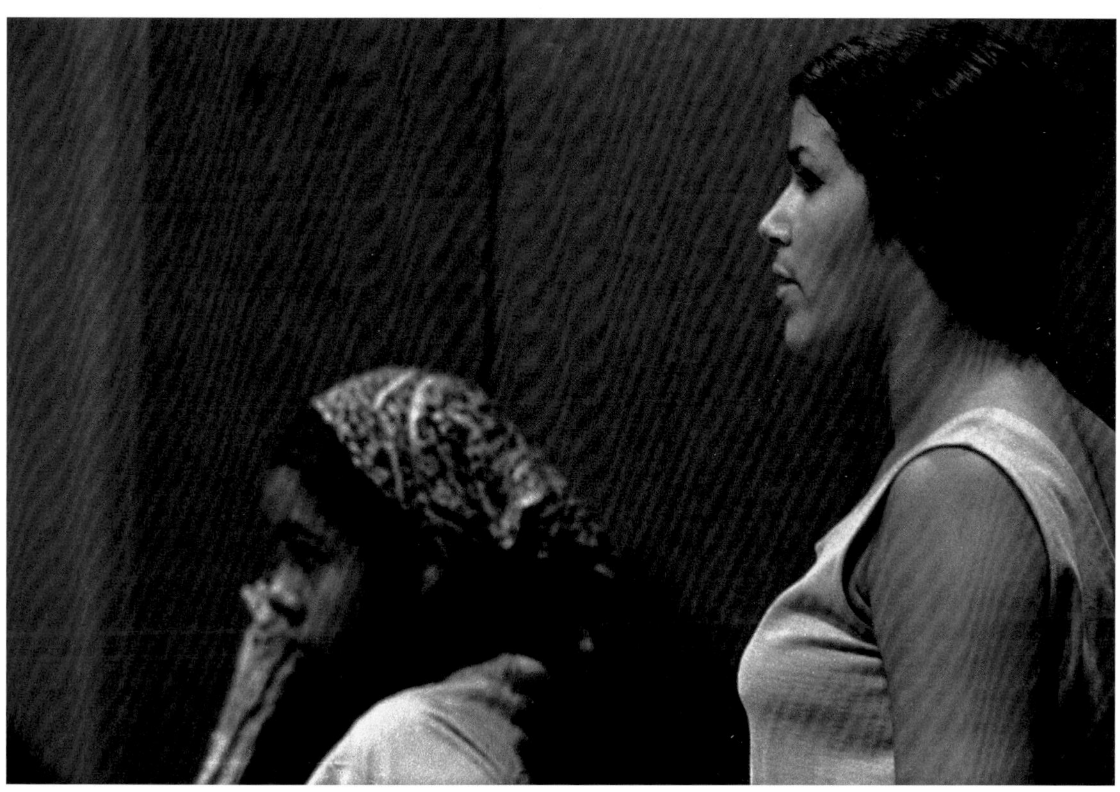

Gloria Cruz, Young Lords Field Marshall
Young Lords Community Outreach, East Harlem, New York, Fall 1969

Following spread
Black Panther Party member, Zayd Malik Shakur, addressing the community meeting
Young Lords Community Outreach, East Harlem, New York, Fall 1969

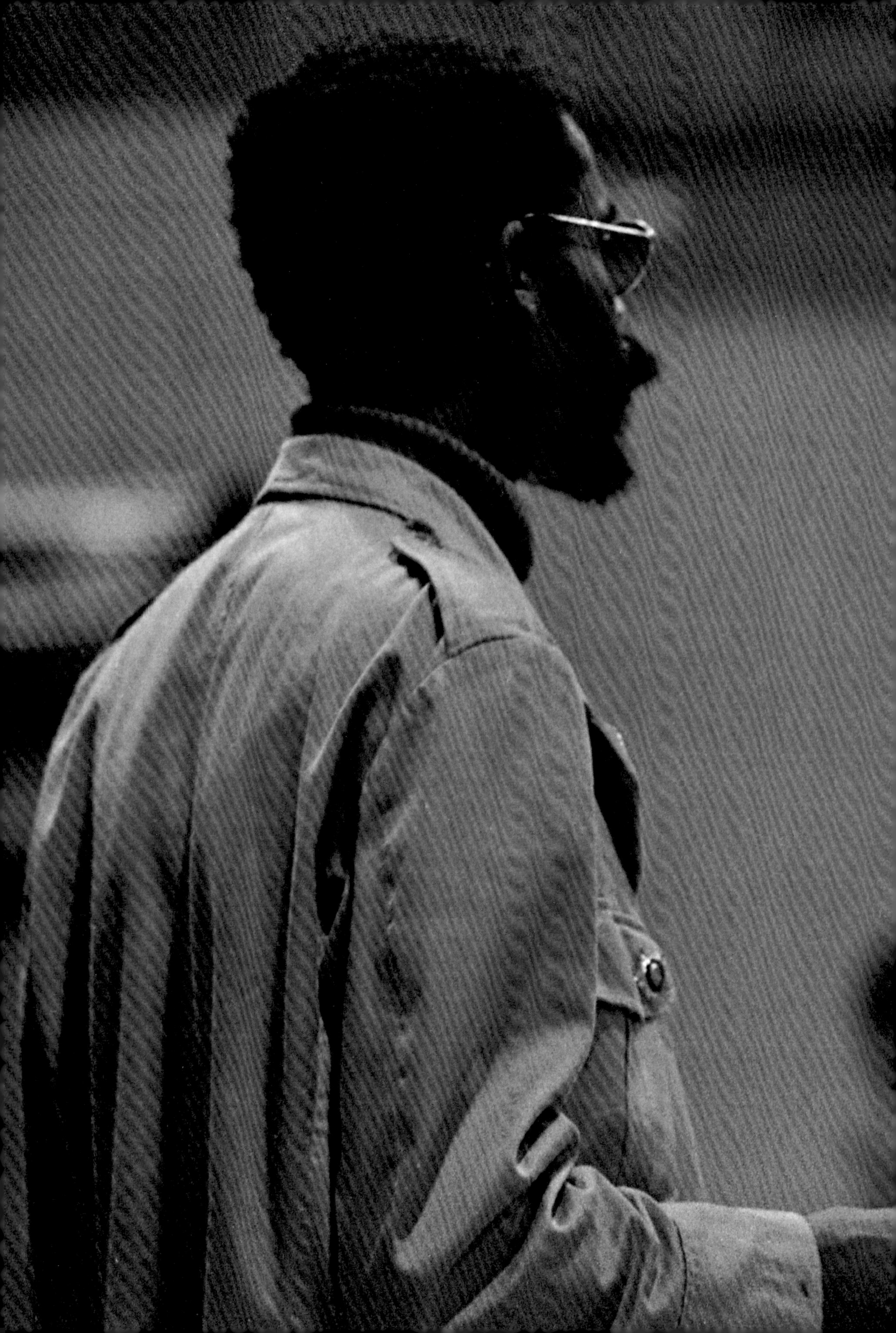

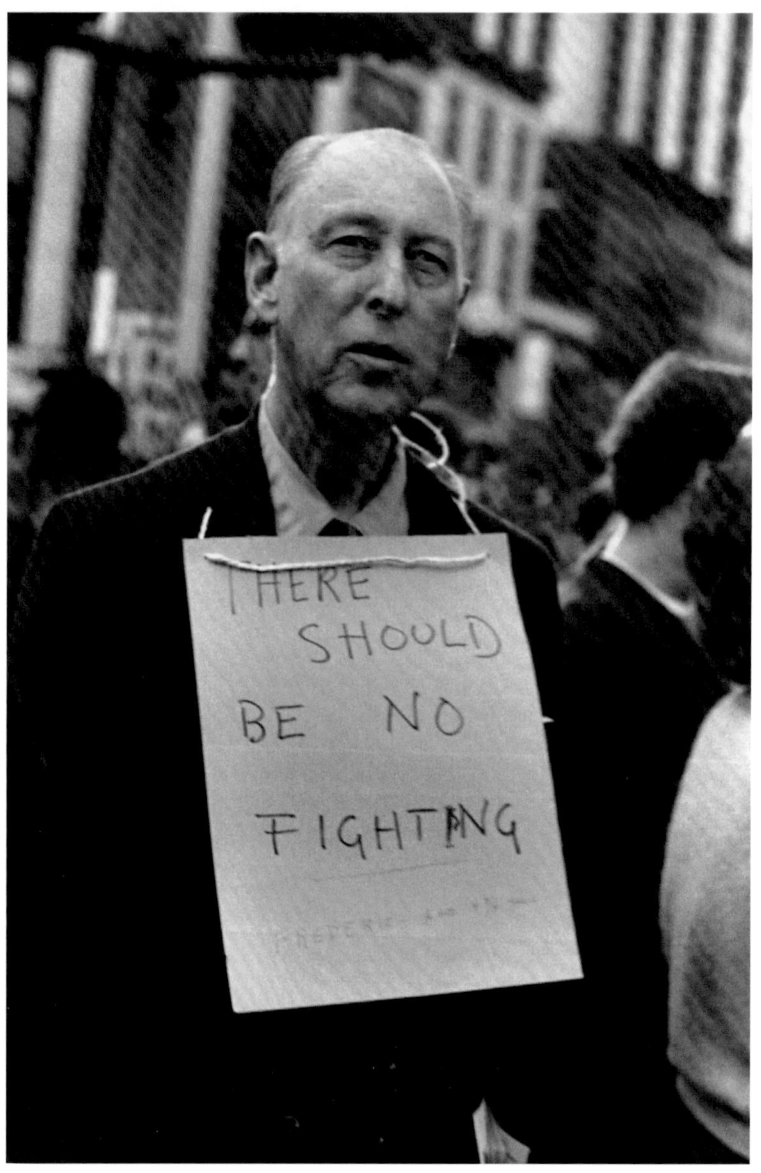

Moratorium to End the War in Vietnam, Midtown, New York, October 15, 1969

October 15, 1969

Moratorium to End the War in Vietnam
Midtown, New York

When I came back from Cuba, I got a day job with Fortune Magazine, part of the Time Life Company. I was a secretary to two young executives in the Advertising Department. My most meaningful moment there was when I "accidentally" broke all the coffee cups and told my bosses that from then on we'd have to go to the coffee cart that came around every morning. They didn't object; in fact, they even bought me coffee. On a particularly cold day, I asked them how they would like to wear a skirt every day. They said they wouldn't and agreed it was fine for me to wear pants to work. It's important to remember that at this time, classified ads were gender specific and skirts, stockings, and high heels were considered proper office attire. Along with two other women I had met on the job, we organized Time/Life/Fortune Employees Against the War in order to have a presence at the giant Moratorium to End the War in Vietnam that took place on October 15, 1969. We first marched up to the President's office, prepared for battle, and demanded use of the auditorium for an organizing meeting. To our surprise, he said "fine".

We had a great turnout. At the demonstration, in front of the Time Life Building on Sixth Avenue, people tabled, handed out leaflets, got petitions signed, passed out black armbands, and talked with passersby. Even my bosses participated and carried a sign saying: "Fortune Employees Against the War." I was proud of them.

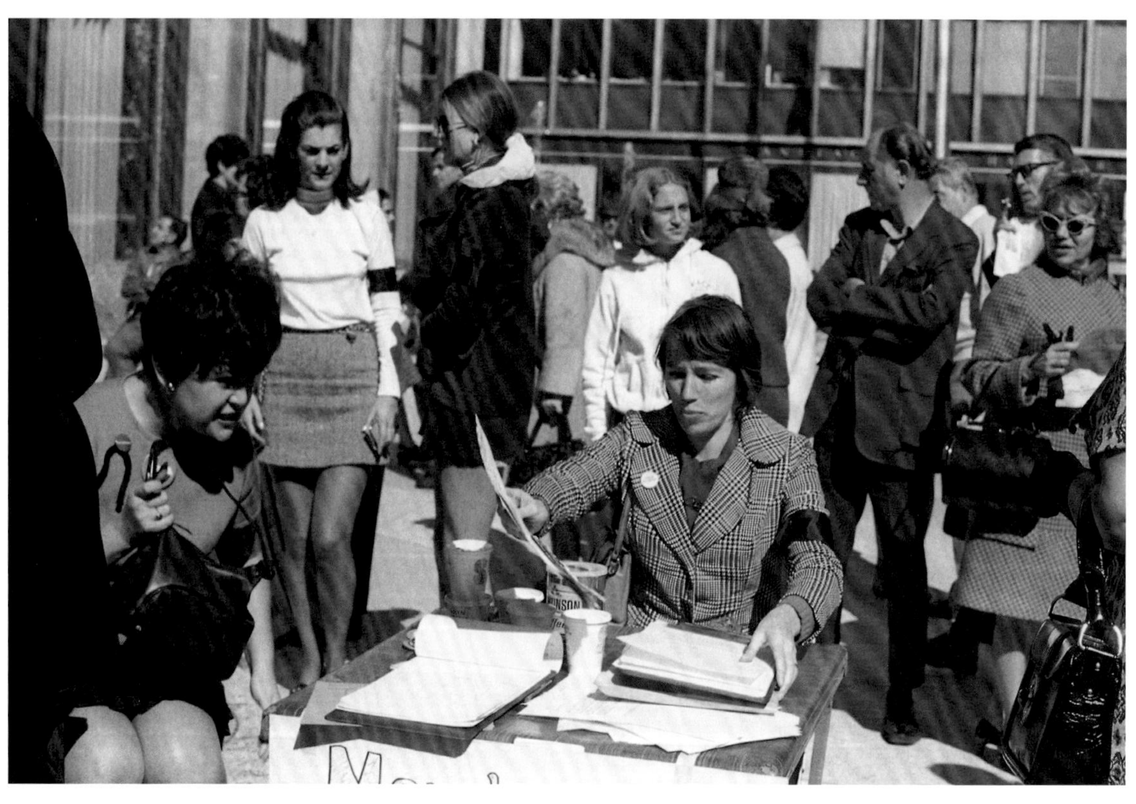

Time Inc. employees organizing
Moratorium to End the War in Vietnam, Midtown, New York, October 15, 1969

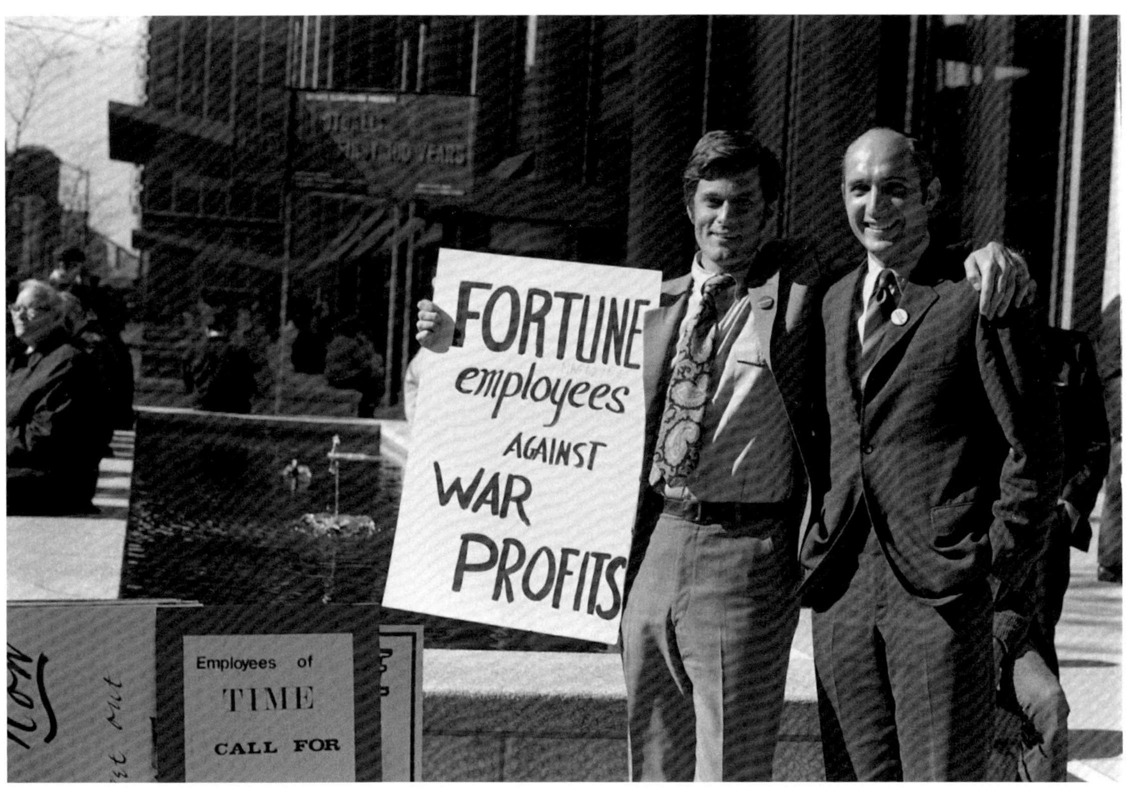

Fortune Magazine Director of Marketing, Howard Kaplan, and his associate
Moratorium to End the War in Vietnam, Midtown, New York, October 15, 1969

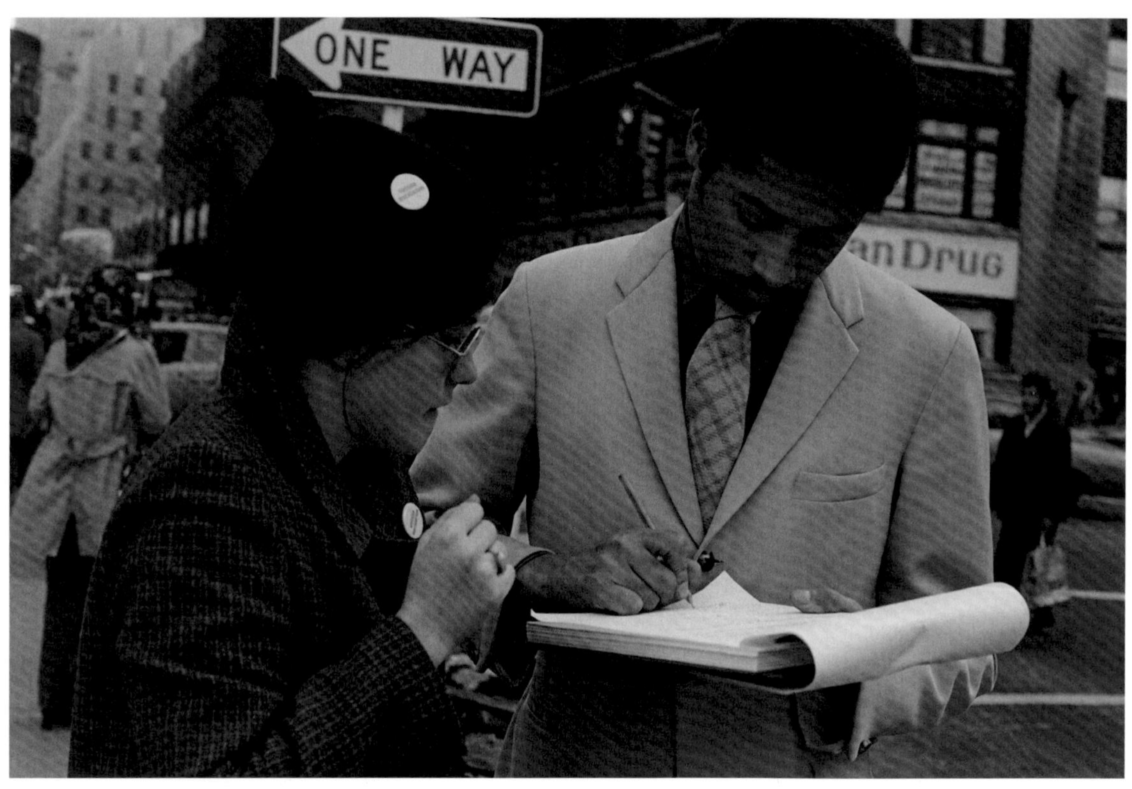

Time Inc. employees getting signatures
Moratorium to End the War in Vietnam, Midtown, New York, October 15, 1969

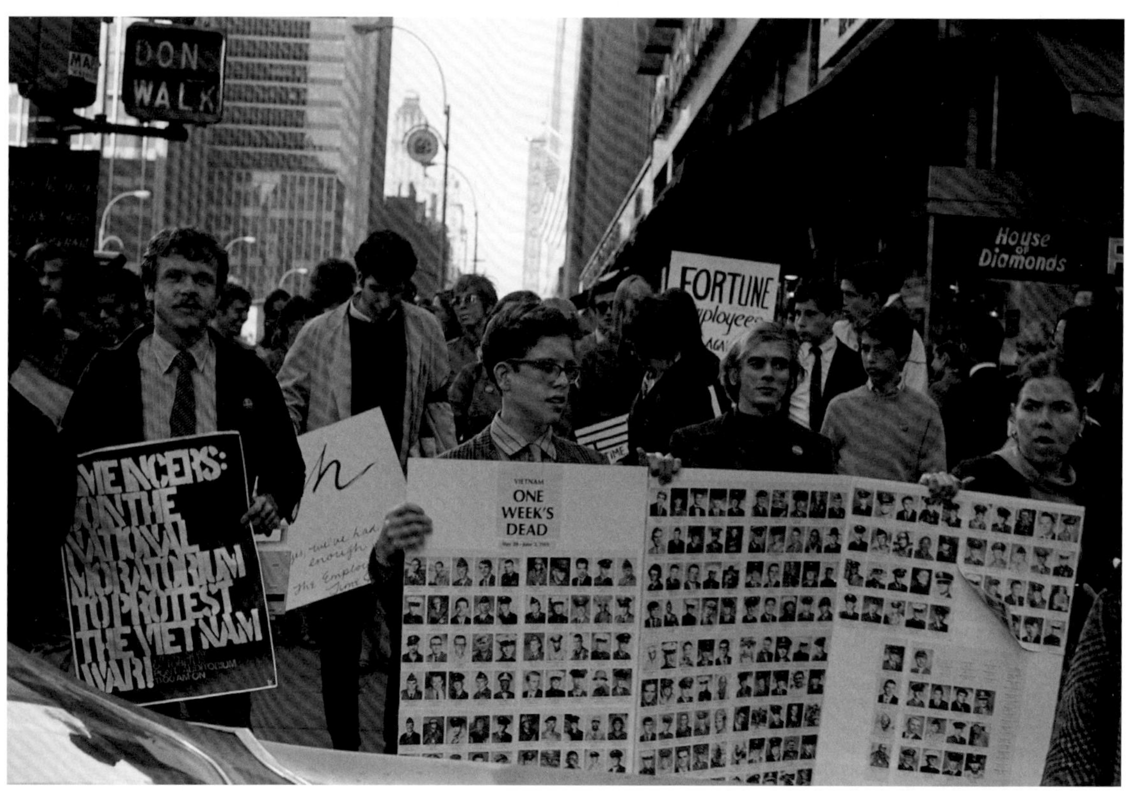

Demonstrators with portraits of *One Week's Dead*
Moratorium to End the War in Vietnam, Midtown, New York, October 15, 1969

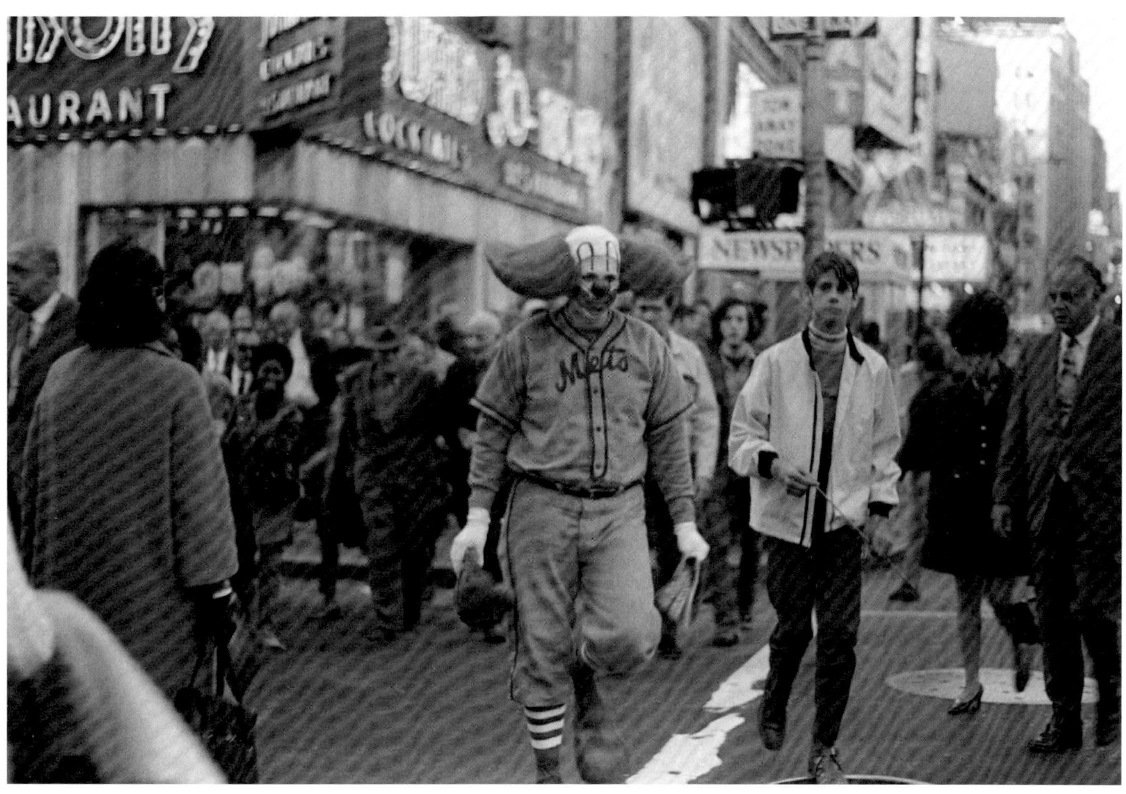

Bozo the Clown
Moratorium to End the War in Vietnam, Midtown, New York, October 15, 1969

Following spread
Protest signs outside the Time Life building, Sixth Avenue
Moratorium to End the War in Vietnam, Midtown, New York, October 15, 1969

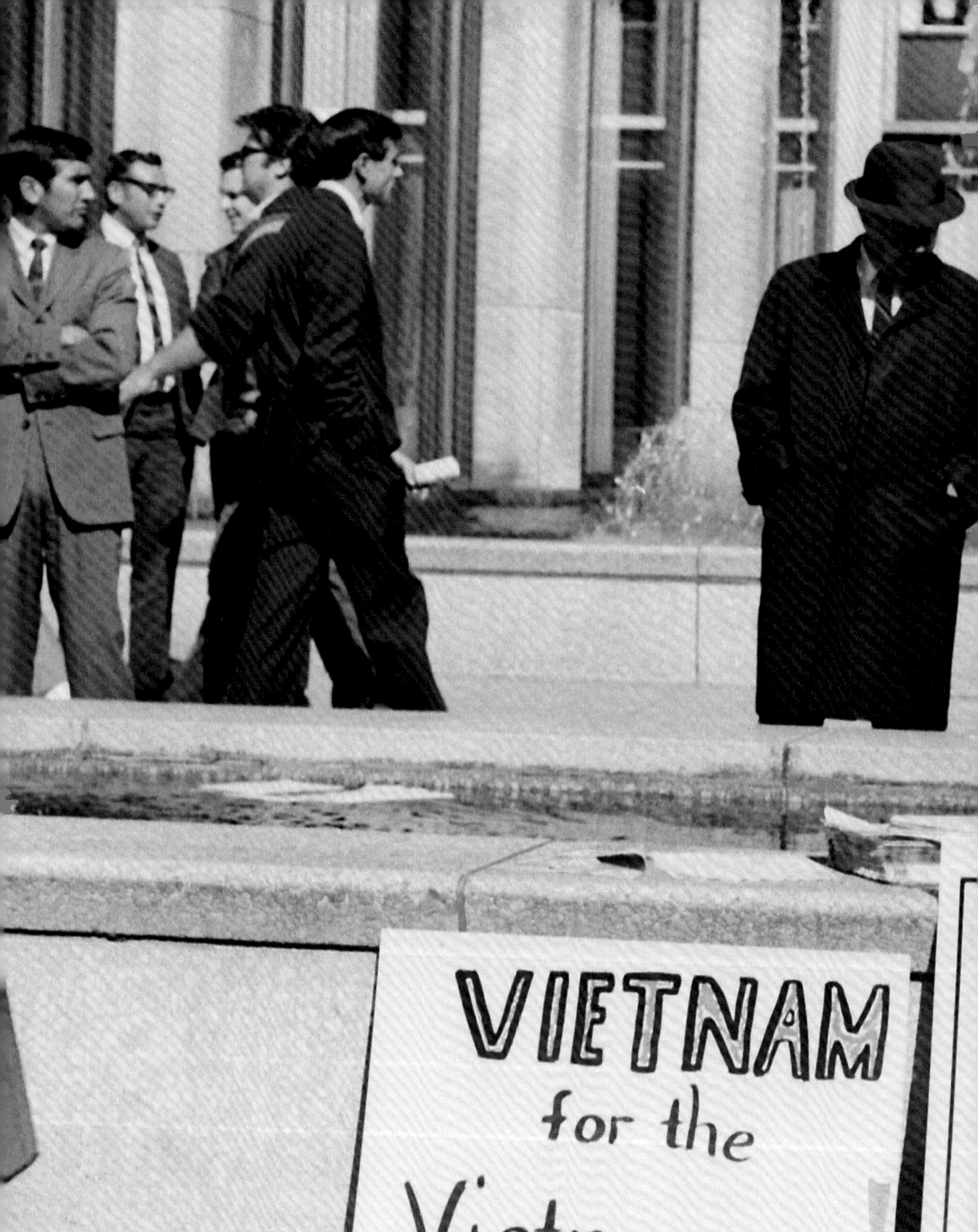
VIETNAM
for the
Vietnamese

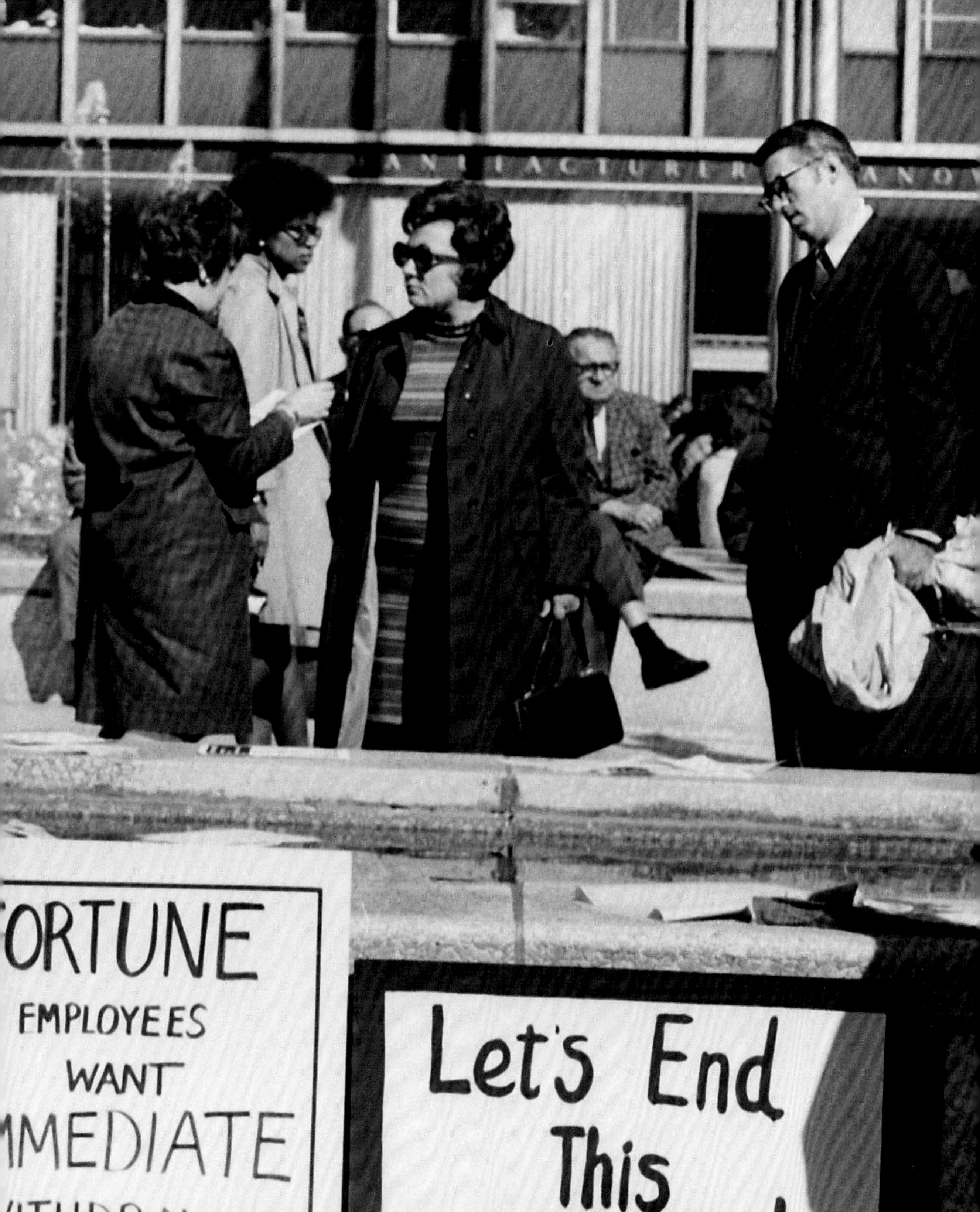
ORTUNE
EMPLOYEES
WANT
MMEDIATE
ITHDRAWAL
FROM
VIETNAM
Let's End
This
HELL !

Free Ericka Huggins and Bobby Seale Protest
New Haven, Connecticut

On November 22, 1969, I went to a women's demonstration in New Haven, Connecticut, organized by the Women's Liberation Movement, the Black Panther Party, and the Young Lords, to free two of their leaders, Bobbie Seale and Ericka Huggins, who had been arrested and charged with murder. This was another long trial that ended without a conviction.

What is notable when I look at my photographs from the demonstration in Connecticut is the intersectionality of the protesters. There are pictures of women from the Black Panther Party, women from the Young Lords, white women, … so many women, seemingly so interconnected, carrying each other's signs and shouting each other's slogans.

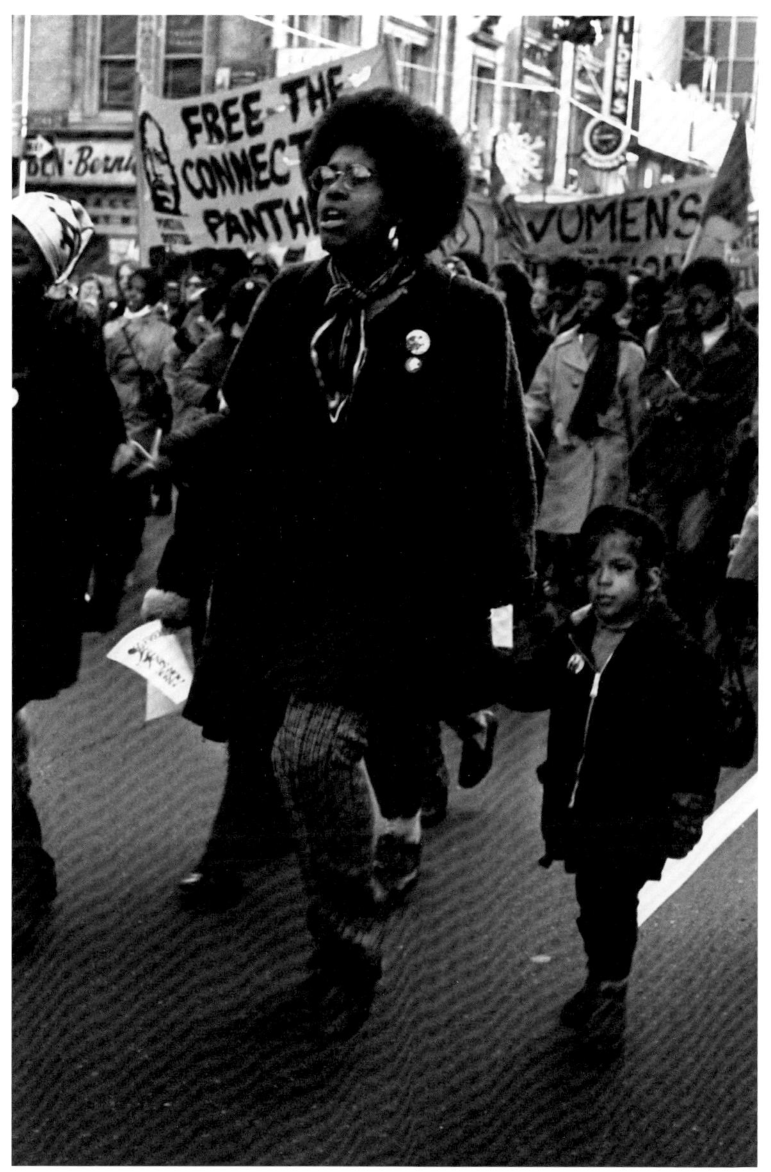

Free Ericka Huggins and Bobbie Seale Protest
New Haven, Connecticut, November 22, 1969

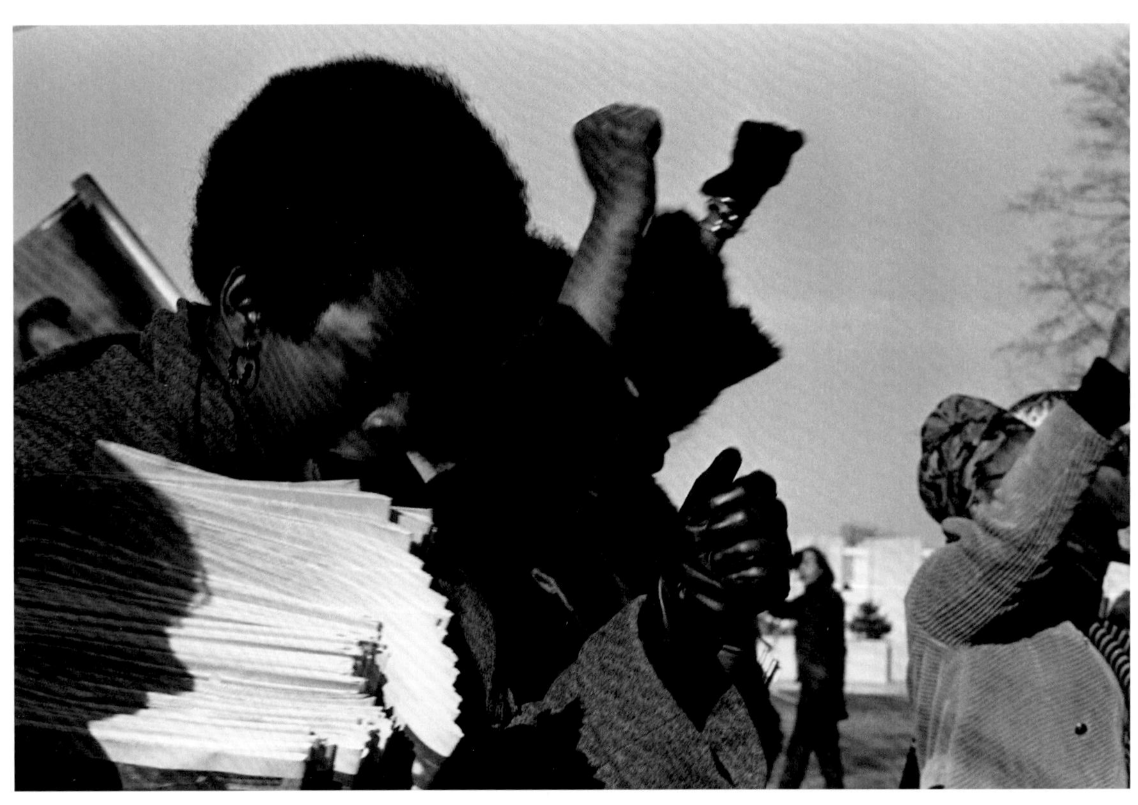

Women from the Black Panther Party
Free Ericka Huggins and Bobbie Seale Protest, New Haven, Connecticut, November 22, 1969

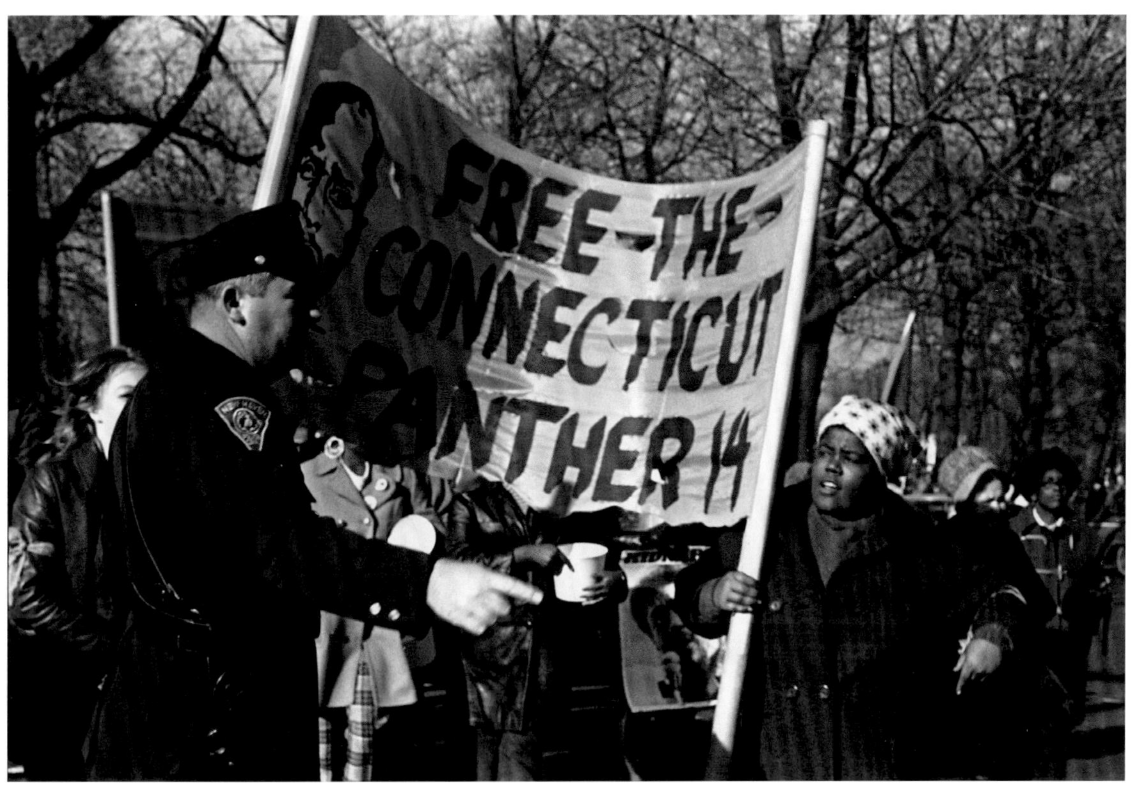

Free Ericka Huggins and Bobbie Seale Protest, New Haven, Connecticut, November 22, 1969

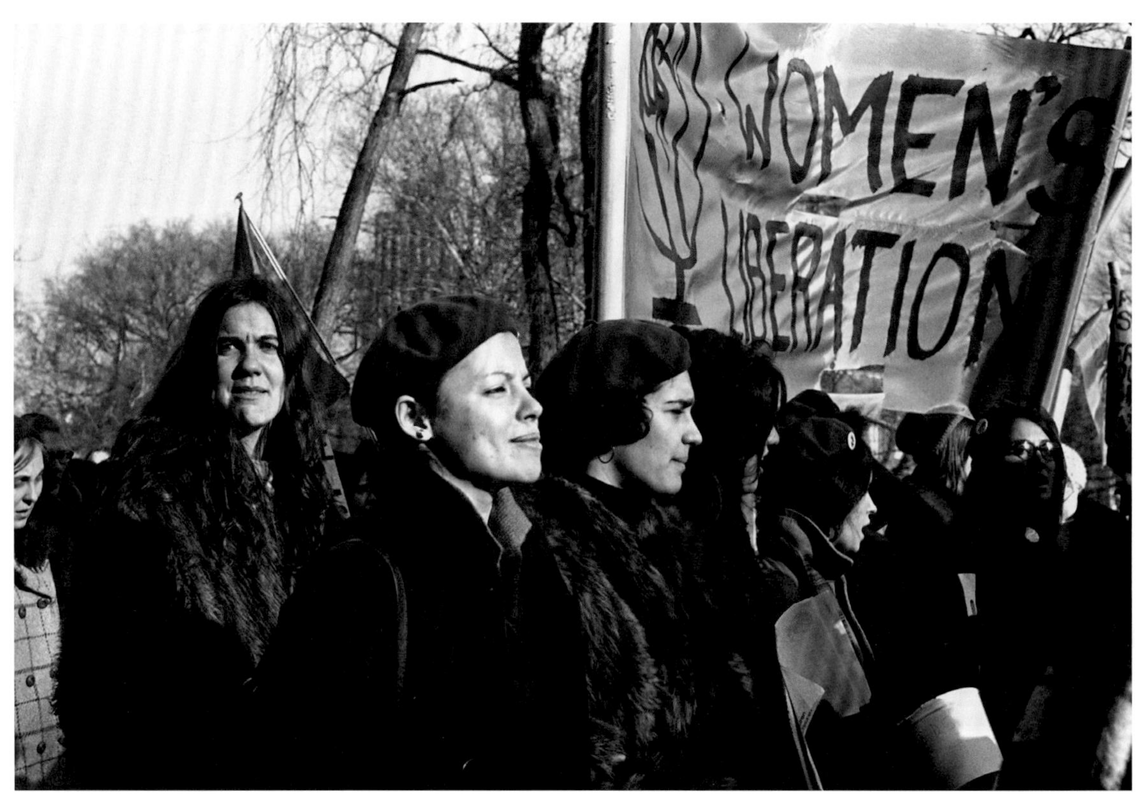

Women from the Young Lords
Free Ericka Huggins and Bobbie Seale Protest, New Haven, Connecticut, November 22, 1969

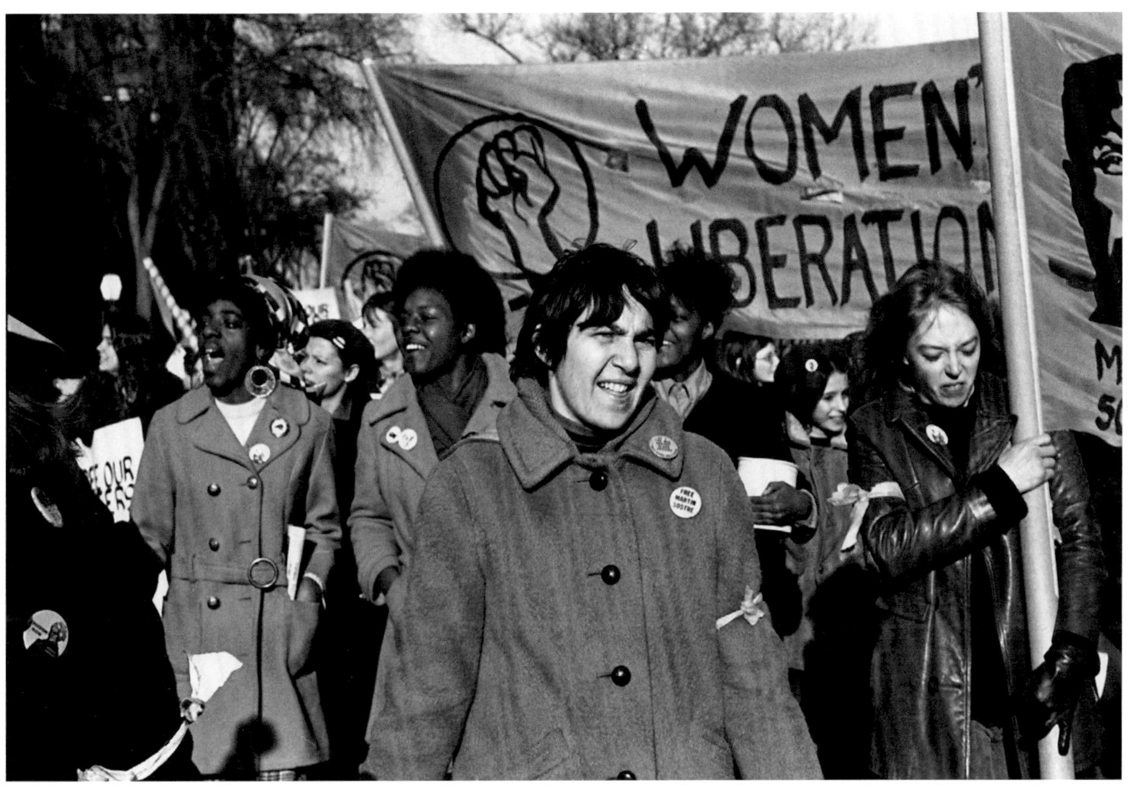

Free Ericka Huggins and Bobbie Seale Protest, New Haven, Connecticut, November 22, 1969

Following spread
Women's demonstration at the court house
Free Ericka Huggins and Bobbie Seale Protest, New Haven, Connecticut, November 22, 1969

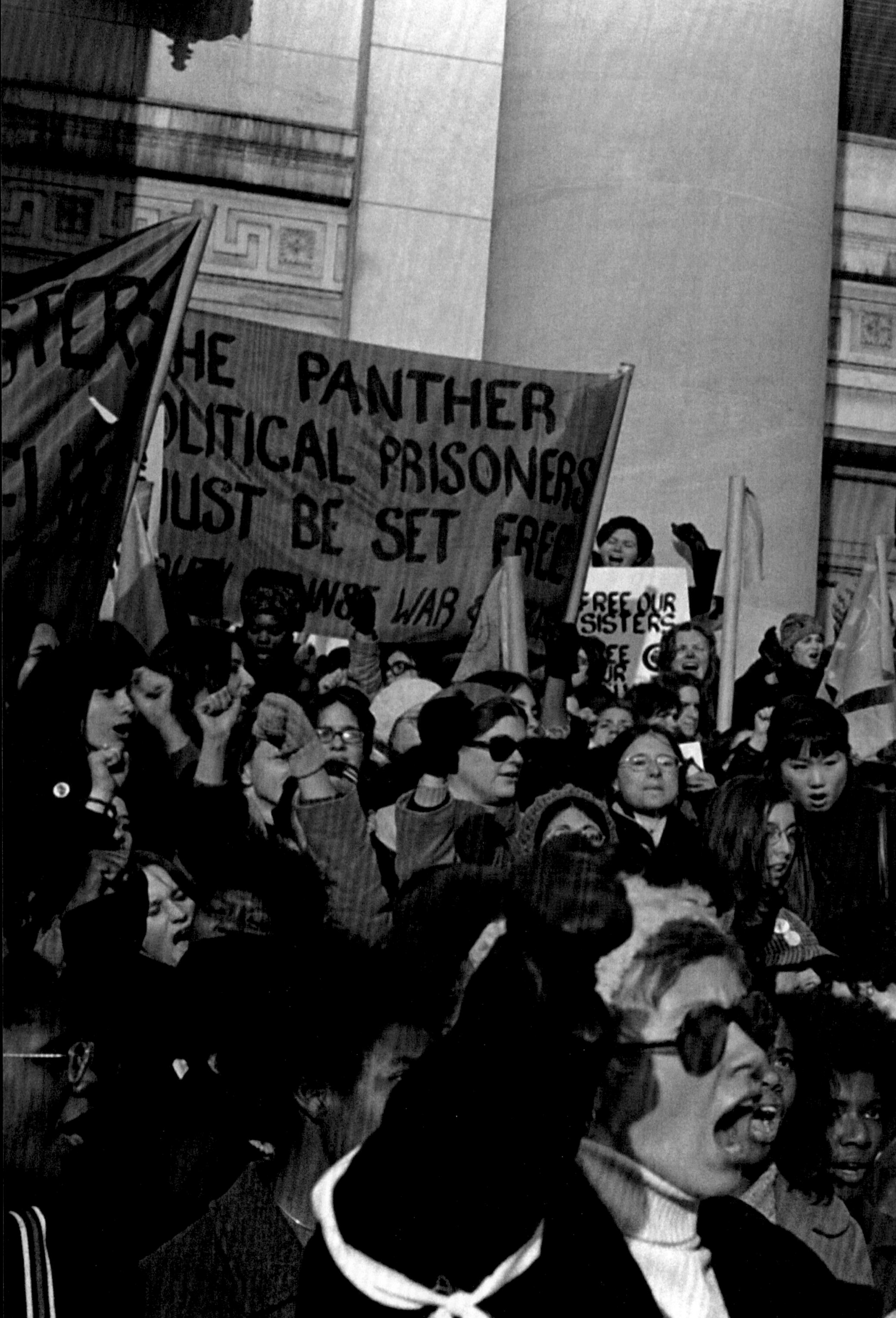
THE PANTHER
POLITICAL PRISONERS
MUST BE SET FREE
FREE OUR
SISTERS

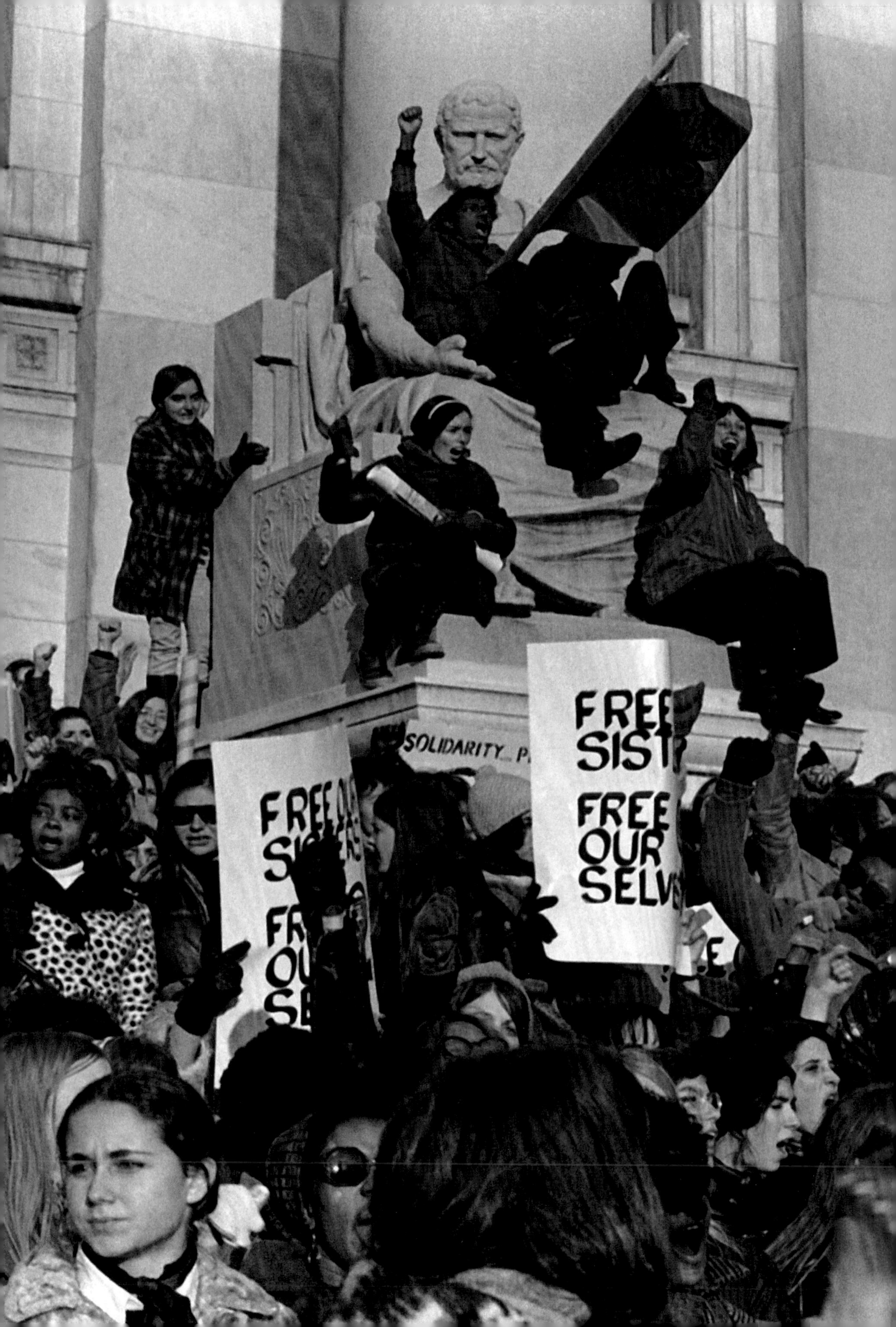

SOLIDARITY P.
FREE
SIST
FREE
OUR
SELVE
FREE
SIS
FREE
OU

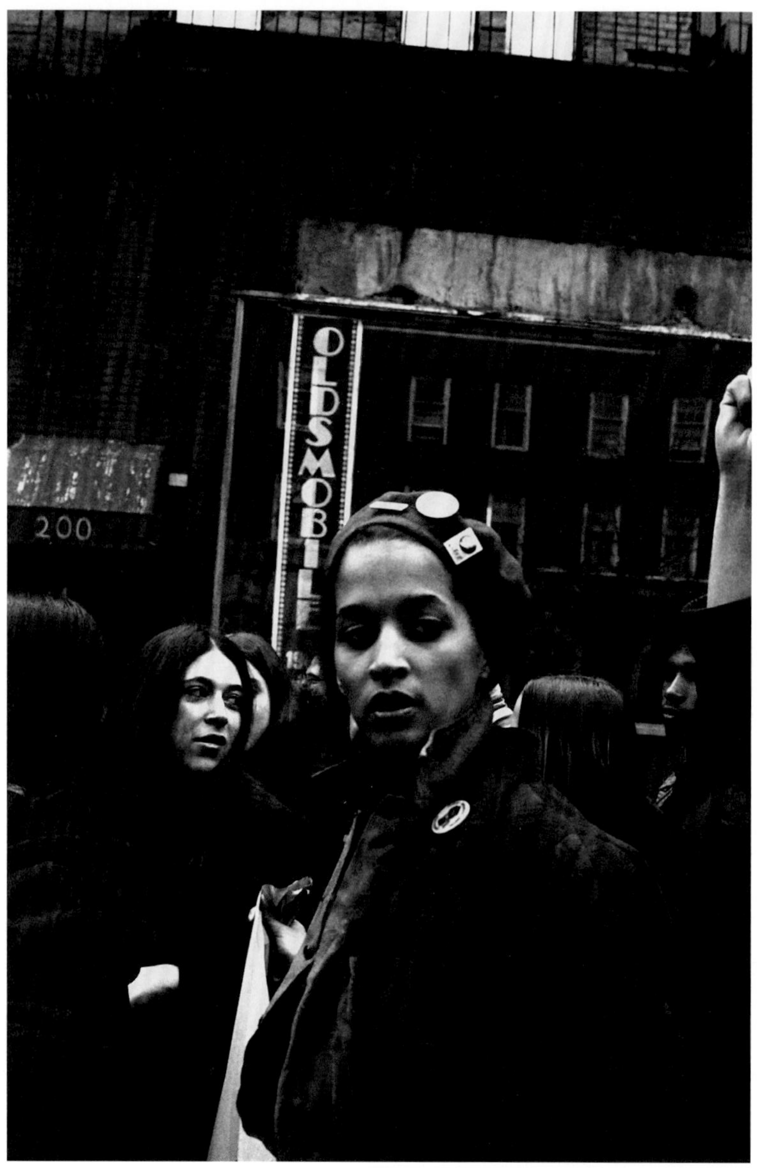

Denise Oliver, member of the Young Lords and the Black Panther Party
Fred Hampton Assassionation Protest, Midtown, New York, December 1969

Fred Hampton Assassination Protest
Midtown, New York

Some of the last photos I took while still in Newsreel were at a demonstration in New York protesting the assassination of Fred Hampton. Hampton was a young, charismatic and effective organizer, head of the Chicago Black Panther Party, and the leader of the Rainbow Coalition. He was successfully organizing gangs, Black, white and Latino communities to come together in unity to fight for better conditions. J. Edgar Hoover particularly targeted the black movement, writing that "we must prevent the rise of a new black messiah." Hampton was J. Edgar Hoover's worst nightmare, the Black messiah he so feared, and was targeted by the FBI and the Chicago Police Department. On December 4, 1969, at 4am in the morning, Hampton and his bodyguard, Mark Clark, who had been secretely drugged by an FBI undercover operative, were coldly assassinated while they were sleeping. A few days after the assassination, demonstrations in Chicago, New York, and elsewhere took place, including this Fred Hampton Assassination Protest, organized by the Young Lords. In 1971, the FBI finally admitted to the assassination and disbanded COINTELPRO.

Following spread
Fred Hampton Assassionation Protest, Midtown, New York, December 1969

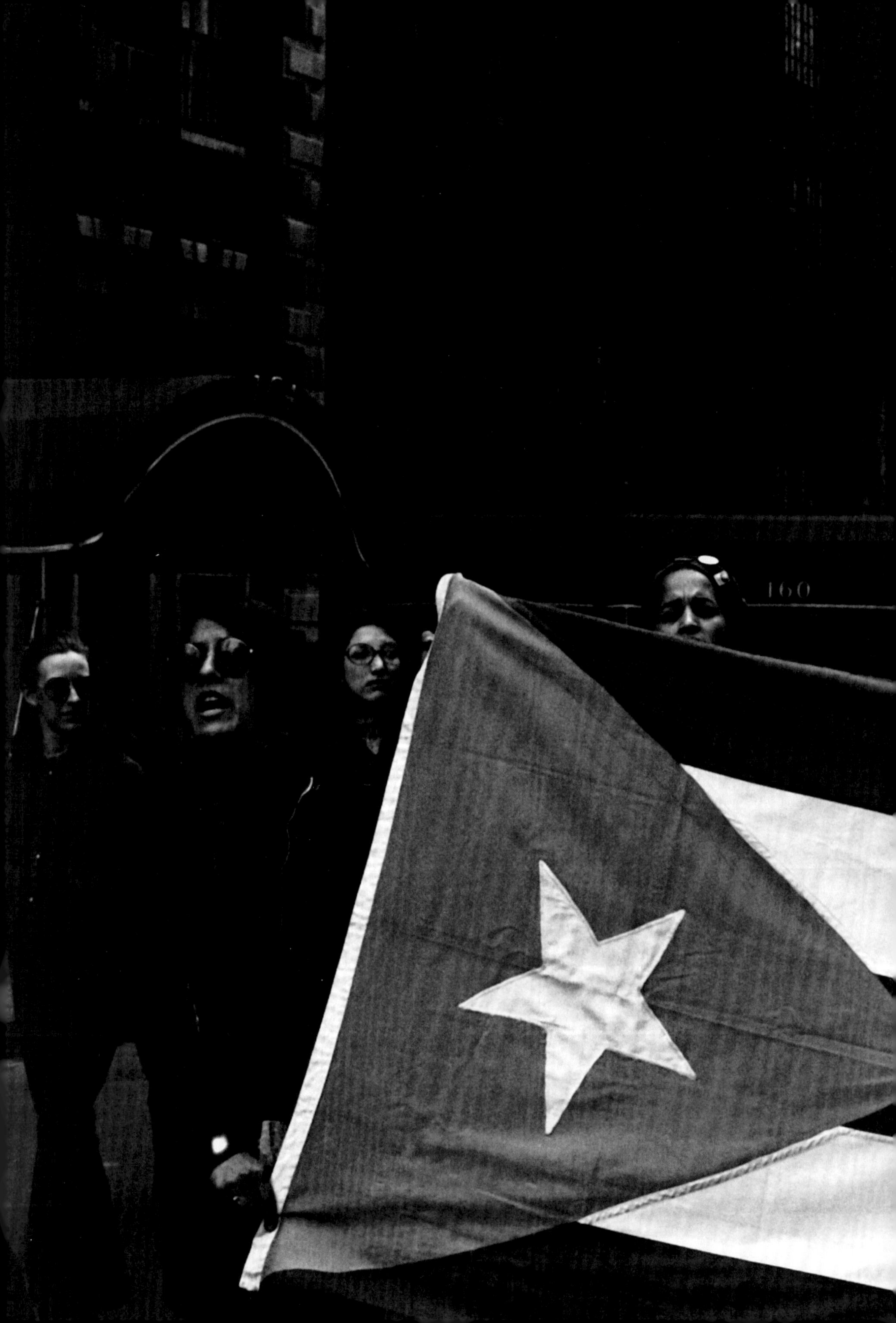

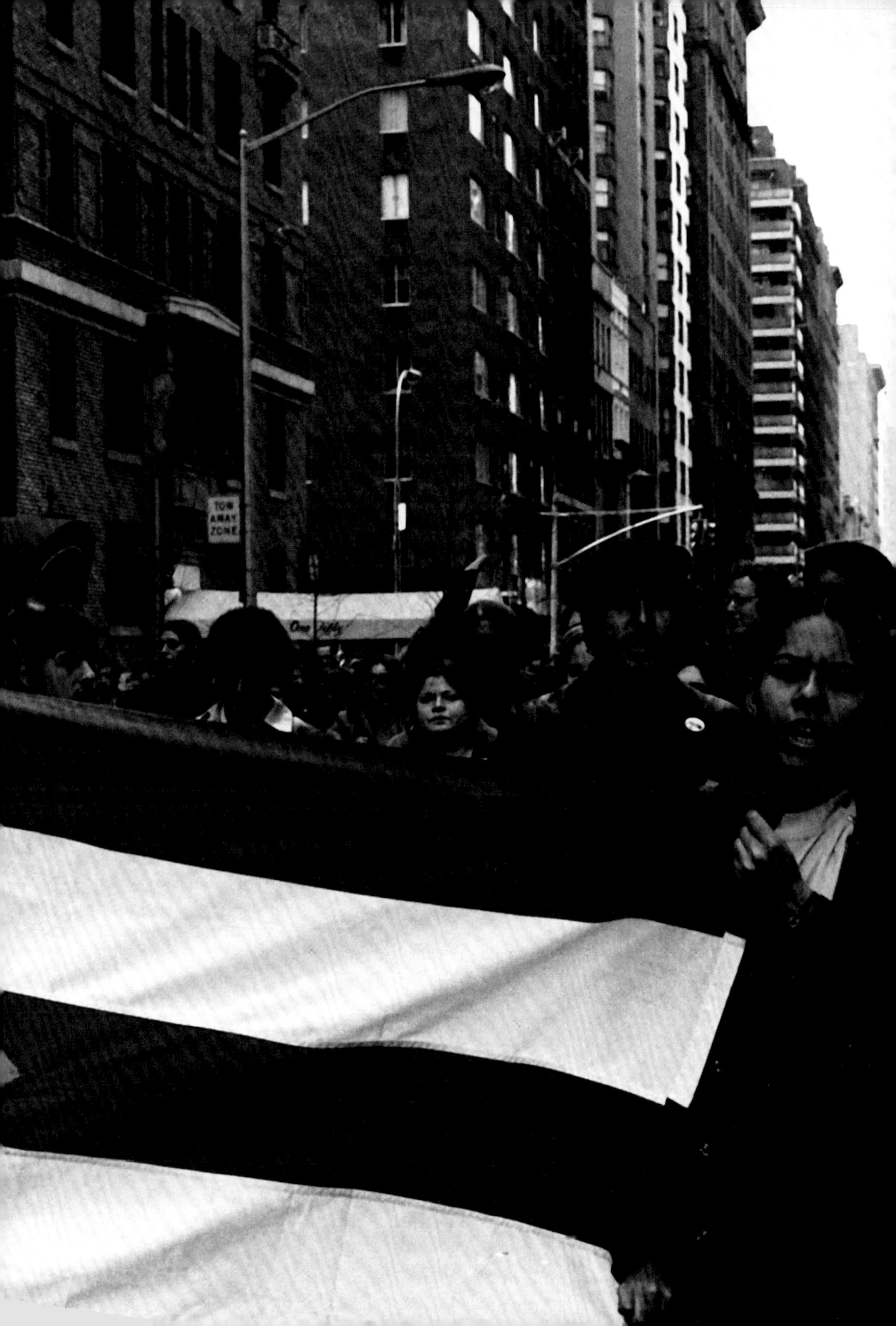

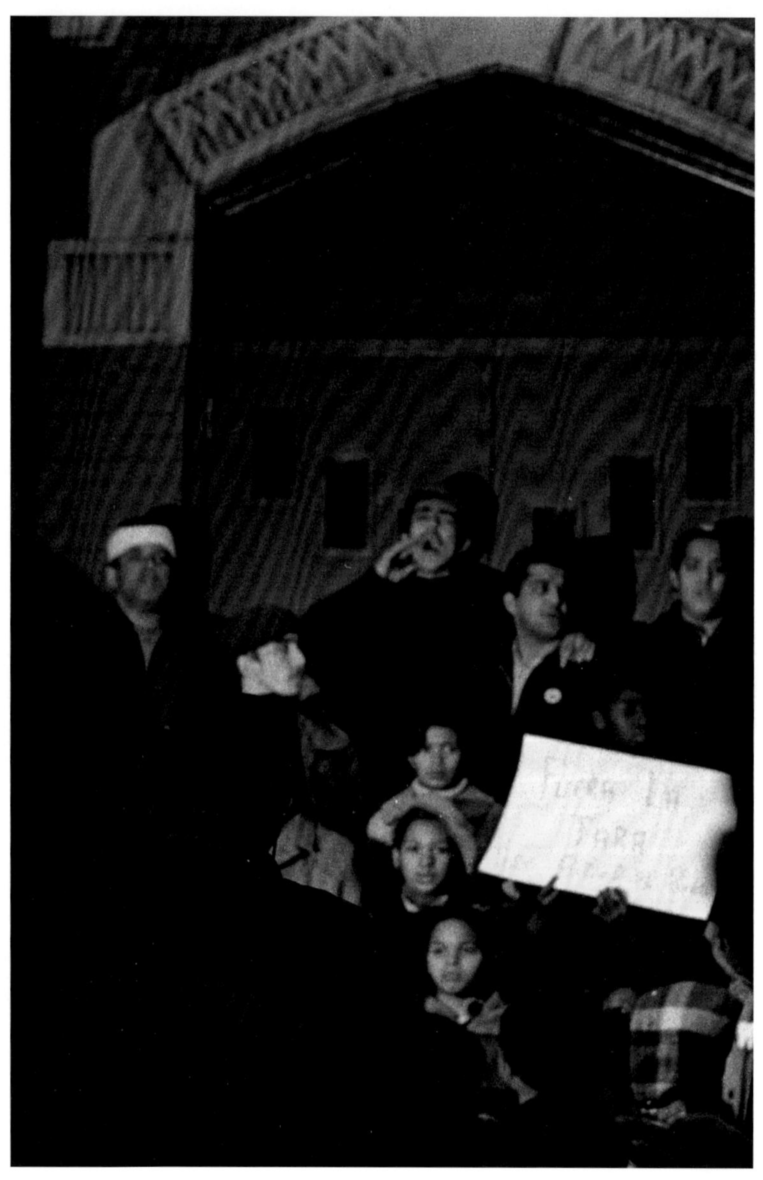

David Perez, Young Lords Minister of Defense
Young Lords Church Occupation, East Harlem, New York
December 28, 1969 - January 9, 1970

Young Lords Church Occupation
East Harlem, New York

Sometime in December 1969, the Young Lords began going to the First United Methodist Church in East Harlem, a Spanish church that was only open for Sunday services, with a congregation that came mostly from outside the community. The Lords had been asking the pastor and the congregation for the use of space to run their community programs. They were refused on each occasion, but on December 28, 1969, they occupied and "liberated" the church, calling it the "Peoples' Church". They held it for eleven days while serving food, doing Tuberculosis testing, giving away free clothing, and providing education and entertainment to everyone who stopped by.

During the church occupation, I wasn't doing much photography because I was working as part of a three-person crew documenting the Young Lords for a Newsreel film, entitled El Pueblo se Levanta. I was helping with the community services in the church by washing dishes, whatever was needed. I was also working a full-time day job. I shot some of the footage for the film and did some of the sound recording. Later, Robert Lacativa, Florence Summergrad and I would huddle around the editing machine, a Movieola, for hours discussing how to put the film together and choosing music for it. Once we had a final edit, I learned to cut negative.

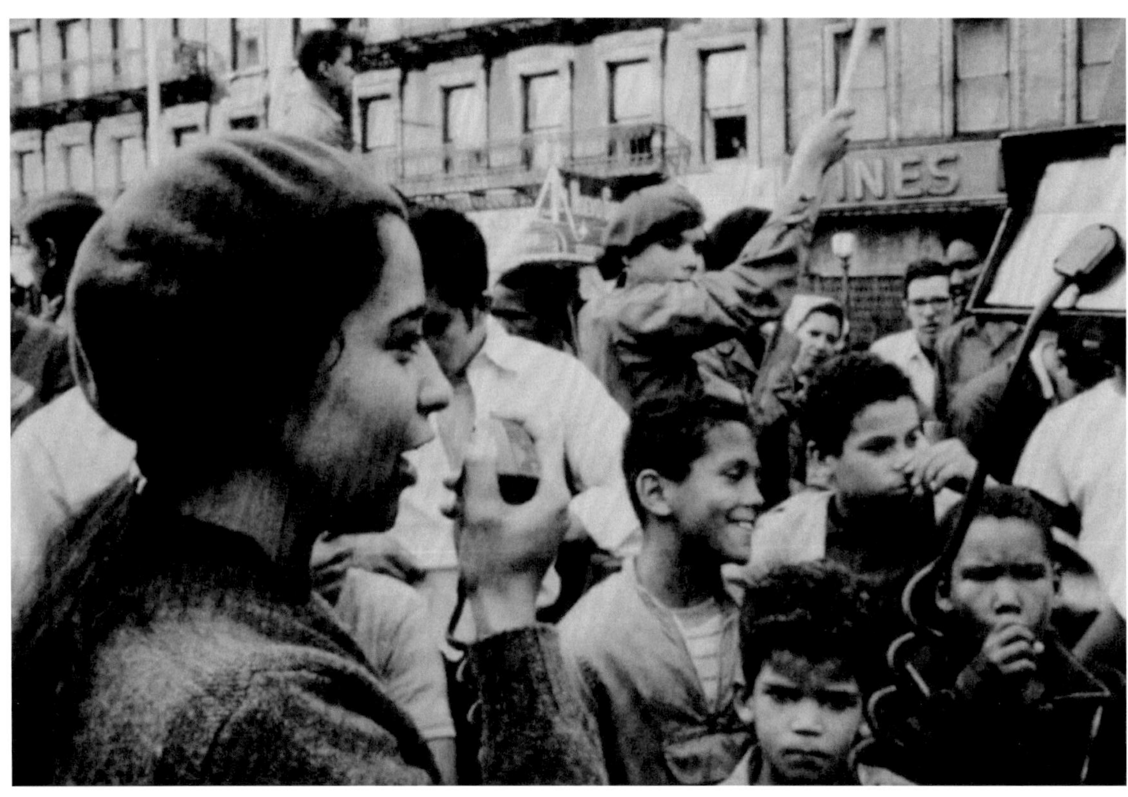

Film still from *El Pueblo Se Levanta* (1971) with Iris Morales, Young Lords Deputy Minister of Education and co-founder of the Women's Caucus

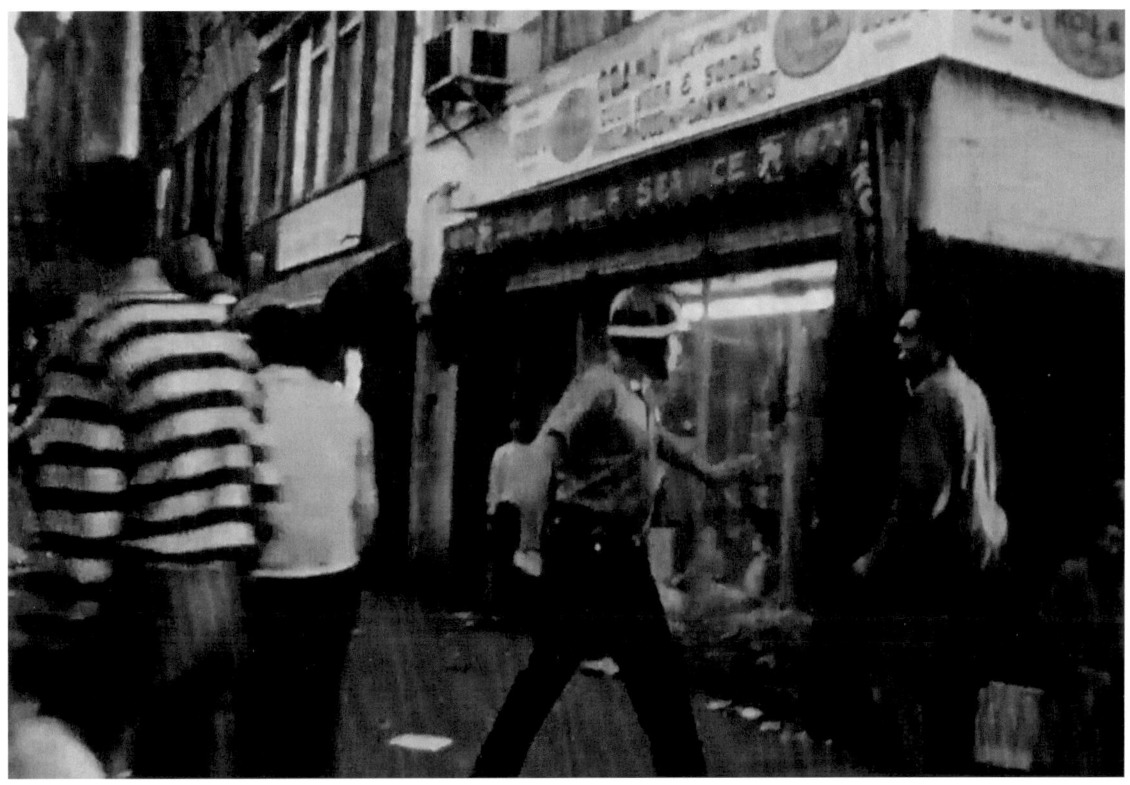

Film still from *El Pueblo Se Levanta* (1971) *showing* police attacking Young Lord outside the Young Lords office

Following spread
Young Lords Church Occupation, East Harlem, New York, December 28, 1969 - January 9, 1970

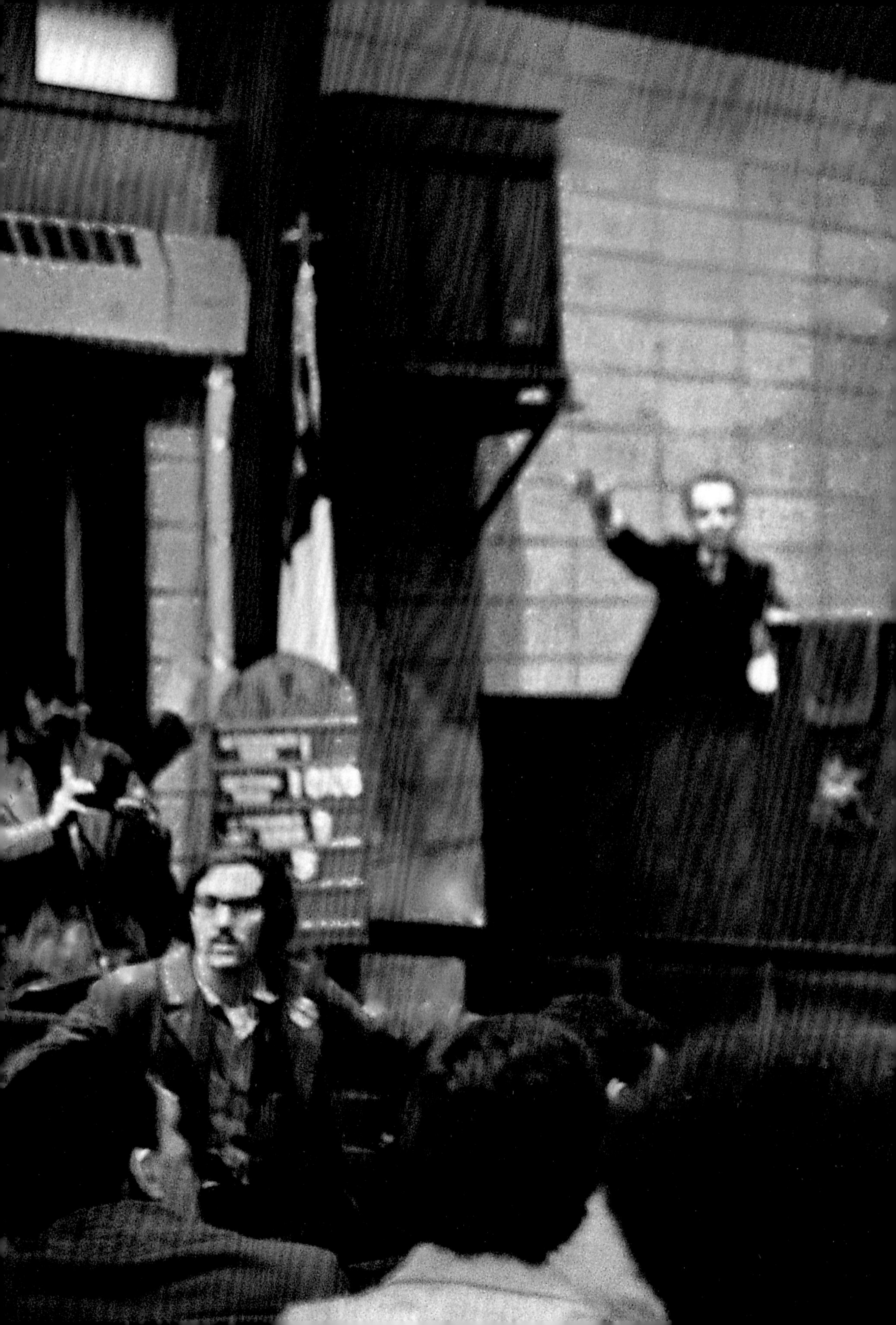

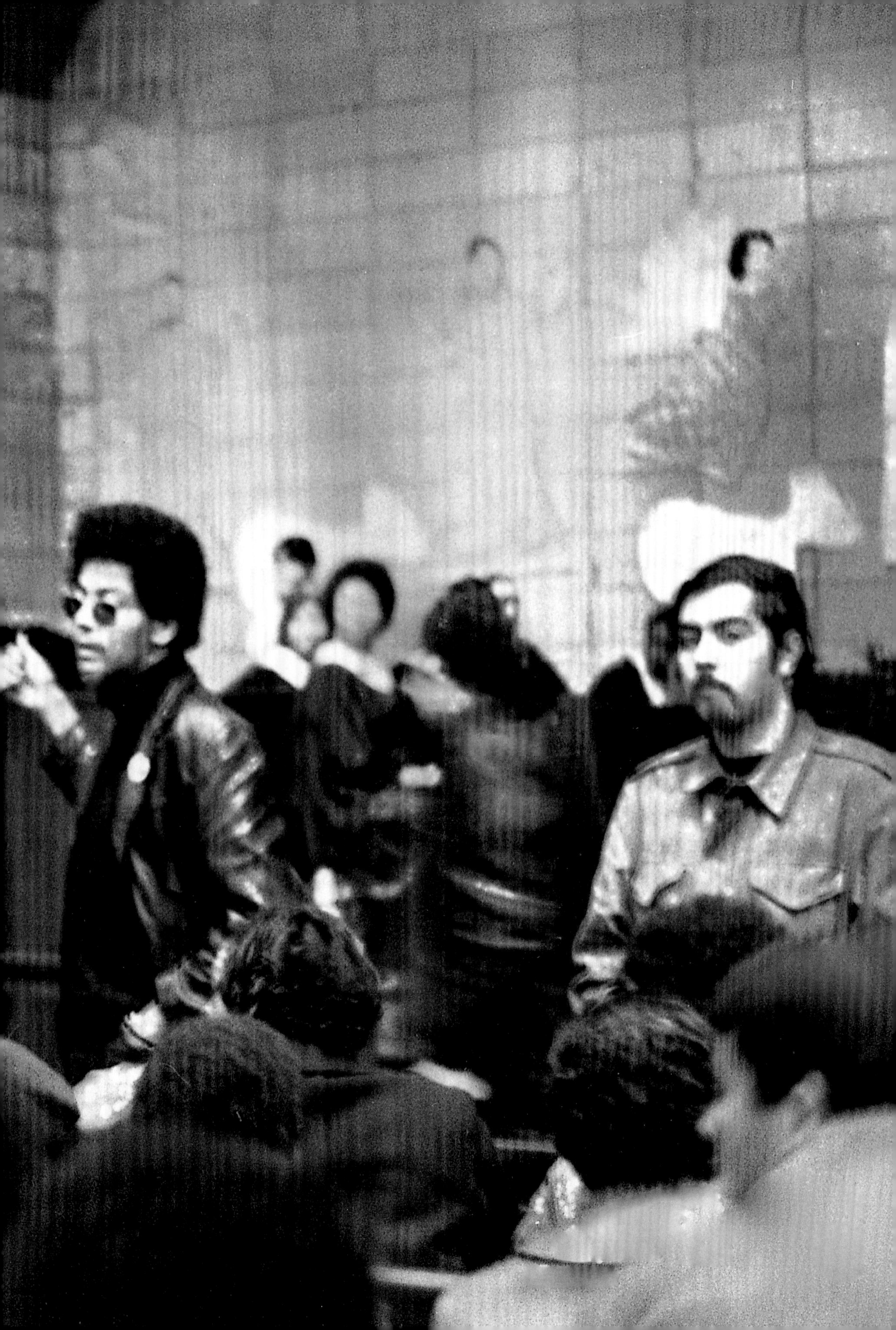

April 4, 1970

Panther 21 Protest
New York City

On April 2, 1969, twenty-one members of the Harlem chapter of the Black Panther Party, including my brother-in-law, known then as Clark Squire, were formally indicted and charged with 156 counts of conspiracy to blow up subway and police stations, five local department stores, six railroads and the New York Botanical Garden. Charges were dropped on some of them, but twelve members (two women and ten men) were formally arrested and jailed with bail set at $100,000 each. The first and only one to post bail was Alice Faye Williams, better known as Afeni Shakur (mother of Tupac). She was also the only one to represent herself in court. Joan Bird spent 15 monts in prison before being released on June 6, 1970, and the other ten weren't released until May 12, 1971. They spent two years in jail on false charges, for which the jury only took forty-five minutes to acquit them. Before the arrests, my sister had given birth to my niece, who for two years had no father. When she went to court with her mom, they searched her diaper. Many lives were thrown into chaos by that trial, the longest in the history of New York State.

On April 4, 1970, about halfway through their incarceration awaiting trial, a demonstration in support of the Panther 21 took place. An integrated crowd of over 4,000 protesters marched from Manhattan across the Queensboro Bridge to the Queensboro Correctional Facility in Long Island City.

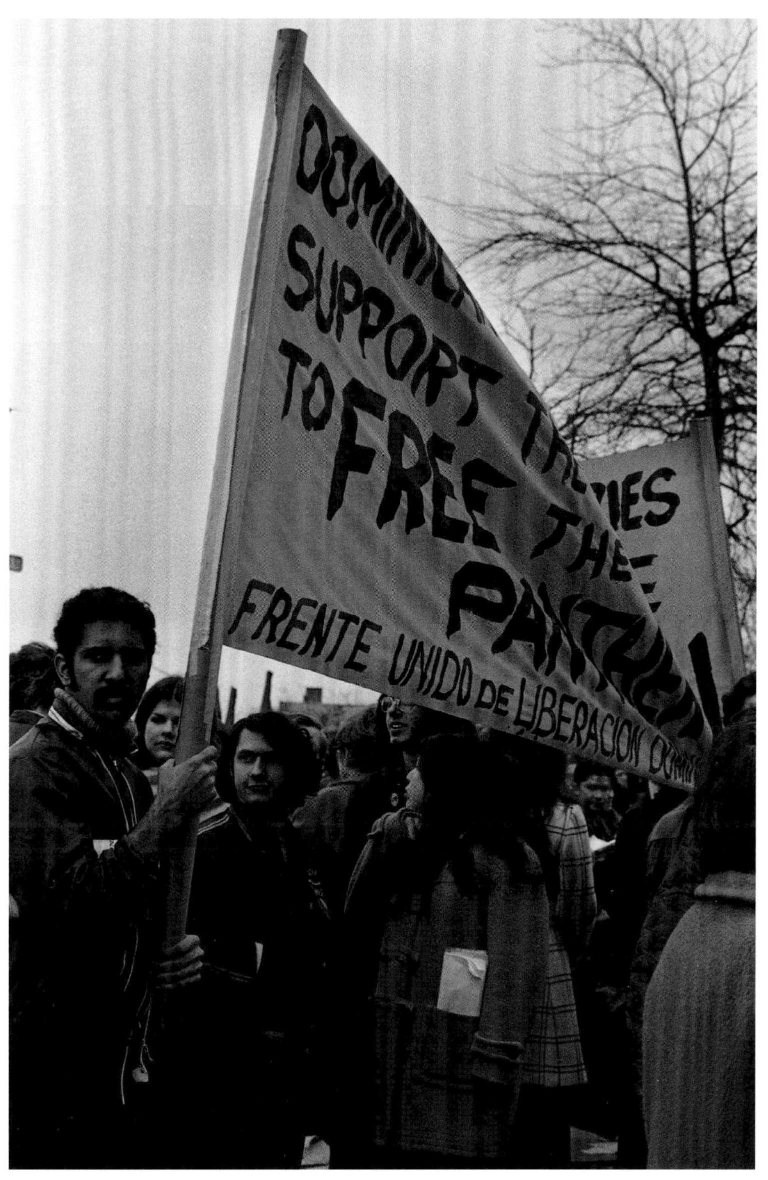

Panther 21 Protest, New York City, April 4, 1970

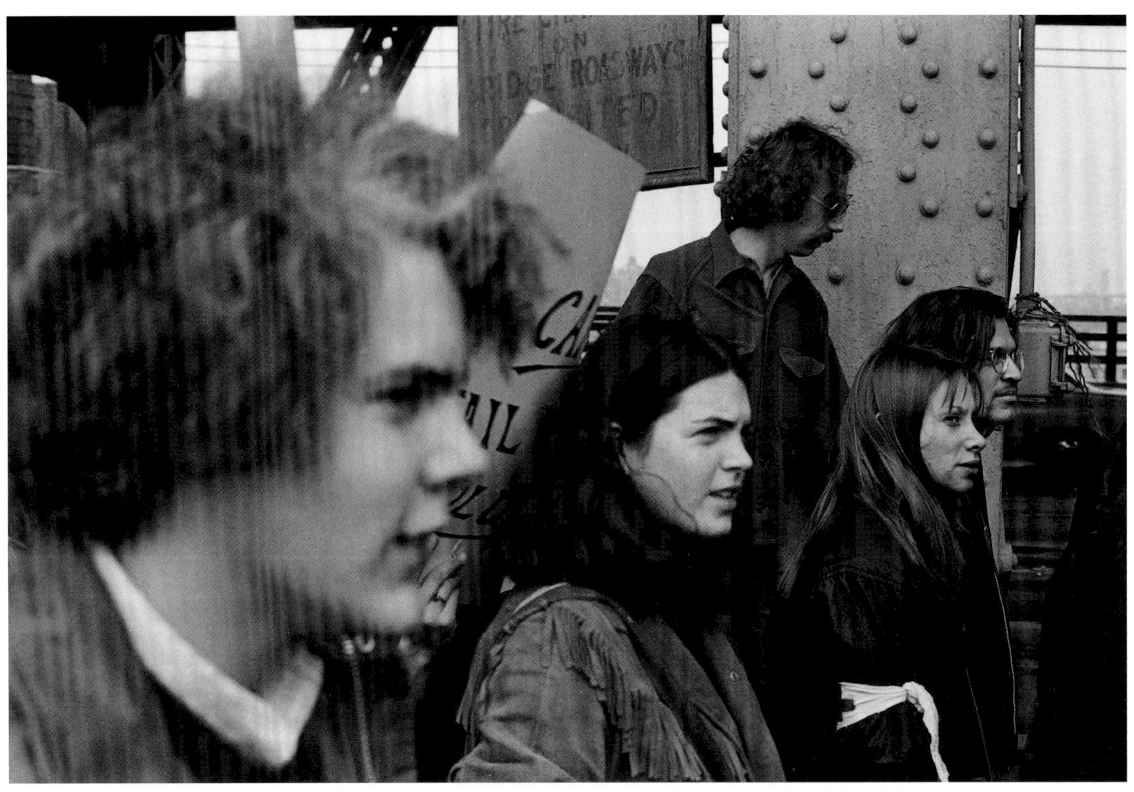

Protesters crossing the Queensboro Bridge on their way to the Queensboro Correctional Facility in Long Island City
Panther 21 Protest, New York City, April 4, 1970

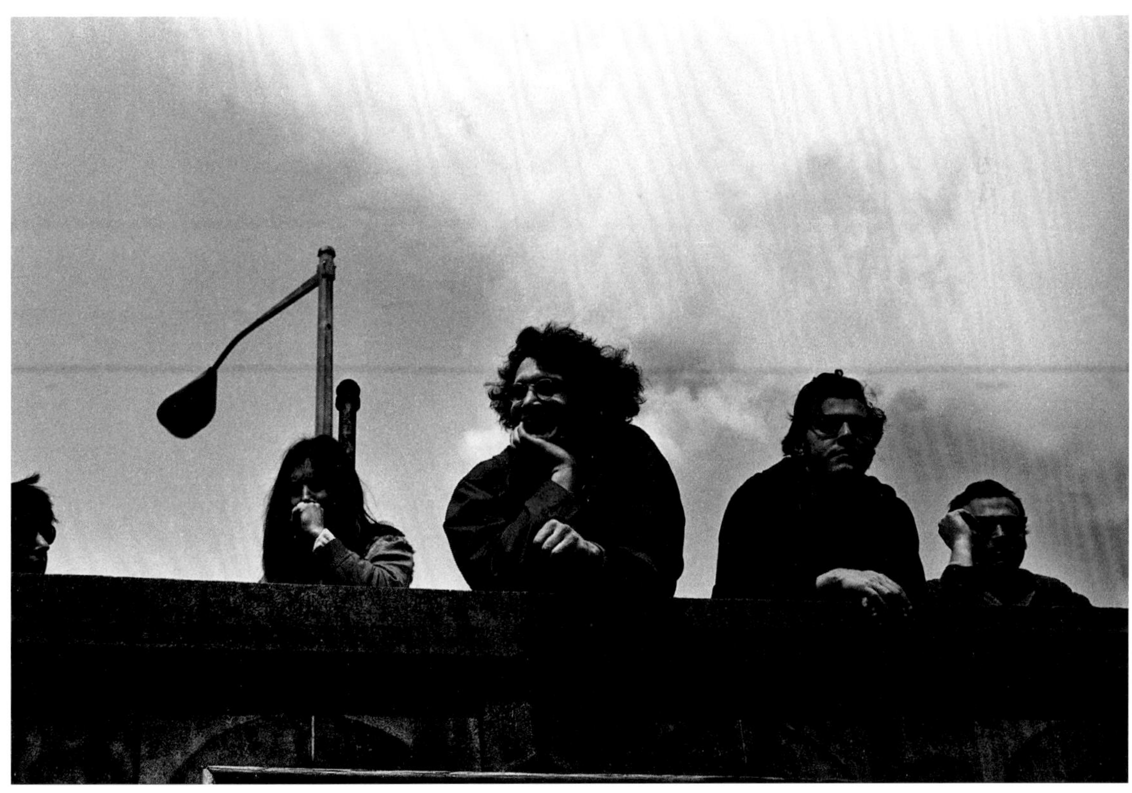

Mike Singer of Newreel observing the protest
Panther 21 Protest, New York City, April 4, 1970

Following spread
Protesters on their way to the Queensboro Correctional Facility in Long Island City
Panther 21 Protest, New York City, April 4, 1970

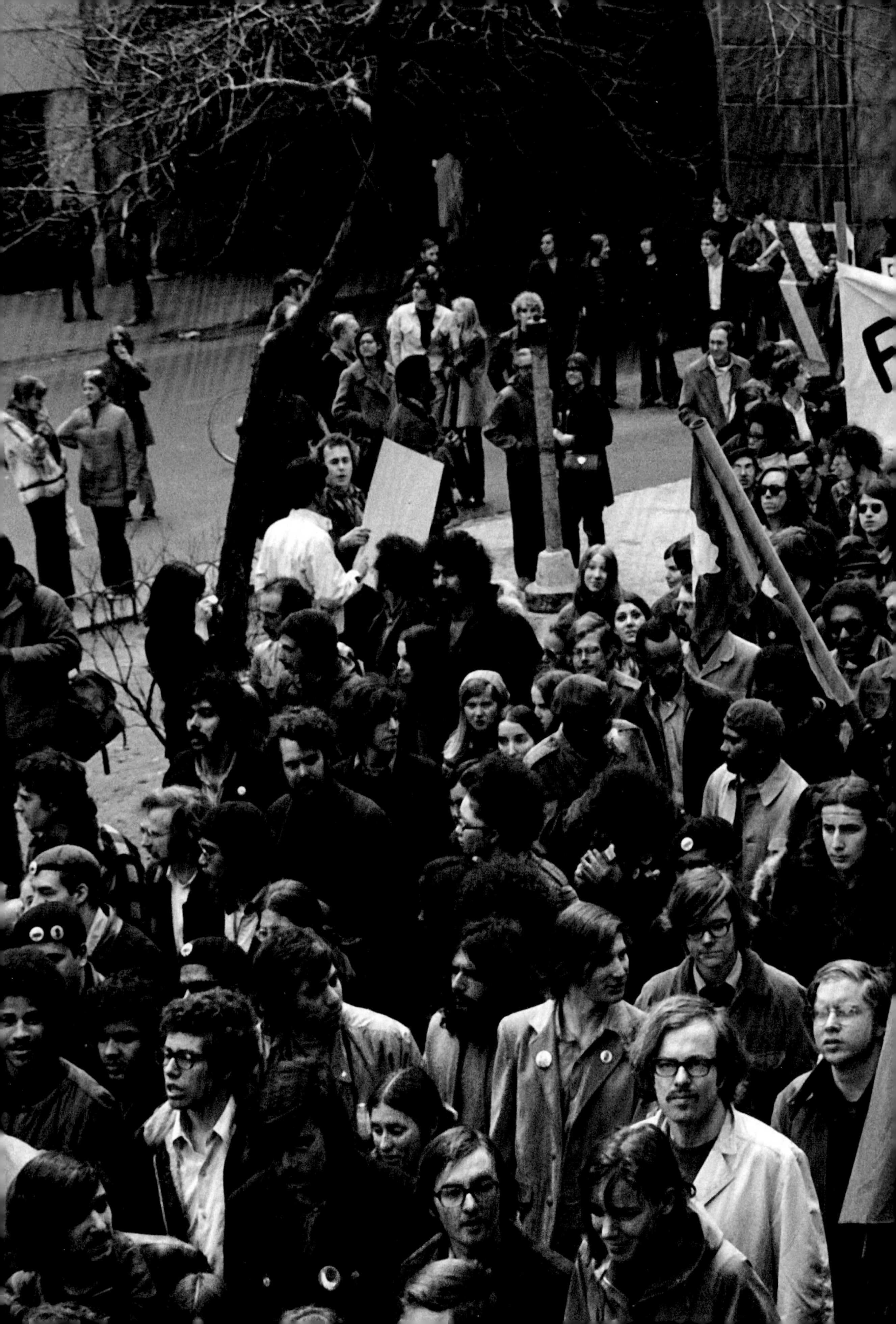

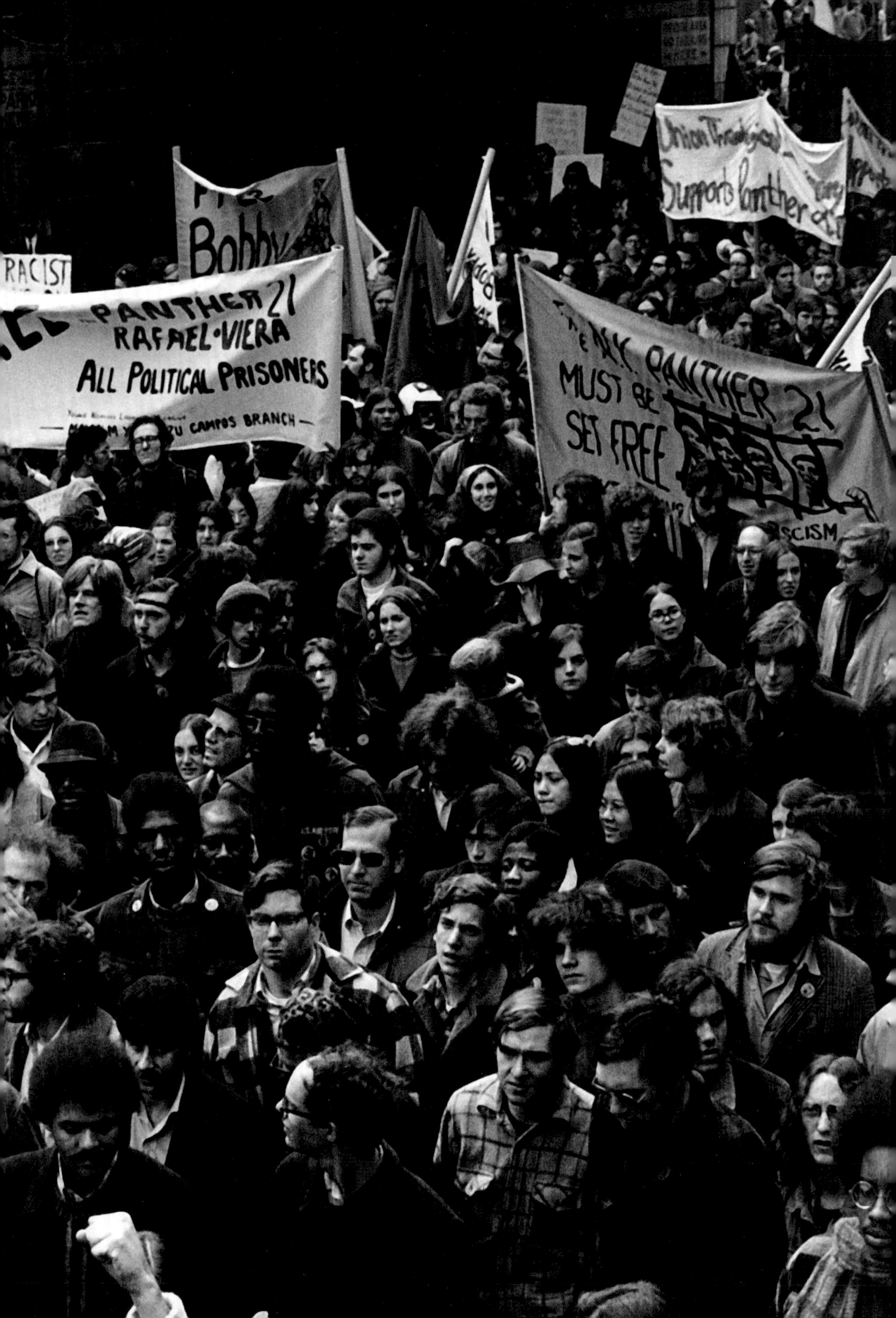

FREE Bobby
RACIST
PANTHER 21
RAFAEL·VIERA
All Political Prisoners
CAMPOS BRANCH
THE N.Y. PANTHER 21
MUST BE
SET FREE
FASCISM
Union Theological
Supports Panther

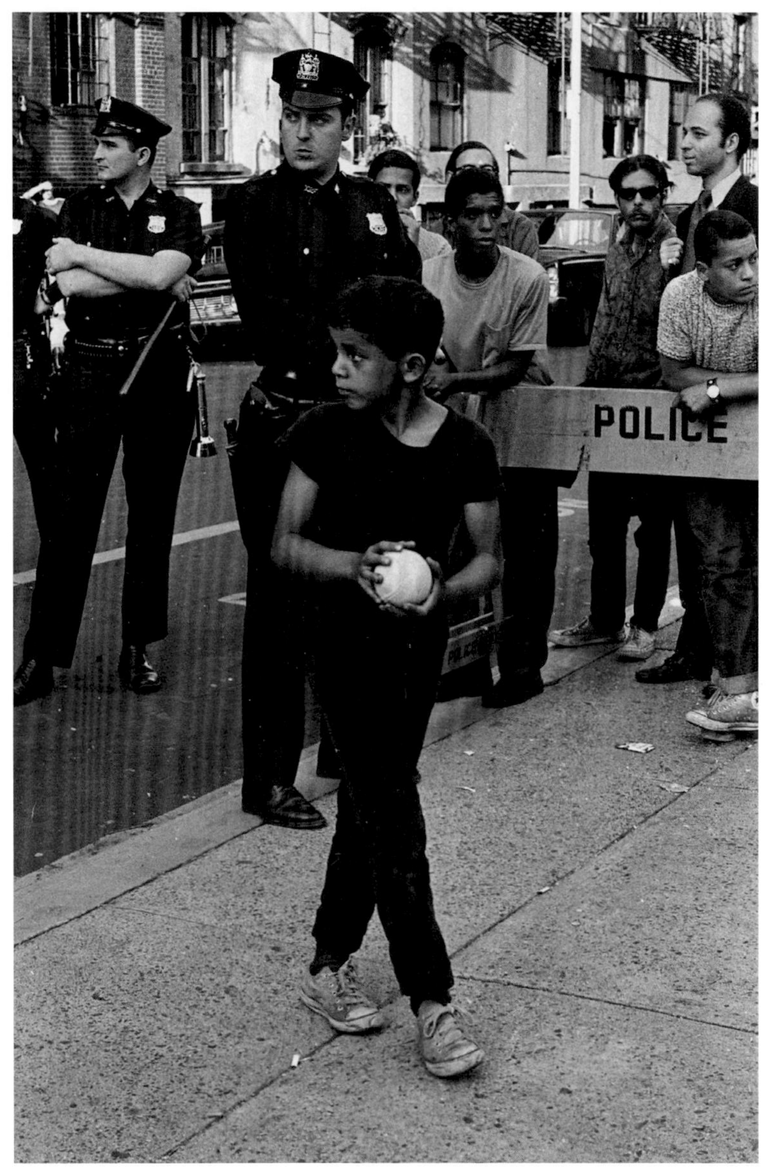

Boy with a ball in front of the 9th Precinct, New York, Summer 1971

Lower East Side Community
Lower East Side, New York

In the early 1970s, the mood changed. New York City lost residents and manufacturing jobs, and many landlords abandoned their buildings. Arson was widespread, often perpetrated by the landlords themselves. A shortage of affordable housing led to record levels of homelessness in the Lower East Side. There was a growing population addicted to heroin, including many Vietnam vets, who took refuge in the vacant buildings and littered lots. Police brutality and corruption were widespread, and officers generally weren't held accountable. Confrontations and assaults were frequent. The COINTELPRO misinformation, infiltration, and raids, brought into stark focus by the assassination of Fred Hampton at the end of 1969, left many on the left divided and in disarray. Some felt there could be no progress without armed struggle. A faction of the SDS radicalized into the Weather Underground, and some members of the Black Panthers, convinced that it was time to "pick up the gun," joined the Black Liberation Army, influenced by the liberation struggles taking place in Africa and Latin America.

Ericka Huggins was still incarcerated and awaiting trial at Niantic State prison, and I was invited to perform there. Afeni Shakur, who had been acquitted of the Panther 21 charges, heard about my upcoming performance and asked if I would sing a song that she and Joan Bird, the other female Panther 21 defendant, had written. I said yes and they met me in the basement of a Newsreel member's townhouse on East 15th Street to teach me the song. On December 13, 1970, I performed for the women prisoners at Niantic State Prison and dedicated the song to Ericka on Afeni and Joan's behalf.

I was living on the Lower East Side then, high on my new consciousness as a radical woman, and trying, as part of Newsreel, to be an ally to the liberation movement. But the movement began splintering in terms of whose organization or party held the correct line. Many of us became divided by sectarianism, thinking our way was the only way. The violence could be felt around us. The Weather Underground accidentally exploded one of their bombs in a Greenwich Village townhouse on March 6, 1970, and on January 27, 1972, two patrolmen were shot and killed on Avenue B by members of the BLA, who claimed responsibility. We knew something had changed. We lost a sense of solidarity.

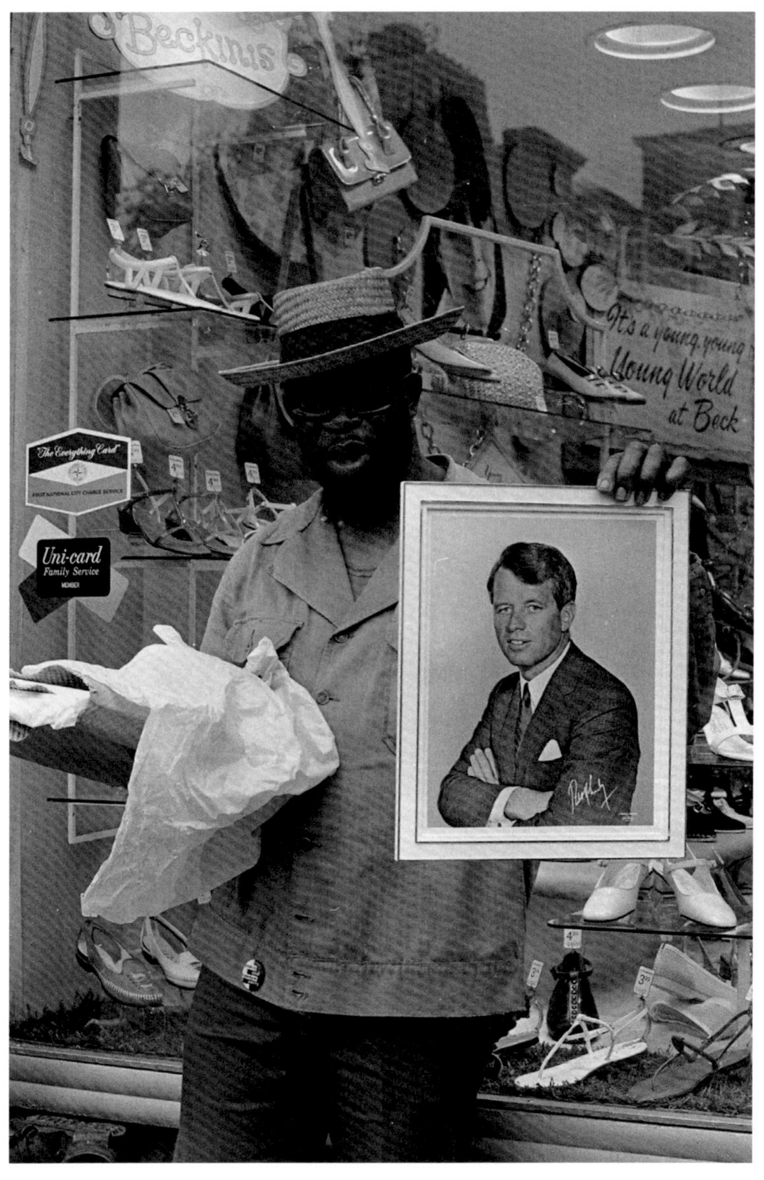

Man holding portrait of Robert F. Kennedy
New York City, Summer 1971

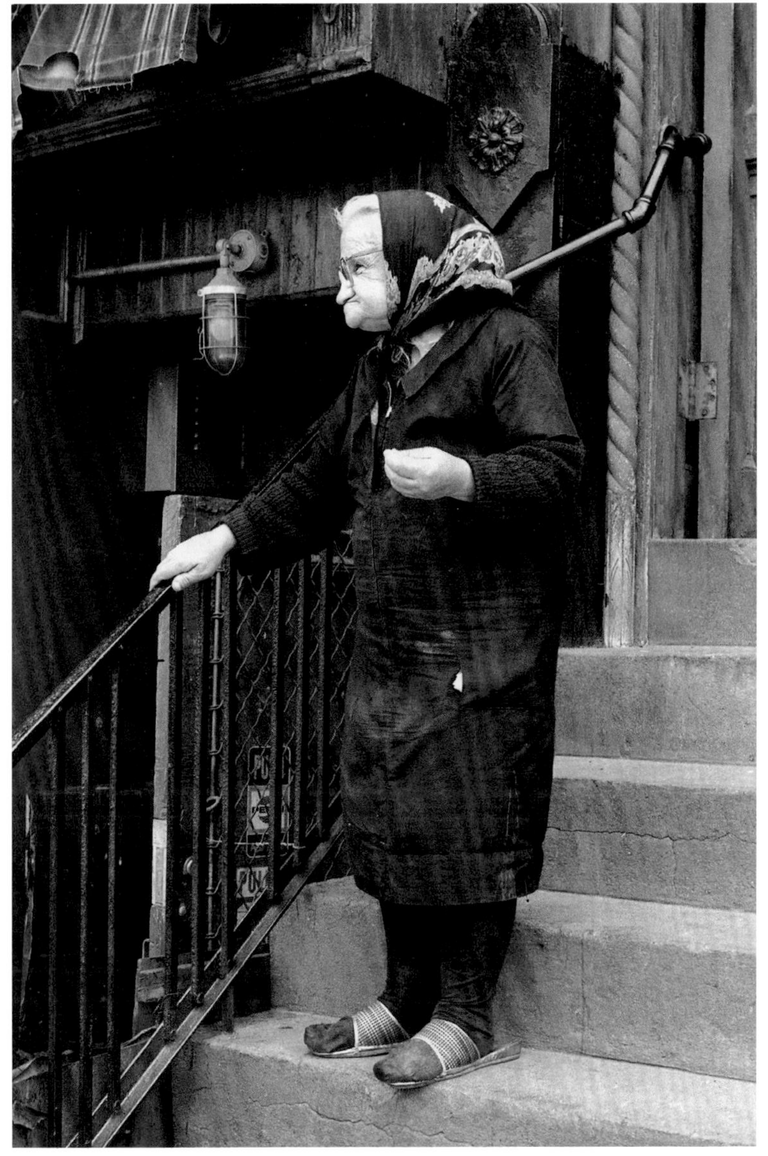

Woman on a stoop, Lower East Side, New York, Summer 1971

Following spread
Boy sitting on a police barricade in front of the 9th Precinct
New York, Summer 1971

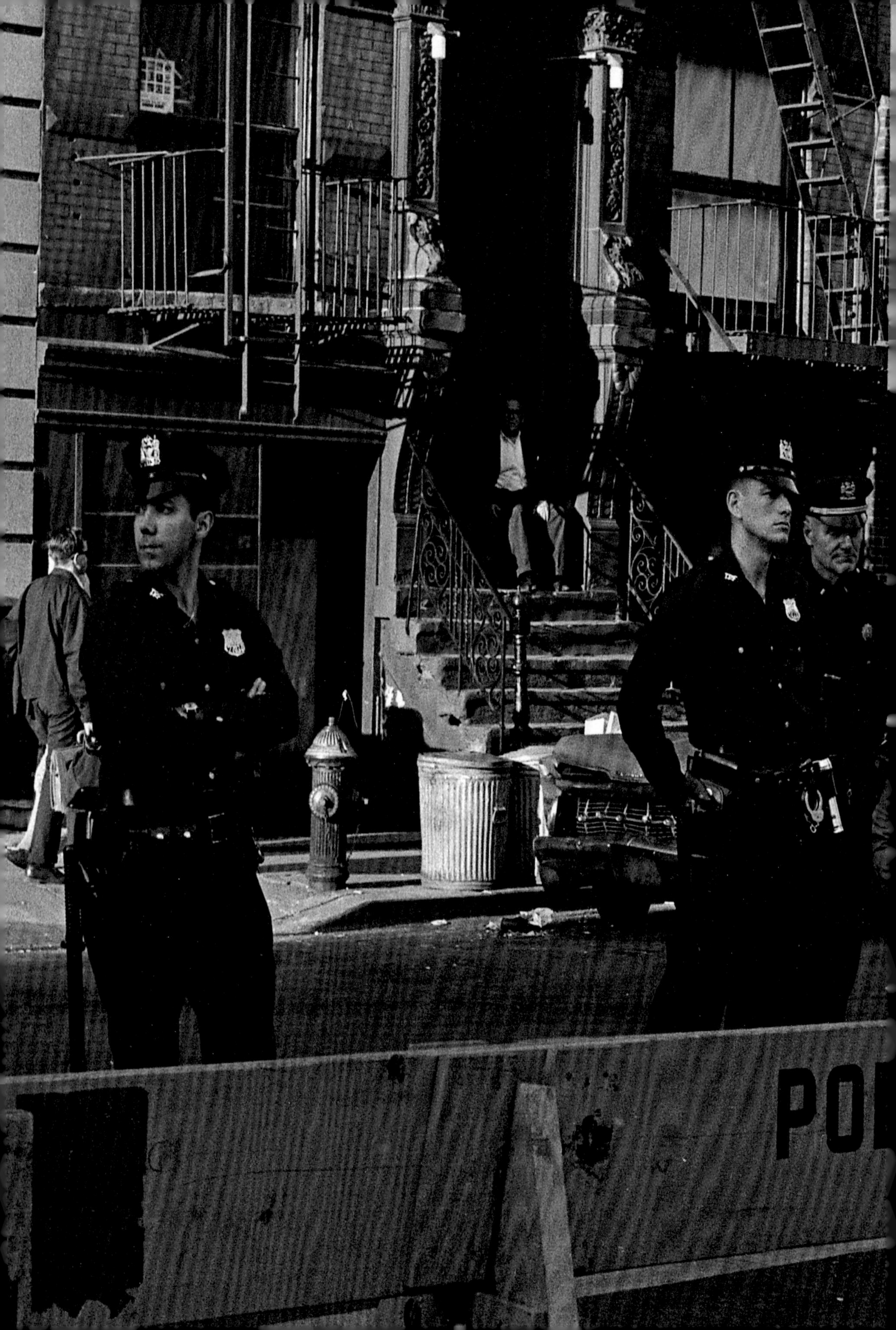

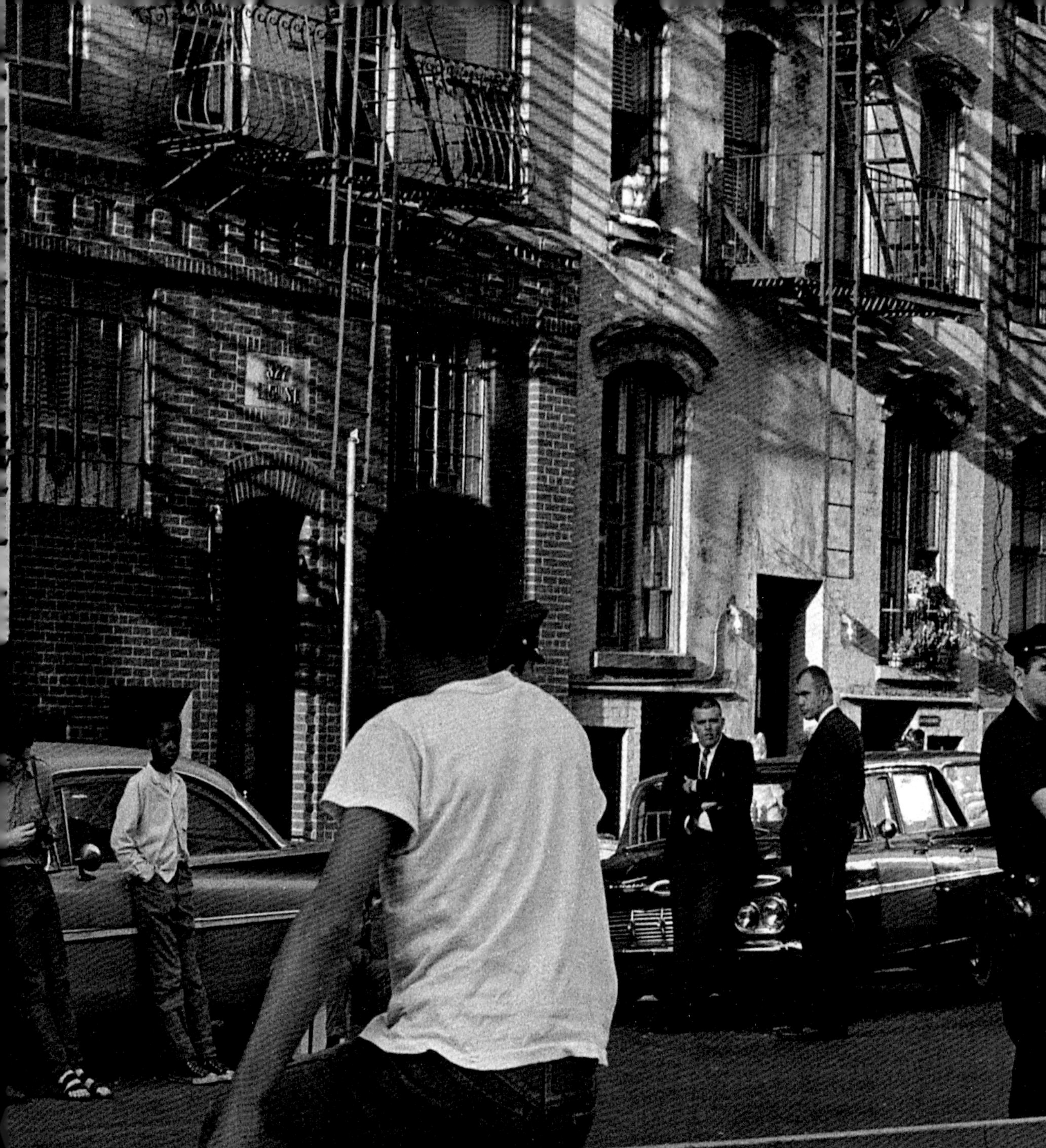

CE LINE
POLICE
DO NOT CROSS
DEPT

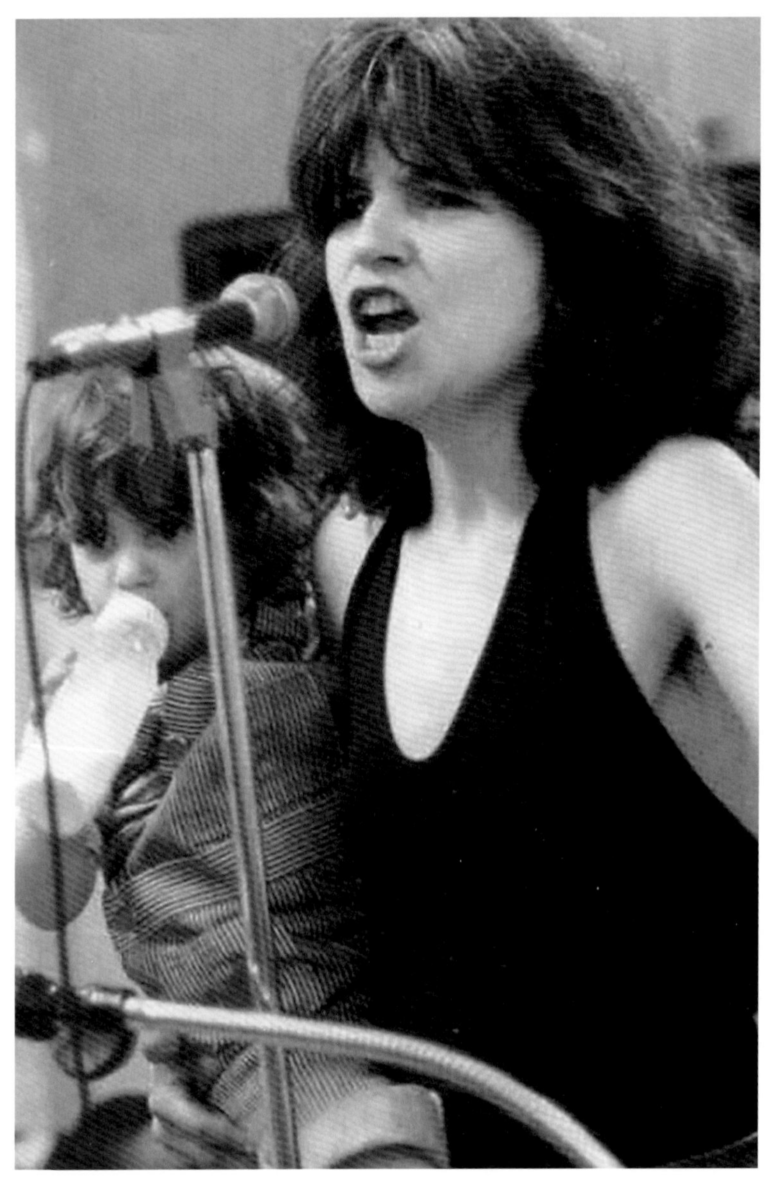

Bev Grant holding her daughter, Leticia
Community center concert, Bronx, New York, Fall 1973

Family
New York

I left Newsreel in 1971. I was pregnant with my first child and had started a band called The Human Condition. I began expressing my activism through songwriting. The band became part of the movement, playing social justice music for many of the communities I'd become familiar with through my work with Newsreel. We played in support of the Vietnam Veterans Against the War or VVAW, the welfare rights movement, Puerto Rican independence, justice and freedom in Haiti, and the African National Congress or ANC against apartheid in South Africa. We stayed together for nineteen years, first as a five-member folk rock band with me as the only woman, and then as a World Music band with five men and five women from multiple backgrounds including Brazilian, Nicaraguan, Puerto Rican, Zimbabwean, and American. We sang in five different languages and had a horn section as well as two percussionists and a trap drummer.

I had another child in 1982. In 1997, I founded the Brooklyn Women's Chorus, which continues to this day. I've been doing cultural work in the labor movement, presenting a multi-cultural show on women's labor history called We Were There.

Rediscovering my photo negatives has opened up a whole new world, putting me in touch with such a seminal period in our history at a time when many of the same struggles are front and center today. Many people I know who were taking photos back then, some of whom were my teachers, lost their negatives because they moved around or followed unrelated paths. I was fortunate to have stayed in the same Brooklyn apartment since 1977, and kept that shoebox full of negatives in a safe place. I've continued to document my family and my music to this day but I find myself more likely to take photos with my phone, which makes it harder for me to think of myself as a photographer.

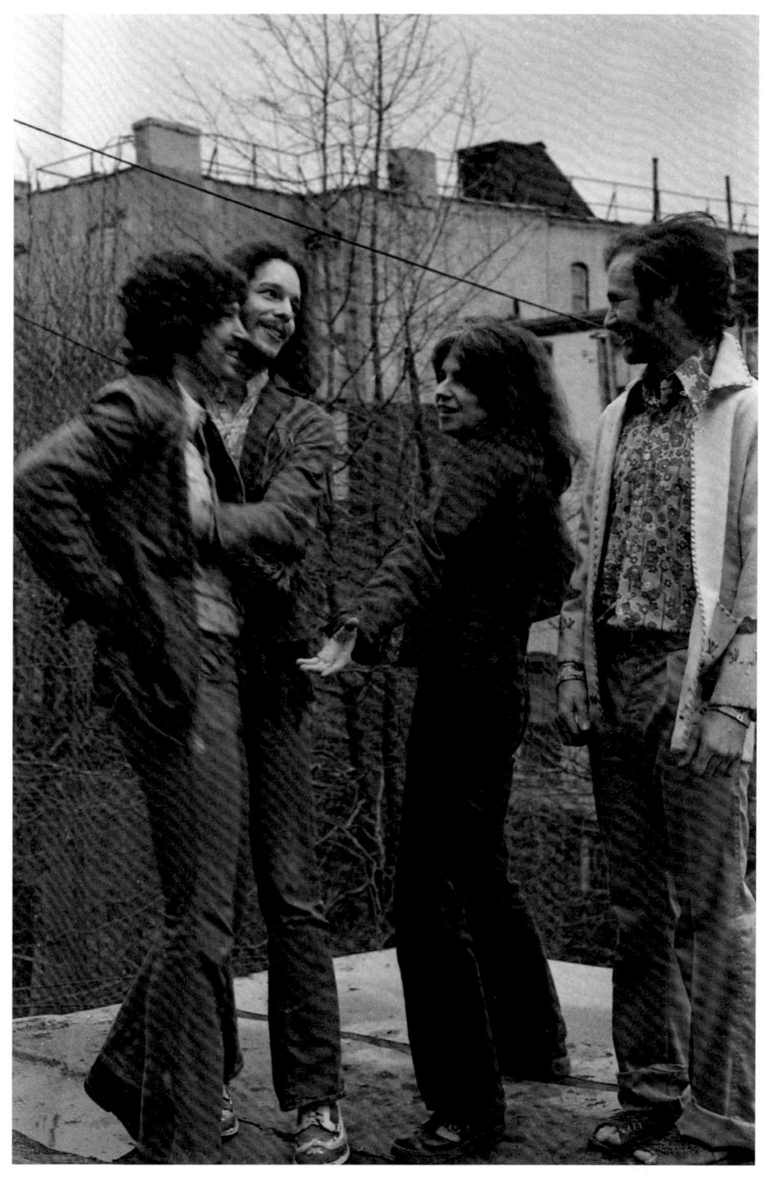

The Human Condition band members, Jerry Ross, Jerry Mitnick, Bev Grant, and Gene Hicks on a roof, Garfield Place, Brooklyn, New York, Fall 1971
Photo by Carol Foresta

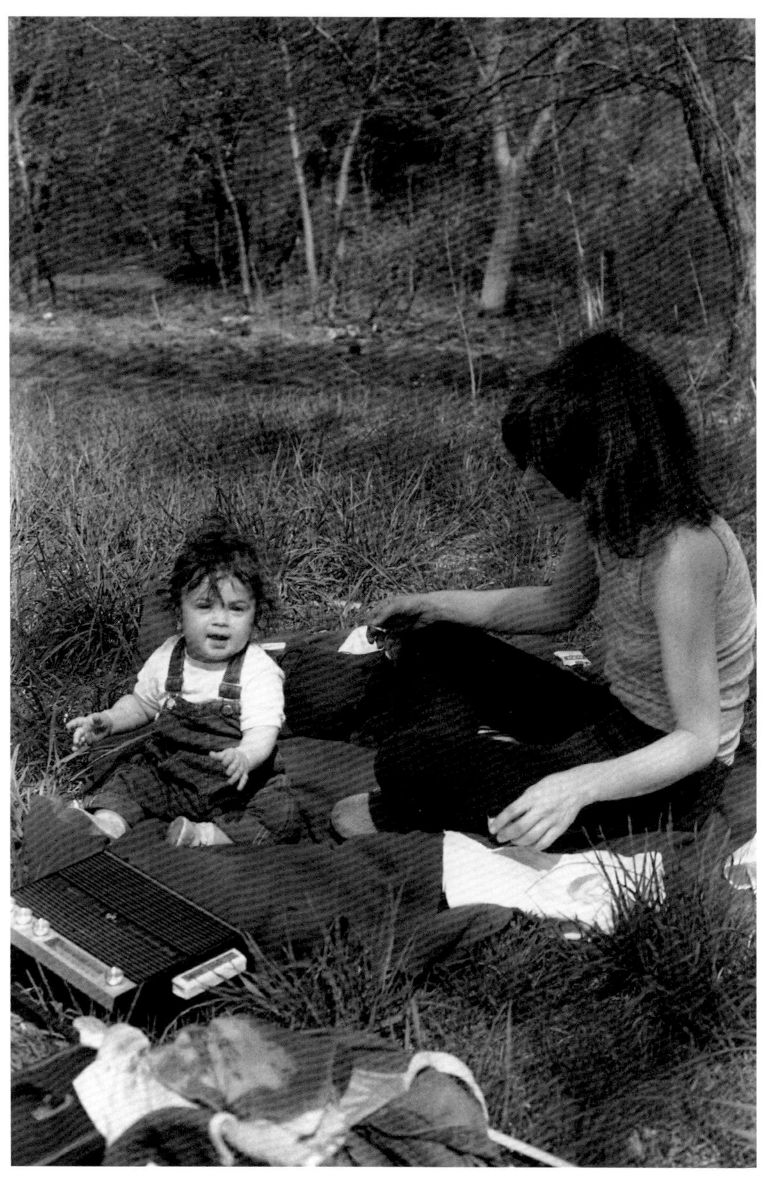

Bev and daughter Leticia, Westchester, New York, Spring 1973

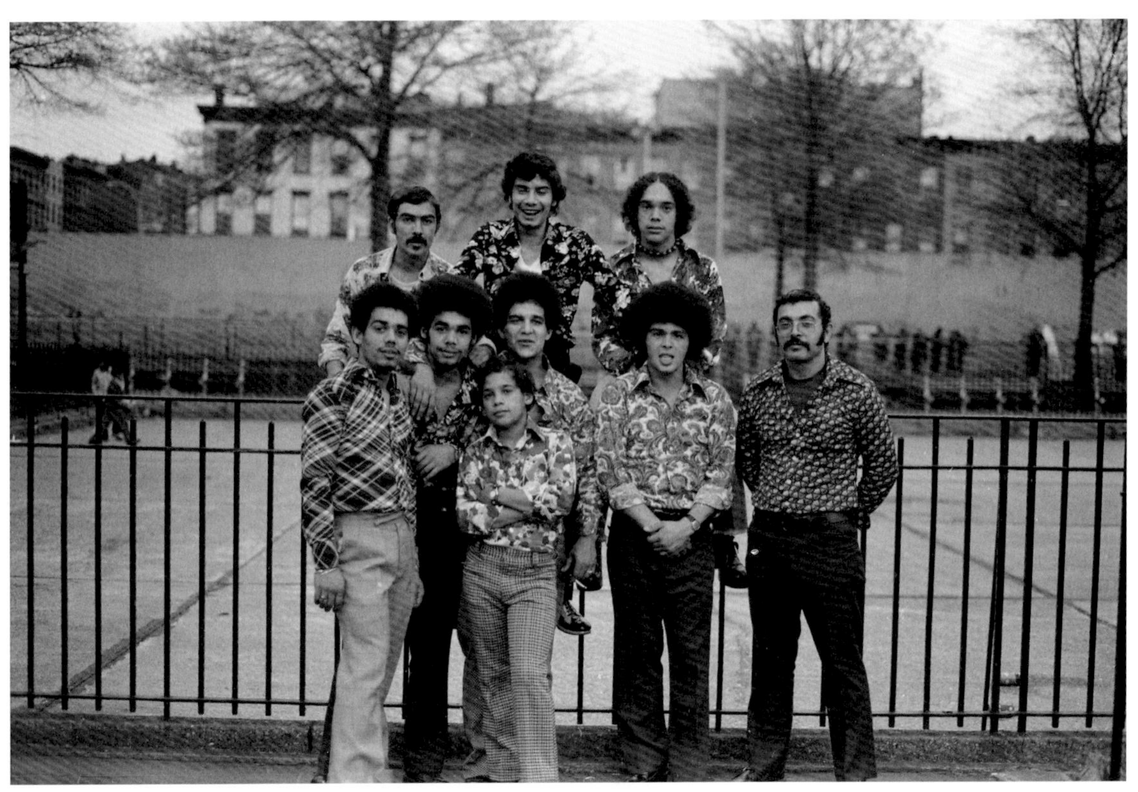

Brothers and cousins in paisley, Hunts Point playground, Bronx, New York, Fall 1972

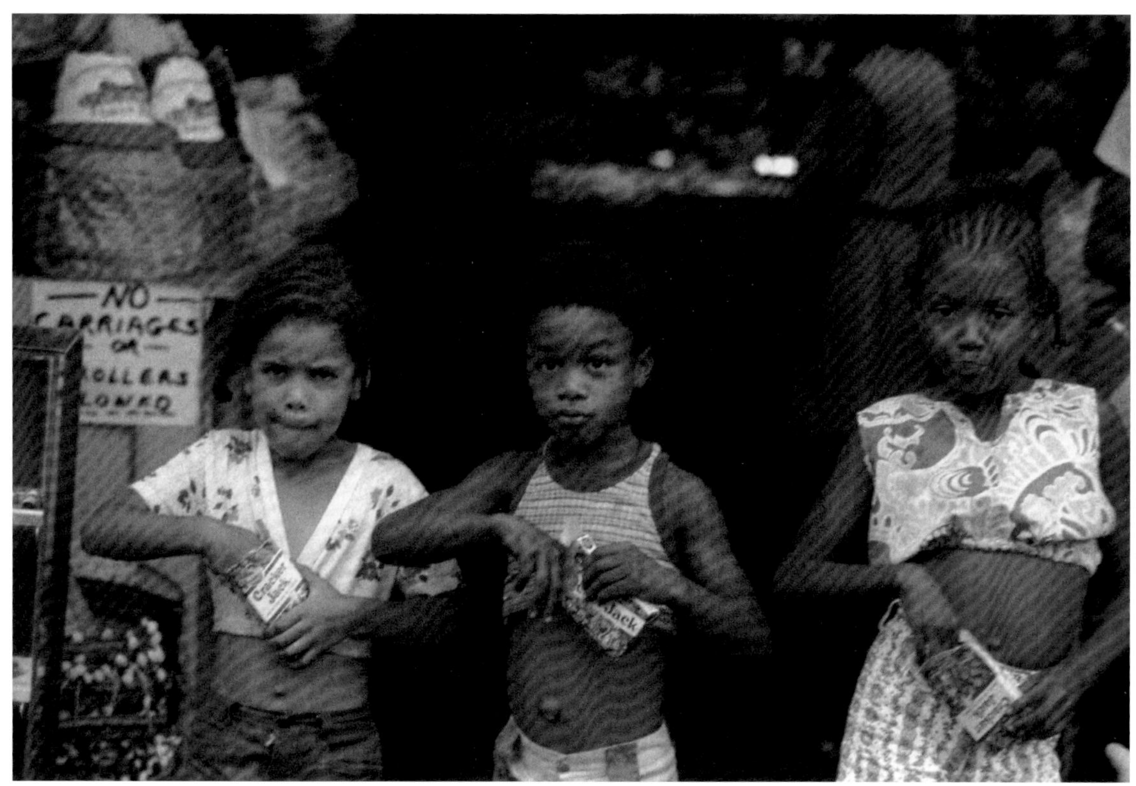

Bev's niece, Sunni Acoli Middleton on the left, Coney Island, New York, Summer 1972

Following spread
Girls on Forsyth Street, New York, Fall 1967

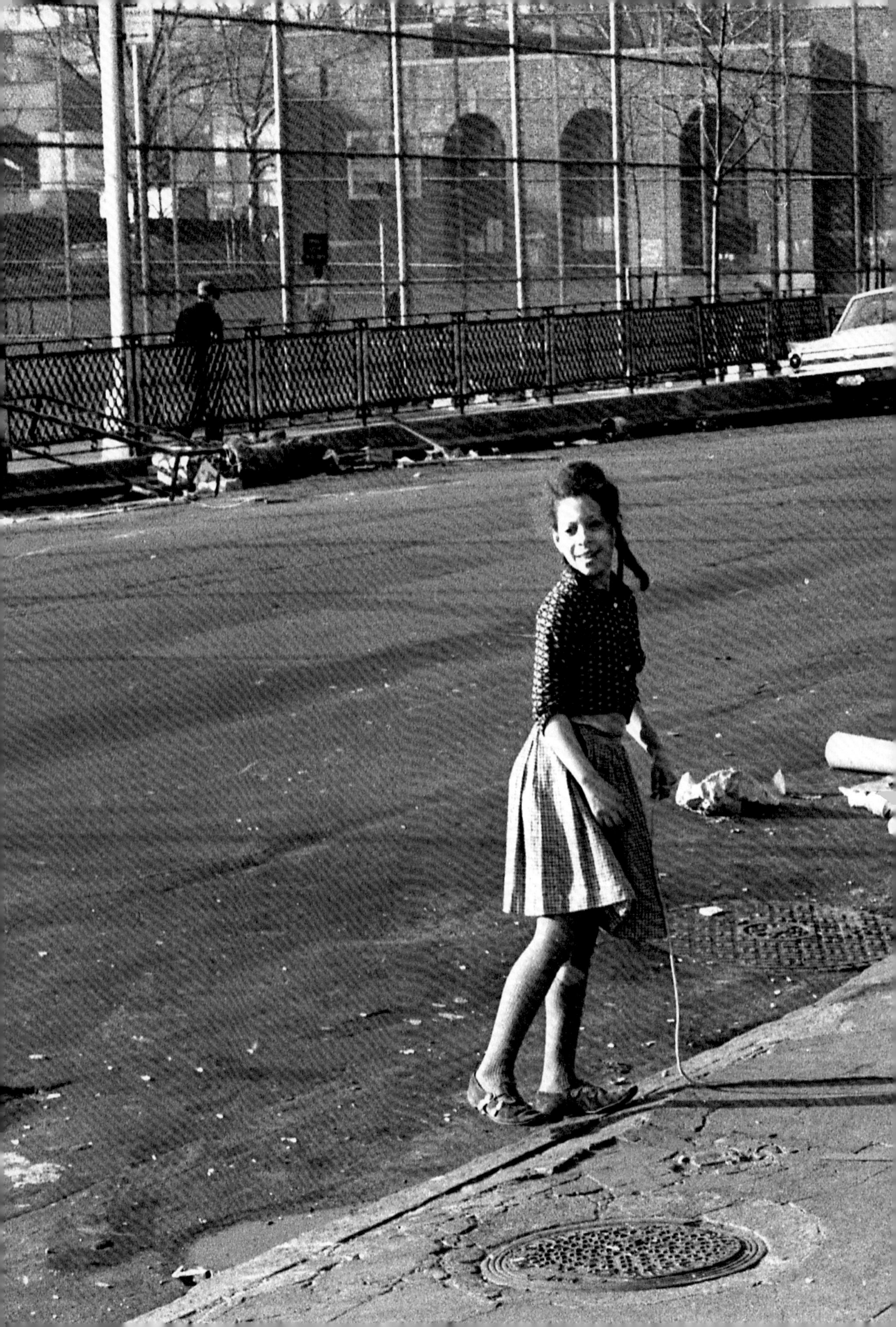

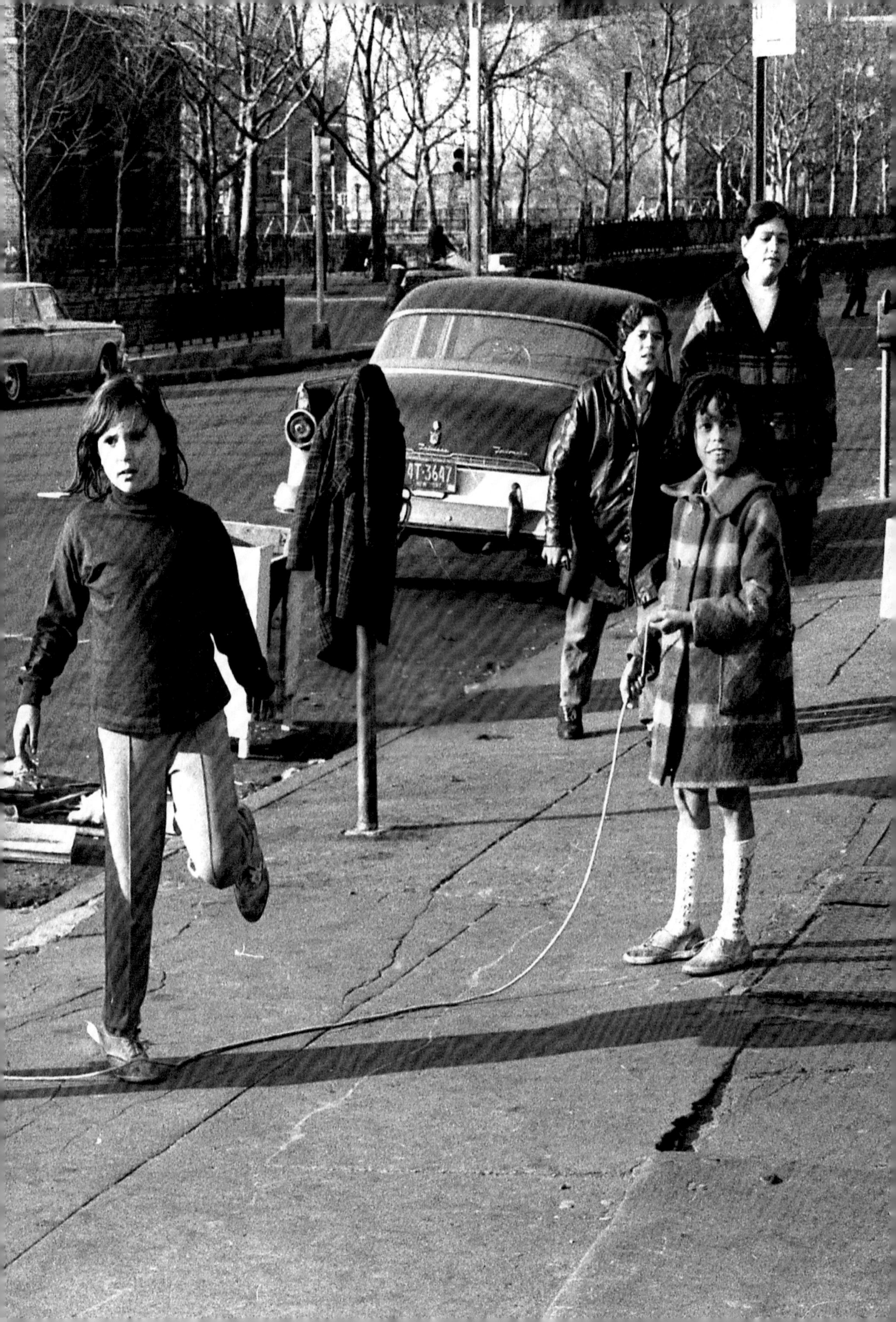

Between Proximity and Diffidence

by Johanna Fernández

The movements of the sixties changed the culture of American society. They transformed the relationship between white people and people of color, especially Black people, introduced gender as an analysis for understanding women's oppression, challenged heteronormativity, eroded support for the Vietnam War, and legitimized critiques of U.S. foreign policy at the

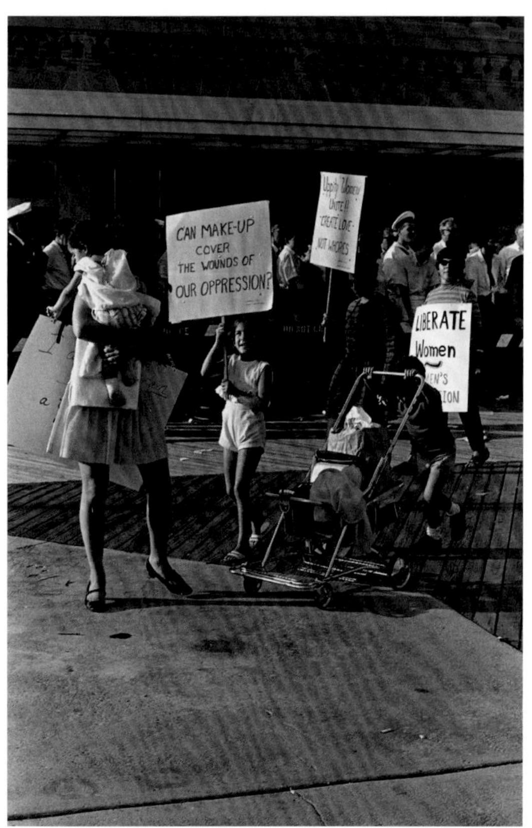

Miss America Pageant Protest
Atlantic City, New Jersey, September 7, 1968

height of the Cold War. A shift in consciousness of this magnitude was only possible through the deliberate actions and ideas of small groups of very committed people acting independently but also in concert with thousands of other small, like-minded collectives across the country. Who were the people behind these small collectives who changed America? Where did they gather? And what strategies did they employ toward their vision of social transformation?

Bev Grant's photographs offer perspective on these questions. Taken at the height of sixties radicalization between 1967 and 1972, the photographs capture some of the most important protests of the period in the anti-war and women's movements and those organized by urban radicals of color. Grant's photographs also document some of the activities of the era's groundbreaking organizations, including New York Radical Women, the Black Panthers, Young Lords, and the Poor People's Campaign, Eastern Contingent. On first encounter, these photos suggest

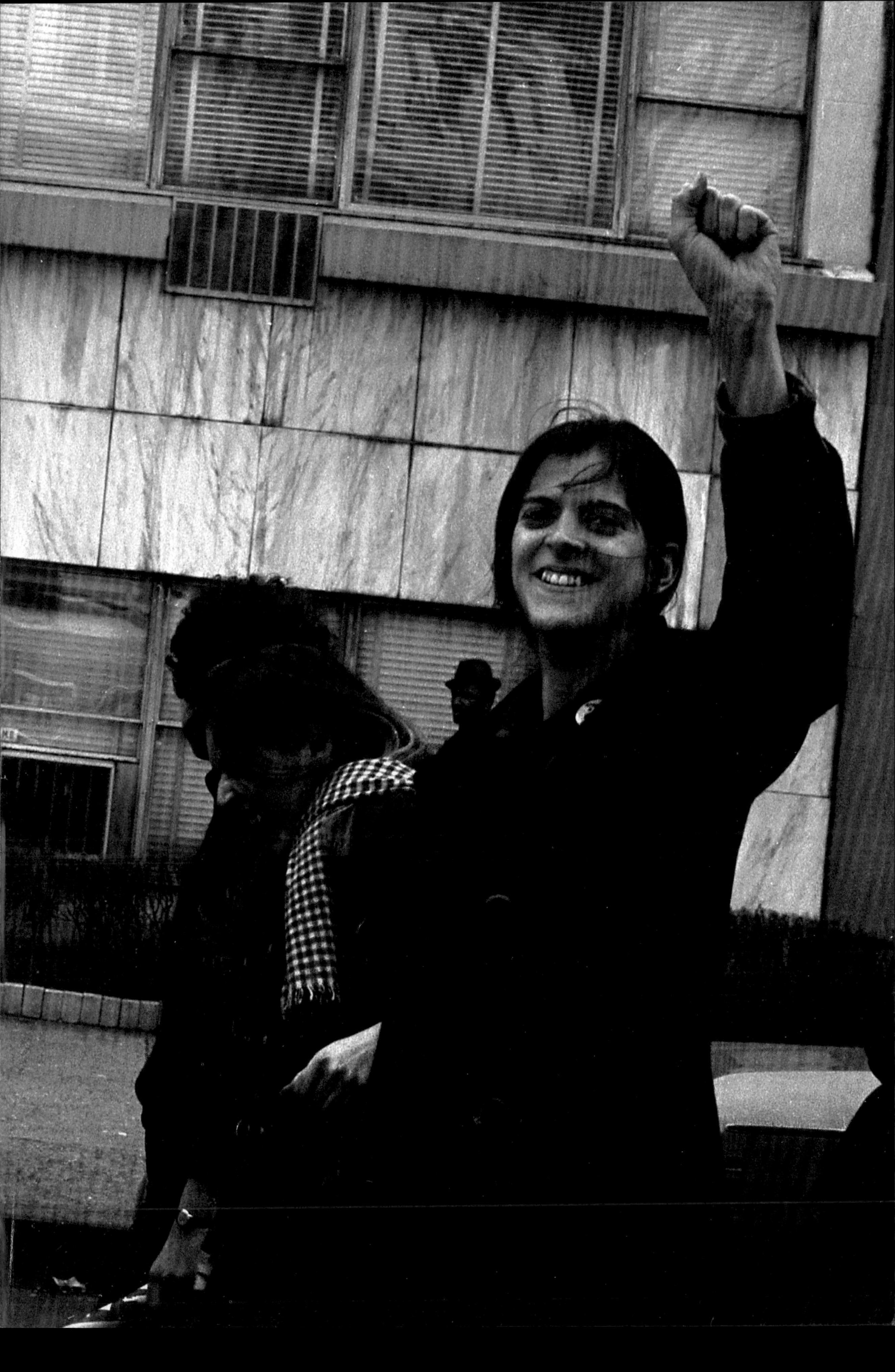

Published in 2021 by OSMOS Books

Editor
Cay Sophie Rabinowitz

Authors
Wiilliam Cordova
Joanna Fernández

Design
Quinn Sherman

Image Postproduction
Kate Steciw

Research
Christian Rattemeyer

Typeface
Maison Neue

Paper
135gsm Magno satin

Printed and bound by
die Keure, Bruges

Cover
Bev Grant and Young Lords Deputy
Minister of Defense, Juan González
Young Lords offices, East Harlem,
New York, Summer 1969
Photographer unknown

Front Endpaper
New York Radical Women organizers
at a planning meeting, SCEF offices,
New York City, Summer 1968

Back Endpaper
Poor People's Campaign,
New York City, May 11, 1968

OSMOS
20 Railroad Avenue
Stamford, New York 12167

osmos.address@gmail.com
www.osmos.online
@osmos.online

First Edition Monograph
Paper bound hardback
7.3 x 10.25 inches
224 pages

North American Distribution
D.A.P. / Distributed Art Publishers
75 Broad St, Suite 630
New York, New York 10004
www.artbook.com

ISBN 978-0-9906980-6-7

Thanks
Ryan Buckley, William Cordova,
Johanna Fernández, Glenda
Garrick, Alison Gingeras, Shirley
Hainer, Remy Holwick, Interference
Archive, Adrienne Resa Jones, Ralph
Rabinowitz, James June Schneider,
Sasha Turrentine, Third World
Newsreel, Charlene Woodworth

The artist would like to thank her
family, friends, galleries, master
printers, studio team, and the folks
at OSMOS for making her work and
this book possible.

Bev Grant photographs are available
for purchase exclusively through
OSMOS.

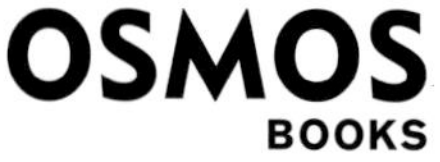

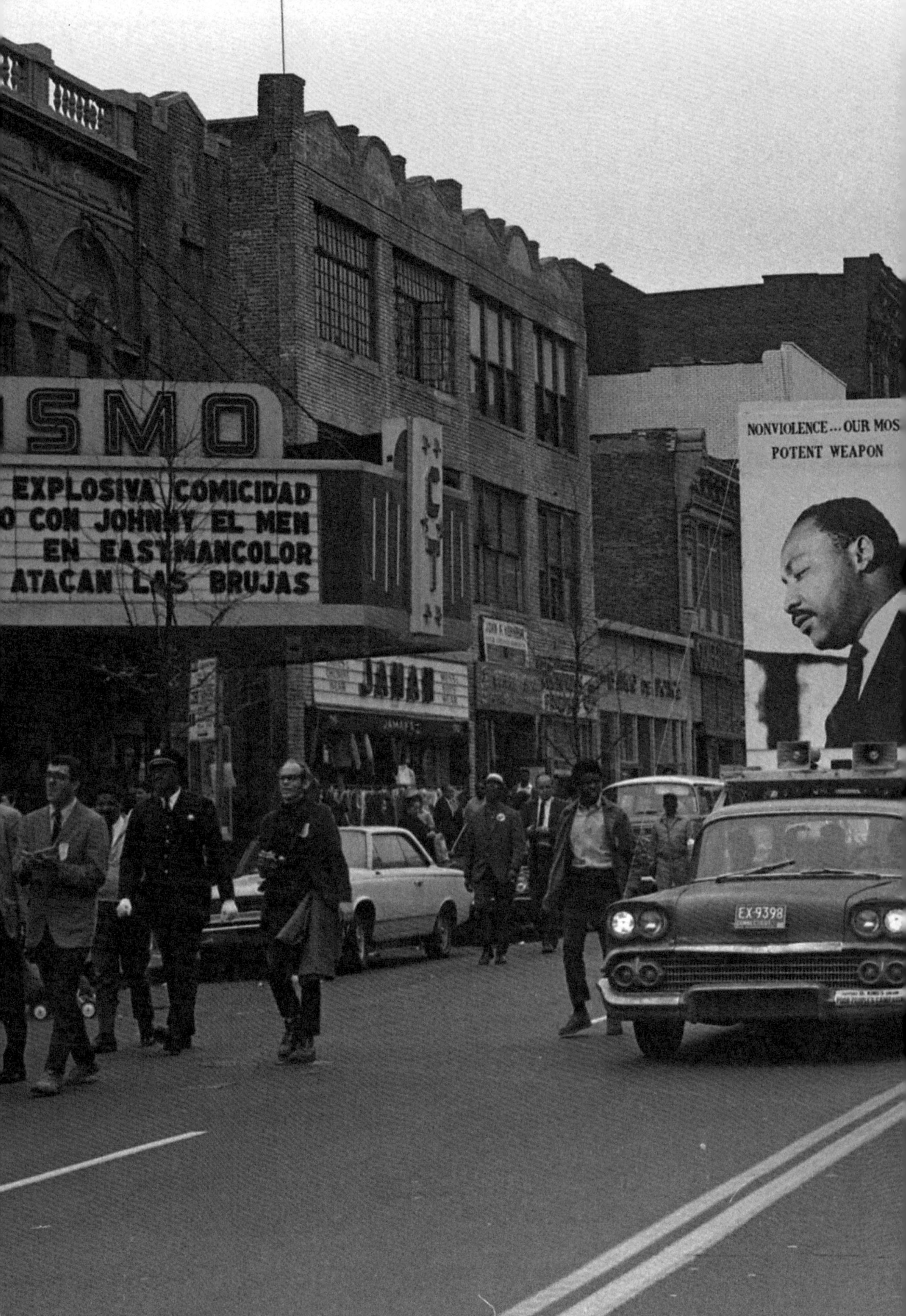
SMO
EXPLOSIVA COMICIDAD
O CON JOHNNY EL MEN
EN EASTMANCOLOR
ATACAN LAS BRUJAS
JAMAL
NONVIOLENCE...OUR MOS
POTENT WEAPON
EX-9398
CONNECTICUT